# GOD: ONE IN ALL AND ALL IN ONE

AF080818

[SOURCE: GOOGLE MERIDIAN WEBSITE – NO INFRINGEMENT INTENDED]
"WE ALL HAVE THE SAME GOD, WE JUST SERVE HIM DIFFERENTLY. RIVERS, LAKES, PONDS, STREAMS, OCEANS ALL HAVE DIFFERENT NAMES, BUT THEY ALL CONTAIN WATER. SO DO RELIGIONS HAVE DIFFERENT NAMES, AND THEY ALL CONTAIN TRUTH, EXPRESSED IN DIFFERENT WAYS, FORMS, AND TIMES." – MUHAMMAD ALI

**BY**
**PRAHALAD RAO**

**BLUEROSE PUBLISHERS**
India | U.K.

Copyright © Prahalad Rao 2025

All rights reserved by author. No part of this publication may be reproduced, stored in a retrieval system or transmitted in any form or by any means, electronic, mechanical, photocopying, recording or otherwise, without the prior permission of the author. Although every precaution has been taken to verify the accuracy of the information contained herein, the publisher assume no responsibility for any errors or omissions. No liability is assumed for damages that may result from the use of information contained within.

BlueRose Publishers takes no responsibility for any damages, losses, or liabilities that may arise from the use or misuse of the information, products, or services provided in this publication.

For permissions requests or inquiries regarding this publication, please contact:

BLUEROSE PUBLISHERS
www.BlueRoseONE.com
info@bluerosepublishers.com
+91 8882 898 898
+4407342408967

ISBN: 978-93-6783-203-5

Cover design: Daksh
Typesetting: Tanya Raj Upadhyay

First Edition: March 2025

# DEDICATION

THIS BOOK IS DEDICATED TO ALL THE RELIGIONS IN THE WORLD WHICH BELIEVE THAT 'GOD IS ONE WITH DIFFERENT FACETS' AND ONENESS OF GOD IS ONE IN ALL AND ALL IN ONE THAT IS HOW THE WORLD IS MOVING FOR BETTERMENT OF THE HUMANS AND ALL OTHER LIVING BEINGS ON 'MOTHER EARTH'

# DISCLAIMER

Views expressed by the author in this book are based on his personal understanding of the past and perception of the present. This book neither intends nor suggests any attribution of whatsoever nature to anyone or to any policy or program or system existing or envisaged nor this book intends or suggests to hurt sentiments of any person or state or political bodies or religious bodies or political or religious leaders or body of any other nature or defame any of them whatsoever and any construction of the writings in this book otherwise is sole to the person so construing. The author or the publisher will not be liable for any civil or criminal proceedings under the laws of the country.

# GRATITUDES

My gratitude to Dr. Sharda, K.Ananth Raman, Royal Hotel, Hyderabad, V.Laxma Reddy, T.S.Murthy, A.R. Venkataraman, P.P.S.Puri, A.S.Dhupia, R.B. Mathur and Lalit Chand, whose guidance, benevolence and humanism in my initial years of service will shine in my heart for ever, C.V.Nair, D. Sankaraguruswamy, Dr. Uddesh Kohli, B.M. Pant, M. Prasad, T.N. Thakur, A.A. Khan, Dr. K. K. Govil and Raji Phillips who gave confidence and lent support to me during my most testing time of life.

My gratitude to senior Indian Administrative Officers (IAS) who headed the organizations, account and audit service officers, eminent engineers, eminent finance & legal experts with whom I had the opportunity to work in one capacity or the other during my thirty years of service in public sector Financial Institutions. Gratitudes to A.K.Sah and Shahzad Bahadur for giving me opportunity to develop my career as a consultant post retirement. My gratitude and special thanks to Dr.J.T.Verghese who offered me chance for continuity of my consultancy job with continued guidance and advice. My association with all of them helped imbibe in me their direction, dedication to the cause of economic development, virtues, values, compassion and affection that became bedrock of my life.

My gratitude to Scholars, Journalists, Thinkers, Philosophers, Historians, Bankers, Economists, Professionals, Socialists and Environmentalists within and outside the country whose writings on Google website helped me to understand the width and depth of subject selected for this book. Author has disclosed the sources of valuable writings relied upon under in the book. No copyright infringement is intended. Author reiterates his grateful thanks to all of them.

My special thanks to Google for providing inspiration with invaluable sources of information that helped me in completing this book.

In particular, my special gratitude to Arun Kumar Sarna who gave me strong standing support during my association with him in service in multi-national consultancy Services Company as well as throughout thereafter.

My gratitude to K. G. Dewan, Sadiq Shafiq and Boben Anto whose ever helping hand remained a sustainable strength to me.

Grateful thanks to M/s BLUE ROSE PUBLISHESERS PRIVATE LIMITED, the Publishers without whose cooperation, guidance and advice, this book wouldn't have reached the readers.

Thanks to my friends, relatives and my family members for their continued encouragement. Their suggestions and support were a great strength for me in completing this book.

15th October, 2024 Prahalad Rao

# Table of Contents

SECTION [1] GOD ............................................................. 1

SECTION [2] ORIGIN OF LIFE ..................................... 19

SECTION [3] MEANING OF LIFE IN LITERATURE ... 32

SECTION [4] RELIGIONS .............................................. 40

SECTION [5] ATHEIST VS AGNOSTIC ....................... 60

SECTION [6] WHO CREATED THE GOD .................... 62

SECTION [7] WHAT HOLY SCRIPTS SAY ................. 88

SECTION [8] WHAT RISHIS AND SAGES SAY ........ 102

SECTION [9] WHICH PATH THE GREAT SAINTS OF DIFFERENT RELIGIONS IN THE WORLD FOLLOWED TO REALIZE THE INNER SPIRIT [GOD]? ........................................................................ 108

SECTION [10] PRESENT DAY PRACTICE ................ 113

SECTION [11] ASTROLOGICAL & RELIGIOUS APPROACH ................................................................. 124

SECTION [12] SELF, EGO & PERSONA ..................... 134

SECTION [13] NEGATIVITY, POSITIVITY & MEDITATION .............................................................. 138

SECTION [14] SOUL ..................................................... 156

SECTION [15] .............................................................. 171

SECTION [18] HUMAN & HUMANITY ..................... 274

SECTION [19] HUMANS TREATMENT OF OTHER LIVING BEINGS ............................................ 288

SECTION [20] GODLY QUALITIES ............................ 336

SECTION [21] WHY HUMANS ARE INDIFFERENT WHEN THEY BELIEVE GOD IS ONE ......................... 363

SECTION [22] THANKFULNESS TO GOD ................. 385

ABOUT THE AUTHOR ............................................... 387

# SECTION [1]
# GOD

"WE NEED TO FIND GOD, AND HE CANNOT BE FOUND IN NOISE AND RESTLESSNESS. GOD IS THE FRIEND OF SILENCE. SEE HOW NATURE — TREES, FLOWERS, GRASS — GROWS IN SILENCE; SEE THE STARS, THE MOON AND THE SUN, HOW THEY MOVE IN SILENCE. WE NEED SILENCE TO BE ABLE TO TOUCH SOULS."

-MOTHER TERESA

In the Title of this book, 'ALL' connotes 'ALL THE RELIGIONS', while ONE connotes GOD who is present in all the religions. World Atlas Website notes 'The 10 Largest Religions in the World' and elucidates each of them as follows:

"After millennia of passing down knowledge through rich oral and written traditions, each of the world's major religions has carried ambitious philosophies through countless eras. Woven throughout these mystical theologies are the epic sagas of humanity's ancestors, who fought every day to uncover their purpose in life, just the same as us. Different approaches often utilize the same foundational myths, such as Eastern religions and the concept of the Dao, or the Abrahamic faith's shared understanding of monotheism. Worth remembering is that humankind has been infatuated with religion for at least as long as people have pursued agriculture, approximately 10 thousand years. By studying these 10 ongoing faiths, one glimpses into an ancient history involving forefathers who gambled their souls on what they believed.

At well over 30% of the global population, Christianity is a religion that resonates with over 2 billion believers. The core of the belief, despite the glaring differences between Protestants, Catholics, and Orthodox, revolves around the 1st-century figure that is Jesus of Nazareth. As an Abrahamic religion, Christians claim a belief in a singular god, who represents himself through three identities: Jesus, the Holy Spirit, and God the Father.

Another essential aspect is the death and resurrection of Jesus, in which humanity is allowed to repent of all misdeeds, and eventually spend the afterlife with their beloved deity. The philosophical values and codes of Christianity have been influential enough to form the backbone of Western institutions, despite a growing acceptance of secularism.

Most active towards the end of the 6th century, the Prophet Muhammad is celebrated by Muslims today for founding the religion of Islam. Roughly 1.8 billion followers populate the world, the majority of which are spread between northern Africa, West Asia, and Indonesia. The prophet desired to repair the Abrahamic religions, which he believed to be corrupted.

Islam is marked by its adherence to discipline, in which abstinence from worldly behaviors as well as observance of daily rites is rigorously demanded. Notable historic discoveries have come from Islamic institutions, in fields such as algebra, surgery, architecture, and even coffee.

The two main branches of Islam that cohabitate the Muslim world are Sunni and Shia, which are said to have been divided 14 hundred years ago over an issue of succession.

The origin of Hinduism, a religion with 1.1 billion followers, is difficult to pin down because it began as an amalgamation of different beliefs. Officially formed between 2300 B.C. and 1500 B.C., the Indus Valley near modern-day Pakistan is the location in which it first blossomed. Typically thought of as the 'religion with 33 million gods,' the majority of Hindus worship one god alone, albeit they accept the existence of other gods. Core values are ones such as Karma and Samsara. Karma dictates that the moral sum of the deeds we produce will be returned to us eventually, through consequence or reward. Samsara is a model for the cyclical nature of life, a symptom of which is reincarnation. Historical contributions to the world include mathematics as well as astronomy and yoga.

A prince who renounced his wealth to pursue wisdom, the Buddha is an eclectic figure from the 5th century B.C. who brought together many different beliefs in order to develop a revolutionary philosophy on human identity and purpose. The goal is to achieve an enlightenment called Nirvana, through meditation, kindness, and hard work. Values revolve around the absence of an 'essential self,' impermanence, and the reality that life is suffering. Therefore, a primary aim for mankind is the elimination of suffering in all its forms. The orange tunic, that the monks famously adorn, represents a fire that burns away impurities. Two different sects exist, the Theravada Buddhists and the East Asian Buddhists, which differ in their selection of texts. At 500 million followers, Buddhism has been lauded for its effective use of an egalitarian philosophy that has worked to dismantle caste systems worldwide.

Shinto, the ever-nebulous religion of Japan, has no settled doctrine or origin story. At its simplest, Shinto beliefs gravitate towards a fluid idea of kami. Kami are the personified concepts of wind, rivers, trees, and other natural elements. Due to the influence of Christianity, the concept of an afterlife was introduced, and some followers believe humans become kami after death. The religion became more concrete in the events surrounding WWII, wherein the Japanese government instituted it as a state religion that aimed to venerate the emperor as a living, human, kami. Otherwise, Shinto beliefs have developed since the 6th century as a nature-focused series of scattered beliefs that merged and then split with Buddhism as well as Confucianism. With 104 million followers and a focus on ancestry and nature, the belief can be understood through indulging in Japanese storytelling; wherein, the horror of 20th-century industry threatens the magic of the world around us.

In 1469, the first Guru of Sikhism was born. Guru Nanak, a northeast Pakistan native, migrated to India and began to record and teaches his revelations during journeys around the Islamic and Hindu world throughout the early 1500s. These revelations are few but substantial: Share with others, earn an honest living, meditate on God's name and resist negative behaviors. Currently, the 25 million followers organize to promote universal egalitarian principles and believe that all faiths ultimately worship a singular divine being. A well-known example of this mindset is the tendency for Sikh temples to have a community kitchen dedicated to serving meals to anyone, for free. Sadly, Sikh history is marked by political difficulty and deadly rebellion against intolerant regimes. Several of the original Gurus, leaders that carry on Nanak's spiritual empowerment, were executed by the state authority of their time.

The original Abrahamic faith, Judaism has been practiced for over 3500 years. Archaeological evidence confirms the existence of two adjacent Jewish kingdoms between 900 and 700 B.C., and the religious texts assume a confederacy of 12 tribes united in faith before that. Each tribe, and subsequent kingdom, claim descent from Abraham.

The faith is monotheistic, in contrast to the ancient Levant's polytheistic history. The devotion to their god, "Yahweh," comes from his commitment to them as a chosen people, while constantly being urged by him to return to pious behaviors. Unlike Christianity and Islam, there is no detailed assumption of the afterlife other than a deep sleep called "Sheol." Roughly 14 million Jews continue to practice the faith today, despite extreme persecution during World War II.

A 'one-size-fits-all' belief, Taoism is a series of principles and axioms that attempts to guide followers towards balance. Two 'persons' sit at the heart of Taoism; the Tao itself, and Laozi, a 6th-century contemporary of Confucius. Laozi and his school decreed that the Tao is indefinable, and only engaged through lived experience. It is a powerful force that runs throughout the universe and encourages "De," which is adherence to the Tao. The Tao is the natural order of the universe and is not worshipped as a god, and it is believed that humans merge with the Tao upon death. By adhering to the lifestyle of De, the 12 million followers of Taoism trust that they will experience less suffering. Inaction and a passive effort to synchronize with this balance is the key differentiation from the more intentional Confucianism.

Despite dancing around spirituality, leading many to consider Confucianism as a philosophy only, the religion establishes a theological understanding of the Universe, albeit an impersonal one. In it, the priority of humankind is to strive to synchronize with the order of the universe in order to achieve oneness with heaven for the tranquility of community and self. This order is defined by "Tiān," a non-speaking 'God of Heaven' which can be best translated as "the way things are." Moreover, Confucianism argues that the way humankind should act is a way that conforms to the most evident morals: charity, obedience to mentors, humility, and compassion. All people are inherently good and must work to realign themselves with that nature. Since its establishment by Confucius and his writings in 500 B.C., the faith currently hosts over 6 million followers.

A melting pot of many of the world's largest faiths, Caodaism is a recent creation originating in 1921 when a vision came to an assembled group of mediums located in Vietnam. Nearly 4.4 million believers align themselves with the core tenets that teach harmony, unity with a monotheistic deity, reincarnation, and anti-materialism. Besides the association with Buddhism, Confucianism, and Taoism, Caodaism asserts the existence of several creator spirits as well as devils led by a being resemblant of Satan; this is a dynamic similar to Abrahamic faiths. Naturally, to achieve heaven, a soul must evolve its spirit through good behavior during successive reincarnations. The belief was influential in Vietnam during the 1930s, not only because of its quick spread, but also due to the anti-colonialist sentiment that it cultivated against the French occupation. In 1997, after being banned for 22 years, the practice of the religion was permitted in Vietnam once again.

The shocking reality about each faith, side to side, is that they tend to possess more similarities than differences. For instance, students of each belief spend years honing their self-control and ability to grow through introspection. Countless tales can be heard of disciples who swear by the fact that these faiths transformed them into proud and more joyful members of society. Furthermore, the scholars of each belief are happy to borrow from each other when the opportunity presents itself. For example, famed Christian theologian C.S. Lewis cleverly integrated the concept of Tao into his own writings. After examining the history and core values of each faith, it is evident that the secret to how they might morph and evolve further is buried in the future………….."

The concept of One God, as the above Article states, is known in all the religions [in Hinduism it is known as the 'Supreme Power' among different Gods it follows, nevertheless the supremacy of one God exists]. Great Saints were born in each religion in the past civilizations having spent their lives as such saints and having placed themselves in a state of their own that aimed at searching for the God through Tapasya [Yoga]

Two persons are walking on the road; one asked the other whether he believed in God. The other person got perplexed and was struggling to answer the question. Then, it struck to his thought, why he should have so struggled when everyone believes the god is within. This compelled him to search for what is within the human where god is said to be residing. He experienced how he could have survived and struggling to search for the god without there being some element which the people believed as LIGHT and, if that LIGHT, were not to be there within him, what could have been the consequence of its absence which he understood to be the 'death'. So, after self-testing and satisfying the existence of an element and its absence leading to death, he asked the other person who put the question him, how he could have asked question without being conscious of the fact there is something within him that made him to ask that question.? The person to whom the question was addressed answered the other person that the very fact the question he is asking would not have been possible for him if there were to be no LIGHT [known as God] within him and he would have been a dead person without existence of the LIGHT within him. The other person realized the fact of LIFE THROUGH THE PRESENCE OF 'LIGHT' within him. Asking a question about god is one part and the other part is such question is self-admitting that because of the presence of that

LIGHT, he could not have asked that question as a dead person.

One can say that the existence of God is undeniable and the religions of the land are bound by their respective Faiths. This brings out two points, first who is God who found a place in every religion either in the form of Idols or in the Holy Scripts. Both these have deepest connection with God according to one's Faith. All the Faiths don't have any doubt or disputes about the existence of God as believed according to their Faiths. This makes us to inquire into ourselves who is God who so believed in every Religion or Faith and such religion or faith is the process of LIFE, what is life is a different matter and has its own meaning and purpose according to the Holy Scripts of each Faith. The basic enquiry is the evolution of the concept of GOD, LIFE and the RELIGION. We have understood to a great extent about the God and Religion based on what has been submitted before. We now need to know 'WHAT IS LIFE?'

**NEW WORLD ENCYCLOPEDIA [WEBSITE] POSTED AN ARTICLE TITLED "MEANING OF LIFE"** which is reproduced below for the benefit of the readers:

"The question of the meaning of life is perhaps the most fundamental "why?" in human existence. It relates to the purpose, use, value, and reason for individual existence and that of the universe.

This question has resulted in a wide range of competing answers and explanations, from scientific to philosophical and religious explanations, to explorations in literature. Science, while providing theories about the

How and What of life, has been of limited value in answering questions of meaning—the Why of human existence. Philosophy and religion have been of greater relevance, as has literature. Diverse philosophical positions include essentialist, existentialist, skeptic, nihilist, pragmatist, humanist, and atheist. The essentialist position, which states that a purpose is given to our life, usually by a supreme being, closely resembles the viewpoint of the Abrahamic religions.

While philosophy approaches the question of meaning by reason and reflection, religions approach the question from the perspectives of revelation, enlightenment, and doctrine. **Generally, religions have in common two most important teachings regarding the meaning of life: 1) the ethic of the reciprocity of love among fellow humans for the purpose of uniting with a Supreme Being, the provider of that ethic; and 2) spiritual formation towards an afterlife or eternal life as a continuation of physical life.** [Emphasis added by the author]

### Scientific Approaches to the Meaning of Life

Science cannot possibly give a direct answer to the question of meaning. There are, strictly speaking, no scientific views on the meaning of biological life other than its observable biological function: to continue. Like a judge confronted with a conflict of interests, the honest scientist will always make the difference between his personal opinions or feelings and the extent to which science can support or undermine these beliefs. That extent is limited to the discovery of ways in which things (including human life) came into being and objectively given, observable laws and patterns that might hint at a certain origin and/or purpose forming the ground for possible meaning.

Life experience of the author shows people asking 'who is God', 'where is God', 'I don't believe in God', 'it is all for saying. These questions are also true for those who are asking them. What such people are speaking is the reflection of their imagination about God. It is good to listen to such questions because they afford opportunity to listeners also to test how firm they stand knowing about God or are they shaken as a result of such questions believing uncertainty entering into the domain of doubts. Those who firmly believe in God attempt to explain as they understood God which may or may not be convincing. This brings a gap between those who deny belief in God and those who believe in God. Those who are for and against on existence of God fail to understand the very essence of Source within them.

This essence of source, in author's understanding, is the SPIRIT [GOD], the Atman or Soul being the personalization in the humans or the other living beings. Without there being the Spirit, the Soul or Atman in humans wouldn't have asked those questions or answered them. The other living beings never expressed anything about the Spirit which capacity exists in the humans. That is, it is the existence of Spirit by virtue of which they are alive for asking or answering. If we deny this basic concept of God, both types of people would not have been a living body. They are living because there is Spirit in them not able to recognize because of their predominant perception in mind, ignorant or blinded to ask this very basis to them.

Fact is that no living body whether human or of any other being on earth can move an inch without the existence of Spirit whether that being is doing well or bad is one's own creation represented by the ego. Also, in almost all religions, traditionally, the new born are named from out of the religious Faiths. In Hinduism various names of God and Saints and Sages are named. For example, Rama, Krishna, Ishwar, Mahadeva, Sita, Lakshmi, Parvathi, Sarswati, Padmavathi, and so on. Author believes, so also may be the case, in other religions. Assuming to be so, for those who question the existence of God whether in Form or Holy Script, need to start their enquiry from their name and its relationship with God or Holy Script or the saints and sages. What is needed is to know oneself how such name is originated and what significance that name embodies. A simple inquiry leads one to the origin of the name and its significance. Because the names so given are the inspiration from the names of God or Holy Script or Sages or Saints. Search for Truth begins from here.

Let us now turn to relationship among the religions and how we understand God on Earth is founded on religiosity. That is, success the humans have made to co-exist among them. Can we say they have attained the status of harmoniousness? Or, should we say it has to a great extent but there still prevails disharmony to a greater extent? Our belief in religion that we should live because of the happy things; we should live because there are people who love us; we should live because people we love back; we live because we want to find out things, and learn, and become able to do things that we would like to do; and we live because others want us to, and we want them to live with us. Religiosity is the condition of being religious, whereas spirituality relates to Spirit within the human and other living beings on Mother Earth (or God) as opposed to the materialistic thinking.

Religion or religiousness can be considered a form of spirituality but spirituality per se is a broader concept. There cannot be existence of the humans and other living beings on Mother Earth without there being the Spirit within everyone and in every other living being. This question is already answered by our Great Saints and Sages who lived through ages and have laid down the path for reaching the Spirit; so there is hardly any need today to search for that path but yet the question remains whether we could be able to find that path? This has also been already proved in the past and being endeavored in the present and will continue to be so in future. This is endless as it will continue be the human effort. The other living beings do have Spirit but lack the capacity to think about that Spirit. This is the difference between the humans and other living beings on Mother Earth. The latter live their life as ordained by that Spirit that is endowed in them.

Who Am I?" What Is My Purpose In Life? Why I Am Here? – Great philosophers and spiritual leaders pondered over these questions and gave variegated answers. Some other such great persons pointed these questions to Spirit within for seeking an answer through meditation and devotion. Many others advocated to the followers and devotees that the purpose of meditation should be to seek answers to such questions. These questions can be answered only by those Great Saints and Sages who realized the inner Spirit. By this, they obtained the entire COSMIC COMPREHENSION otherwise said as known only to God. Such Saints and Sages freed themselves from their physical existence on the earth to attain that Divineness.

Author's personal view is that the questions referred to cannot be addressed by the humans, howsoever, learned and knowledgeable, to the Spirit, the human having born with Atman (Soul) within him or her on the earth to perform the obligated duties as ordained by God. Asking such questions to seek answers from Spirit existing in the human and other living being and the human having the capacity of reasoning, by that very human in his or her physical form existing on the earth, is something like trying to know the predetermined not knowable, therefore, he would come to know himself or herself of who he or she was, what was purpose of him or her in life, why he or she was here and what he or she had done in his or her life, just before his or her departure from the earth, all of which has happened by what the Spirit contemplated for him or her when he or she was born. These are inscribed in him and her neither visible to nor ascertainable by him or her. Human duty is be in action which is life. This is the Ultimate. Every human should express his or her gratitude to the Spirit every day. That is what a human being could do having come to earth in human form and having done his or her duty on the earth, whether righteous or unrighteous answerable by him or her.

The humans and other living beings on Mother Earth do quarrel every day which is born because of selfishness. This is the source of quarrel whether among humans or other living beings. The principal causes of quarrel Posted on: June 16, 2012 – [https://calamur.org/gargi/2012/06/16/the-principa-causes-of-quarrel/ ] are stated as under:

**"So that in the nature of man, we find three principal causes of quarrel. First, competition; secondly, diffidence; thirdly, glory. The first maketh men invade for gain; the second, for safety; and the third, for reputation. The first use violence, to make themselves masters of other men's persons, wives, children, and cattle; the second, to defend them; the third, for trifles, as a word, a smile, a different opinion, and any other sign of undervalue, either direct in their persons or by reflection in their kindred, their friends, their nation, their profession, or their name."**

The Top 20 Reasons People Quarrel - By Frank Sonnenberg- [Source: https://www.franksonnenbergonline.com/blog/the-top-20-reasons-people-quarrel/

"20 Root Causes of Conflict

From communication breakdowns to divergent values, 20 root causes of conflict fuel the flames of discord. Understanding these fundamental triggers is essential for managing interpersonal relationships…

**Insensitive.** Some people are self-centered and focus solely on their own needs.

**Demeaning.** Some folks look down their nose at people and treat them with disrespect.

**Moody.** Some people run hot and cold. You're never sure which one of them will show up that day.

**Narrow-minded.** Some folks with different cultural backgrounds and life experiences may find themselves facing misunderstandings and disagreements.

**Judgmental.** Some people have inflated egos and scrutinize everything that people do.

**Competitive.** Some folks always have to win — even if it's at someone's expense.

**Opinionated.** Some people are unabashedly outspoken. They constantly share their opinions, even if it's *not* welcomed.

**Spendthrift.** Some folks with different perspectives on saving and spending can give rise to bickering about money.

**Ungrateful.** Some people are unappreciative and take everything for granted.

**Selfish.** Some folks are opportunists. They only show up when they need something.

**Egotistical.** Some people always have to be right — even when they're not.

**Unjust.** Some folks show preferential treatment — which results in unfair treatment toward others.

**Uncommunicative.** Some people are icy, behaving in a distant and detached manner.

**Dishonest.** Some folks can't be trusted. They distort facts, stretch the truth, and withhold key information.

**Unreliable.** Some people are so unpredictable; you're never sure whether you can count on them.

**Jealous.** Some folks have an axe to grind with people who are successful.

**Greedy.** Some people are like sharks. All the oceans in the world won't satisfy these eating machines.

**Stubborn.** Some folks are closed-minded and tend to reject anything new.

**Power-hungry.** Some folks are addicted to power — and will go to any length to secure more.

**Unaligned.** Some people, driven by diverse values or priorities, quarrel due to the pronounced disparities in their perspective.

We can't expect others to abandon their values any more than we would forsake our own.

It's Time to Stop Quarreling

➢ Identifying the causes of conflict is half the solution; doing something about it is the other half. Avoiding arguments doesn't require rocket science. It simply requires genuine desire and unwavering commitment.

➢ Keep these thoughts in mind:

➢ Listen not just to hear, but to truly understand.

- ➢ Be patient. Your relationship depends on it.
- ➢ Park your ego at the door. *What* is right is a lot more important than *who* is right.
- ➢ Be respectful. Judge ideas not people.
- ➢ Be open-minded and seek to understand other people's perspectives.
- ➢ Practice empathy by putting yourself in others' shoes.
- ➢ Embrace selflessness and be prepared to give of yourself.
- ➢ Discover shared interests. Aim for mutual success rather than a zero-sum outcome.
- ➢ Never win at the expense of a relationship.

Most of the things that we quarrel about are senseless, and usually the result of blowing off pent-up frustration, flaunting one's self-importance, or wanting to be right. Next time you find yourself in a conflict, ask yourself if it's worth fighting about. I'll bet your response will be a resounding, *No*! The fact is, we quarrel about simple things that are inconsequential in the grand scheme of our lives. So, if you're looking for a good fight, fight to fortify your relationships. As Anne Frank said, "I think it's odd that grown-ups quarrel so easily and so often and about such petty matters. Up to now I always thought bickering was just something children did and that they outgrew it."

# SECTION [2] ORIGIN OF LIFE

**What is the origin of life?**

The question "What is the origin of life?" is addressed in the sciences in the areas of cosmogony (for the origins of the universe) and abiogenesis (for the origins of biological life). Both of these areas are quite hypothetical—cosmogeny, because no existing physical model can accurately describe the very early universe (the instant of the Big Bang), and abiogenesis, because the environment of the young earth is not known, and because the conditions and chemical processes that may have taken billions of years to produce life cannot (as of yet) be reproduced in a laboratory. It is therefore not surprising that scientists have been tempted to use available data both to support and to oppose the notion that there is a given purpose to the emergence of the cosmos.

**What is the nature of life?**

Towards answering "What is the nature of life (and of the universe in which we live)?," scientists have proposed various theories or worldviews over the centuries. They include, but are not limited to, the heliocentric view by Copernicus and Galileo, through the mechanistic clockwork universe of René Descartes and Isaac Newton, to Albert Einstein's theory of general relativity, to the quantum mechanics of Heisenberg and Schrödinger in an effort to understand the universe in which we live.

Near the end of the twentieth century, equipped with insights from the gene-centered view of evolution, biologists began to suggest that in so far as there may be a primary function to life, it is the survival of genes. In this approach, success isn't measured in terms of the survival of species, but one level deeper, in terms of the successful replication of genes over the eons, from one species to the next, and so on. Such positions do not and cannot address the issue of the presence or absence of a purposeful origin, hence meaning.

**What is valuable in life?**

Science may not be able to tell us what is most valuable in life in a philosophical sense, but some studies bear on related questions. Researchers in positive psychology study factors that lead to life satisfaction (and before them less rigorously in humanistic psychology), in social psychology factors that lead to infants thriving or failing to thrive, and in other areas of psychology questions of motivation, preference, and what people value. Economists have learned a great deal about what is valued in the marketplace; and sociologists examine value at a social level using theoretical constructs such as value theory, norms, anomie, etc.

**What is the purpose of, or in, (one's) life?**

Natural scientists look for the purpose of life within the structure and function of life itself. This question also falls upon social scientists to answer. They attempt to do so by studying and explaining the behaviors and interactions of human beings (and every other type of animal as well). Again, science is limited to the search for elements that promote the purpose of a specific life form (individuals and societies), but these findings can only be suggestive when it comes to the overall purpose and meaning.

**Analysis of teleology based on science**

Teleology is a philosophical and theological study of purpose in nature. Traditional philosophy and Christian theology in particular have always had a strong tendency to affirm teleological positions, based on observation and belief. Since David Hume's skepticism and Immanuel Kant's agnostic conclusions in the eighteenth century, the use of teleological considerations to prove the existence of a purpose, hence a purposeful creator of the universe, has been seriously challenged. Purpose-oriented thinking is a natural human tendency which Kant already acknowledged, but that does not make it legitimate as a scientific explanation of things. In other words, teleology can be accused of amounting to wishful thinking.

The alleged "debunking" of teleology in science received a fresh impetus from advances in biological knowledge such as the publication of Charles Darwin's On the Origin of Species (i.e., natural selection). Best-selling author and evolutionary biologist Richard Dawkins puts forward his explanation based on such findings. Ironically, it is also science that has recently given a new impetus to teleological thinking by providing data strongly suggesting the impossibility of random development in the creation of the universe and the appearance of life (e.g., the "anthropic principle.[Author adds: Teleology or finality is a branch of causality giving the reason or an explanation for something as a function of its end, its purpose, or its goal, as opposed to as a function of its cause. James Wood, in his Nuttall Encyclopaedia, explained the meaning of teleology as "the doctrine of final causes, particularly the argument for the being and character of God from the being and character of His w... <u>Wikipedia</u>]

## Philosophy of the Meaning of Life

While scientific approaches to the meaning of life aim to describe relevant empirical facts about human existence, philosophers are concerned about the relationship between ideas such as the proper interpretation of empirical data. Philosophers have considered such questions as: "Is the question 'What is the meaning of life?' a meaningful question?"; "What does it really mean?"; and "If there are no objective values, then is life meaningless?" Some philosophical disciplines have also aimed to develop an understanding of life that explains, regardless of how we came to be here, what we should do, now that we are here.

Since the question about life's meaning inevitably leads to the question of a possible divine origin to life, philosophy and theology are inextricably linked on this issue. Whether the answer to the question about a divine creator is yes, no, or "not applicable," the question will come up. Nevertheless, philosophy and religion significantly differ in much of their approach to the question. Hence, they will be treated separately.

### Essentialist views

René Descartes

Essentialist views generally start with the assumption that there is a common essence in human beings, human nature, and that this nature is the starting point for any evaluation of the meaning of life. In classic philosophy, from Plato's idealism to Descartes' rationalism, humans have been seen as rational beings or "rational animals." Conforming to that inborn quality is then seen as the aim of life.

Reason, in that context, also has a strong value-oriented and ethical connotation. Philosophers such as Socrates, Plato, Descartes, Spinoza, and many others had views about what sort of life is best (and hence most meaningful). Aristotle believed that the pursuit of happiness is the Highest Good, and that such is achievable through our uniquely human capacity to reason. The notion of the highest good as the rational aim in life can still be found in later thinkers like Kant. A strong ethical connotation can be found in the Ancient Stoics, while Epicureanism saw the meaning of life in the search for the highest pleasure or happiness.

All these views have in common the assumption that it is possible to discover, and then practice, whatever is seen as the highest good through rational insight, hence the term "philosophy"—the love of wisdom. With Plato, the wisdom to discover the true meaning of life is found in connection with the notion of the immortal soul that completes its course in earthly life once it liberates itself from the futile earthly goals. In this, Plato prefigures a theme that would be essential in Christianity, that of God-given eternal life, as well as the notion that the soul is good and the flesh evil or at least a hindrance to the fulfillment of one's true goal. At the same time, the concept that one has to rise above deceptive appearances to reach a proper understanding of life's meaning has links to Eastern and Far Eastern traditions.

In medieval and modern philosophy, the Platonic and Aristotelian views were incorporated in a worldview centered on the theistic concept of the Will of God as the determinant factor for the meaning of our life, which was then seen as achieving moral perfection in ways pleasing to God. Modern philosophy came to experience considerable struggle in its attempt to make this view compatible with the rational discourse of a philosophy free of any prejudice. With Kant, the given of a God and his will fell away as a possible rational certainty. Certainty concerning purpose and meaning were moved from God to the immediacy of consciousness and conscience, as epitomized in Kant's teaching of the categorical imperative. This development would gradually lead to the later supremacy of an existentialist discussion of the meaning of life, since such a position starts with the self and its choices, rather than with a purpose given "from above." The emphasis on meaning as destiny, rather than choice, would one more time flourish in the early nineteenth century's German Idealism, notably in the philosophy of Hegel where the overall purpose of history is seen as the embodiment of the Absolute Spirit in human society.

**Existentialist views**

Main article: Existentialism

Sketch of Søren Kierkegaard

Existentialist views concerning the meaning of life are based on the idea that it is only personal choices and commitments that can give any meaning to life since, for an individual, life can only be his or her life, and not an abstractly given entity. By going this route, existentialist thinkers seek to avoid the trappings of dogmatism and pursue a more genuine route. That road, however, is inevitably filled with doubt and hesitation. With the refusal of committing oneself to an externally given ideal comes the limitation of certainty to that alone which one chooses.

Presenting essentialism and existentialism as strictly divided currents would undoubtedly amount to a caricature; hence such a distinction can only be seen as defining a general trend. It is very clear, however, that philosophical thought from the mid-nineteenth century on has been strongly marked by the influence of existentialism. At the same time, the motives of dread, loss, uncertainty, and anguish in the face of an existence that needs to be constructed "out of nothing" have become predominant. These developments also need to be studied in the context of modern and contemporary historical events leading to the World Wars.

A universal existential contact with the question of meaning is found in situations of extreme distress, where all expected goals and purposes are shattered, including one's most cherished hopes and convictions. The individual is then left with the burning question whether there still remains an even more fundamental, self-transcending meaning to existence. In many instances, such existential crises have been the starting point for a qualitative transformation of one's perceptions.

Søren Kierkegaard invented the term "leap of faith" and argued that life is full of absurdity and the individual must make his or her own values in an indifferent world. For Kierkegaard, an individual can have a meaningful life (or at least one free of despair) if the individual relates the self in an unconditional commitment despite the inherent vulnerability of doing so in the midst our doubt. Genuine meaning is thus possible once the individual reaches the third, or religious, stage of life. Kierkegaard's sincere commitment, far remote from any ivory tower philosophy, brings him into close contact with religious-philosophical approaches in the Far East, such as that of Buddhism, where the attainment of true meaning in life is only possible when the individual passes through several stages before reaching enlightenment that is fulfillment in itself, without any guarantee given from the outside (such as the certainty of salvation).

Although not generally categorized as an existentialist philosopher, Arthur Schopenhauer offered his own bleak answer to "what is the meaning of life?" by determining one's visible life as the reflection of one's will and the Will (and thus life) as being an aimless, irrational, and painful drive. The essence of reality is thus seen by Schopenhauer as totally negative, the only promise of salvation, deliverance, or at least escape from suffering being found in world-denying existential attitudes such as aesthetic contemplation, sympathy for others, and asceticism.

Twentieth-century thinkers like Martin Heidegger and Jean-Paul Sartre are representative of a more extreme form of existentialism where the existential approach takes place within the framework of atheism, rather than Christianity. Gabriel Marcel, on the other hand, is an example of Christian existentialism. For Paul Tillich, the meaning of life is given by one's inevitable pursuit of some ultimate concern, whether it takes on the traditional form of religion or not. Existentialism is thus an orientation of the mind that can be filled with the greatest variety of content, leading to vastly different conclusions.

Skeptical and nihilist views

Main articles: Skepticism and Nihilism

**Skepticism**

Skepticism has always been a strong undercurrent in the history of thought, as uncertainty about meaning and purpose has always existed even in the context of the strongest commitment to a certain view. Skepticism can also be called an everyday existential reality for every human being, alongside whatever commitments or certainties there may be. To some, it takes on the role of doubt to be overcome or endured. To others, it leads to a negative conclusion concerning our possibility of making any credible claim about the meaning of our life.

Skepticism in philosophy has existed since antiquity where it formed several schools of thought in Greece and in Rome. Until recent times, however, overt skepticism has remained a minority position. With the collapse of traditional certainties, skepticism has become increasingly prominent in social and cultural life. Ironically, because of its very nature of denying the possibility of certain knowledge, it is not a position that has produced major thinkers, at least not in its pure form.

The philosophy of Ludwig Wittgenstein and logical positivism, as well as the whole tradition of analytical philosophy represent a particular form of skepticism in that they challenge the very meaningfulness of questions like "the meaning of life," questions that do not involve verifiable statements.

**Nihilism**

Whereas skepticism denies the possibility of certain knowledge and thus rejects any affirmative statement about the meaning of life, nihilism amounts to a flat denial of such meaning or value. Friedrich Nietzsche characterized nihilism as emptying the world and especially human existence of meaning, purpose, comprehensible truth, or essential value. The term nihilism itself comes from the Latin nihil, which means "nothing."

Nihilism thus explores the notion of existence without meaning. Though nihilism tends toward defeatism, one can find strength and reason for celebration in the varied and unique human relationships it explores. From a nihilist point of view, morals are valueless and only hold a place in society as false ideals created by various forces. The characteristic that distinguishes nihilism from other skeptical or relativist philosophies is that, rather than merely insisting that values are subjective or even unwarranted, nihilism declares that nothing is of value, as the name implies.

**Pragmatist views**

Main article: Pragmatism

Pragmatic philosophers suggest that rather than a truth about life, we should seek a useful understanding of life. William James argued that truth could be made but not sought. Thus, the meaning of life is a belief about the purpose of life that does not contradict one's experience of a purposeful life. Roughly, this could be applied as:

"The meaning of life is those purposes which cause you to value it." To a pragmatist, the meaning of life, your life, can be discovered only through experience.

Pragmatism is a school of philosophy which originated in the United States in the late 1800s. Pragmatism is characterized by the insistence on consequences, utility and practicality as vital components of truth. Pragmatism objects to the view that human concepts and intellect represent reality, and therefore stands in opposition to both formalist and rationalist schools of philosophy. Rather, pragmatism holds that it is only in the struggle of intelligent organisms with the surrounding environment that theories and data acquire significance. Pragmatism does not hold, however, that just anything that is useful or practical should be regarded as true, or anything that helps us to survive merely in the short-term; pragmatists argue that what should be taken as true is that which most contributes to the most human good over the longest course. In practice, this means that for pragmatists, theoretical claims should be tied to verification practices—i.e., that one should be able to make predictions and test them—and that ultimately the needs of humankind should guide the path of human inquiry.

**Humanistic views**

Main article: Humanism

Human purpose is determined by humans, completely without supernatural influence. Nor does knowledge come from supernatural sources; it flows from human observation, experimentation, and rational analysis preferably utilizing the scientific method: the nature of the universe is what we discern it to be. As are ethical values, which are derived from human needs and interests as tested by experience.

Enlightened self-interest is at the core of humanism. The most significant thing in life is the human being, and by extension, the human race and the environment in which we live. The happiness of the individual is inextricably linked to the well-being of humanity as a whole, in part because we are social animals which find meaning in relationships, and because cultural progress benefits everybody who lives in that culture.

When the world improves, life in general improves, so, while the individual desires to live well and fully, humanists feel it is important to do so in a way that will enhance the well-being of all. While the evolution of the human species is still (for the most part) a function of nature, the evolution of humanity is in our hands and it is our responsibility to progress it toward its highest ideals. In the same way, humanism itself is evolving, because humanists recognize that values and ideals, and therefore the meaning of life, are subject to change as our understanding improves.

The doctrine of humanism is set forth in the "Humanist Manifesto" and "A Secular Humanist Declaration."

**Atheistic views**

Main article: Atheism

Atheism in its strictest sense means the belief that no God or Supreme Being (of any type or number) exists, and by extension that neither the universe nor its inhabitants were created by such a Being. Because atheists reject supernatural explanations for the existence of life, lacking a deistic source, they commonly point to blind abiogenesis as the most likely source for the origin of life. As for the purpose of life, there is no one particular atheistic view. Some atheists argue that since there are no gods to tell us what to value, we are left to decide for ourselves. Other atheists argue that some sort of meaning can be intrinsic to life itself, so the existence or non-existence of God is irrelevant to the question (a version of Socrates' Euthyphro dilemma). Some believe that life is nothing more than a byproduct of insensate natural forces and has no underlying meaning or grand purpose. Other atheists are indifferent towards the question, believing that talking about meaning without specifying "meaning to whom" is an incoherent or incomplete thought (this can also fit with the idea of choosing the meaning of life for oneself).

# SECTION [3] MEANING OF LIFE IN LITERATURE

Insight into the meaning of life has been a central preoccupation of literature from ancient times. Beginning with Homer through such twentieth-century writers as Franz Kafka, authors have explored ultimate meaning through usually indirect, "representative" depictions of life. For the ancients, human life appeared within the matrix of a cosmological order. In the dramatic saga of war in Homer's Illiad, or the great human tragedies of Greek playwrights such as Sophocles, Aeschylus, and Euripides, inexorable Fate and the machinations of the Gods are seen as overmastering the feeble means of mortals to direct their destiny.

In the Middle Ages, Dante grounded his epic Divine Comedy in an explicitly Christian context, with meaning derived from moral discernment based on the immutable laws of God. The Renaissance humanists Miguel de Cervantes and William Shakespeare influenced much later literature by more realistically portraying human life and beginning an enduring literary tradition of elevating human experience as the grounds upon which meaning may be discerned. With notable exceptions—such as satirists such as François-Marie Voltaire and Jonathan Swift, and explicitly Christian writers such as John Milton—Western literature began to examine human experience for clues to ultimate meaning. Literature became a methodology to explore meaning and to represent truth by holding up a mirror to human life.

In the nineteenth century Honoré de Balzac, considered one of the founders of literary realism, explored French society and studied human psychology in a massive series of novels and plays he collectively titled The Human Comedy. Gustave Flaubert, like Balzac, sought to realistically analyze French life and manners without imposing preconceived values upon his object of study.

Novelist Herman Melville used the quest for the White Whale in Moby-Dick not only as an explicit symbol of his quest for the truth but as a device to discover that truth. The literary method became for Melville a process of philosophic inquiry into meaning. Henry James made explicit this important role in "The Art of Fiction" when he compared the novel to fine art and insisted that the novelist's role was exactly analogous to that of the artist or philosopher:

"As people feel life, so they will feel the art that is most closely related to it. ... Humanity is immense and reality has a myriad forms; ... Experience is never limited and it is never complete; it is an immense sensibility, a kind of huge spider-web, of the finest silken threads, suspended in the chamber of consciousness.[5]

Realistic novelists such as Leo Tolstoy and especially Fyodor Dostoevsky wrote "novels of ideas," recreating Russian society of the late nineteenth century with exacting verisimilitude, but also introducing characters who articulated essential questions concerning the meaning of life. These questions merged into the dramatic plot line in such novels as Crime and

Punishment and The Brothers Karamazov. In the twentieth century Thomas Mann labored to grasp the calamity of the First World War in his philosophical novel The Magic Mountain. Franz Kafka, Jean Paul Sartre, Albert Camus, Samuel Beckett, and other existential writers explored in literature a world where tradition, faith, and moral certitude had collapsed, leaving a void. Existential writers preeminently addressed questions of the meaning of life through studying the pain, anomie, and psychological dislocation of their fictional protagonists. In Kafka's Metamorphosis, to take a well-known example, an office functionary wakes up one morning to find himself transformed into a giant cockroach, a new fact he industriously labors to incorporate into his routine affairs.

The concept of life having a meaning has been both parodied and promulgated, usually indirectly, in popular culture as well. For example, at the end of Monty Python's The Meaning of Life, a character is handed an envelope wherein the meaning of life is spelled out: "Well, it's nothing very special. Uh, try to be nice to people, avoid eating fat, read a good book every now and then, get some walking in, and try to live together in peace and harmony with people of all creeds and nations." Such tongue-in-cheek representations of meaning are less common than film and television presentations that locate the meaning of life in the subjective experience of the individual. This popular post-modern notion generally enables the individual to discover meaning to suit his or her inclinations, marginalizing what are presumed to be dated values, while somewhat inconsistently incorporating the notion of the relativity of values into an absolute principle.

Assessment

Probably the most universal teachings concerning the meaning of life, to be followed in virtually all religions in spite of much diversity of their traditions and positions, are: 1) the ethic of reciprocity among fellow humans, the "Golden Rule," derived from an ultimate being, called God, Allah, Brahman, Taiji, or Tian; and 2) the spiritual dimension of life including an afterlife or eternal life, based on the requirement not to indulge in the external and material aspect of life. Usually, the connection of the two is that the ethic of reciprocity is a preparation in this world for the elevation of spirituality and for afterlife. It is important to note that these two constitutive elements of any religious view of meaning are common to all religious and spiritual traditions, although Jainism's ethical teachings may not be based on any ultimate divine being and the Confucianist theory of the continual existence of ancestors together with descendants may not consider afterlife in the sense of being the other world. These two universal elements of religions are acceptable also to religious literature, the essentialist position in philosophy, and in some way to some of the existentialist position.

Scientific theories can be used to support these two elements, depending upon whether one's perspective is religious or not. For example, the biological function of survival and continuation can be used in support of the religious doctrine of eternal life, and modern physics can be considered not to preclude some spiritual dimension of the universe. Also, when science observes the reciprocity of orderly relatedness, rather than random development, in the universe, it can support the ethic of reciprocity in the Golden Rule. Of course, if one's perspective is not religious, then science may not be considered to support religion. Recently, however, the use of science in support of religious claims has greatly increased, and it is evidenced by the publication of many books and articles on the relationship of science and religion. The importance of scientific investigations on the origin and nature of life, and of the universe in which we live, has been increasingly recognized, because the question on the meaning of life has been acknowledged to need more than religious answers, which, without scientific support, are feared to sound irrelevant and obsolete in the age of science and technology. Thus, religion is being forced to take into account the data and systematic answers provided by science. Conversely, the role of religion has become that of offering a meaningful explanation of possible solutions suggested by science.

It is interesting to observe that humanists, who usually deny the existence of God and of afterlife, believe that it is important for all humans to love and respect one another: "Humanists acknowledge human interdependence, the need for mutual respect and the kinship of all humanity."[6] Also, much of secular literature, even without imposing preconceived values, describes the beauty of love and respect in the midst of hatred and chaos in human life. Also, even a common sense discussion on the meaning of life can argue for the existence of eternal life, for the notion of self-destruction at one's death would appear to make the meaning of life destroyed along with life itself. Thus, the two universal elements of religions seem not to be totally alien to us.

Christian theologian Millard J. Erickson sees God's blessing for humans to be fruitful, multiply, and have dominion over the earth (Genesis 1:28) as "the purpose or reason for the creation of humankind."[7] This biblical account seems to refer to the ethical aspect of the meaning of life, which is the reciprocal relationship of love involving multiplied humanity and all creation centering on God, although, seen with secular eyes, it might be rather difficult to accept the ideal of such a God-given purpose or meaning of life based on simple observation of the world situation." [Source: https://www.newworldencyclopedia.org/entry/Meaning_of_life]

Author is of the view that the origin of life as narrated in the foregoing Articles cannot be precisely deciphered and has to be understood as stated therein. Author believes the path followed by the rishis in Hinduism as well as revealed in Islam and Christianity are the only paths to know oneself about the origin of life, these having been based on spirituality rather than any scientifically demonstrated. The Articles on the subject matter as seen by the author, though are in detail but none is conclusive. It cannot be so also because the subject comes within the realm of Spirituality and the Holy Scripts of Saints and Sages. The spirituality is to person per se.

It is open to every one for seeking the path for spiritual Enlightment and is dependent upon the degree of commitment, dedication and devotion. These kinds of people exist today in our country and presumably in other countries in the world that are following the path to trace the source of spiritual Enlightenment. Based on their attainment to the extent the circumstances permitted them, they continue to preach to the devotees that open up an opportunity to interact with them to better understand.

With due respects to the learned writers cited before on the Meaning of Life, the author wishes to submit that the Spirit in the body of every living being including human is the manifestation of God. The Soul is Life in every living being including the human and is personal to the Being. The womb is the place where the Life is ascertainable according to the modern methods. When the baby is born through the process of the womb, its first call to Mother Earth is crying. That means the baby is born with Life bestowed upon it by the Spirit present in the baby. The Life cannot exist without the Spirit whether among the humans or other living beings on Mother Earth. The day the Spirit leaves the body whether of the humans or of other living beings on Mother Earth, the Being is said to be dead. It is respectfully submitted that the the Life before it enters the womb is beyond the comprehension of the humans, howsoever the human is learned.

Such capacity to comprehend about the Life existed and continues to exist among the Prophets, Sages and Saints who have acquired it through the process of the Spirituality. That is the spiritual process and, as noted before, until it manifests in the womb blessed with the

Spirit, the humans are not capable to say anything about the Life and their capability to say so comes to know about Life in womb through the prevalent scientific and medical methodologies. The entire spectrum of Life lies within the domain of the Spirit and once the Spirit bestows the Life in any Being, it assumes the character of Soul as Life which is personal to every Being on Mother Earth. The Souls which are specific to their birth are innumerable but the Spirit [God] is One in One and All.

# SECTION [4] RELIGIONS

## South Asian religions

### Hinduism

For Hindus, the purpose of life is described by the purusharthas, the four ends of human life. These goals are, from lowest to highest importance: Kāma (sensual pleasure or love), Artha (wealth), Dharma (righteousness or morality) and Moksha (liberation from the cycle of reincarnation). Dharma connotes general moral and ethical ideas such as honesty, responsibility, respect, and care for others, which people fulfill in the course of life as a householder and contributing member of society. Those who renounce home and career practice a life of meditation and austerities to reach Moksha.

Hinduism is an extremely diverse religion. Most Hindus believe that the soul—the true "self" of every being, called the ātman—is eternal. According to the monistic/pantheistic theologies of Hinduism (such as the Advaita Vedanta school), the ātman is ultimately indistinct from Brahman, the supreme spirit. Brahman is described as "The One without a Second"; hence these schools are called "non-dualist." The goal of life according to the Advaita school is to realize that one's ātman (soul) is identical to Brahman, the supreme soul. The Upanishads state that whoever becomes fully aware of the ātman as the innermost core of one's own self realizes their identity with Brahman and thereby reaches Moksha (liberation or freedom).[2]

Other Hindu schools, such as the dualist Dvaita Vedanta and other bhakti schools understand Brahman as a Supreme Being who possesses personality. On these conceptions, the ātman is dependent on Brahman, and the meaning of life is to achieve Moksha through love towards God and on God's grace.

Whether non-dualist (Advaita) or dualist (Dvaita), the bottom line is the idea that all humans are deeply interconnected with one another through the unity of the ātman and Brahman, and therefore, that they are not to injure one another but to care for one another.

**Islam**

What is Islam?

Islam is one of the world's major religions, followed by over 1.9 billion people globally. It is a faith based on the principles of monotheism, the belief in one Allah, and was revealed to the world through the Prophet Muhammad ﷺ in the 7th century.

The foundation of the religion of Islam was laid in Mecca, Arabia by the Prophet Muhammad ﷺ himself. Today, Islam is spreading quickly around the world. Also, it's one of the largest religions in the Middle East, Central Asia and South Asia. Indonesia, as it happens, leads with the largest number of Muslims in any Muslim-majority country worldwide.

What does Islam mean?

Islam, which in Arabic means "submission," calls for believers to submit to the will of Allah and live according to His guidance.

The word "Islam" comes from the Arabic root "Salam" which means peace, purity, and submission. A Muslim, therefore, is someone who practices this submission and follows the teachings of Islam.

How did Islam begin?

History of Islam began in the early 7th century in Mecca (modern-day Saudi Arabia) with the last Prophet of Allah, Hazrat Muhammad ﷺ, who is the last of prophets عليهم السلام in a long line of messengers sent by Allah throughout the history of mankind. Muhammad ﷺ received revelations from Allah Almighty through the Angel Jibreel over 23 years.

These revelations were compiled into the Quran, the holy book of Islam. The focus of these divine revelations was Tawheed - belief in one Allah or monotheism, Risalat - finality of prophethood, social justice, and moral conduct which form the basis of Islamic teachings.

Who is Allah (God)?

Some people believe that Muslims worship a God that is different from the one worshipped by Christians and Jews. This concept is false. Allah is simply the Arabic word for God. Muslims worship the same God who created the universe and all humanity: the God of Noah, Abraham, Moses, David and Jesus عليهم السلام.

In Islam, Allah Almighty is the one and only God. This is Tawheed and one has to believe in it to be a Muslim. So, according to the Islamic ideology, Allah is the Creator and Sustainer of the universe. Unlike other faiths, Muslims believe that Allah is beyond any human characteristics and cannot be represented in any physical form. He has no image and he cannot be seen.

Moreover, Allah Almighty is all alone in the reign over the entire universe. The essence of Islamic monotheism is that Allah is unique, eternal, and omnipotent, with no partners or equals.

Islam Basic Beliefs - What do Muslims believe?

The basic Islam beliefs of Oneness of Allah and Prophethood of Muhammad ﷺ are the same for Muslims around the world. However, there are other important beliefs as declared in the Holy Quran. So, to be a Muslim one has to hold a set of core beliefs. These include:

- Belief in one God (Allah).
- Belief in angels.
- Belief in the revealed books (including the Quran, Torah, and Bible).
- Belief in the prophets, from Hazrat Adam عَلَيْهِ ٱلسَّلَامُ to Hazrat Muhammad ﷺ.
- Belief in the Day of Judgment and the life after death.
- Belief in divine decree, meaning Allah's knowledge and control over all things.

What are the Five Pillars of Islam?

The holy Prophet Muhammad ﷺ based Islam religion on five basic pillars. These can also be called the Foundations of Islam. These pillars are the foundation of Muslim worship and practice, fostering a sense of community and discipline. Since, the Five Pillars of Islam are the core practices; every Muslim is required to follow them.

Shahada (Faith)

The declaration that "there is no deity worthy of being worshipped except Allah and Muhammad ﷺ is His messenger." This declaration testifies that Allah Almighty exists and he is dissimilar and superior to his creation and that none is worthy of worship but Him. The Shahada also testifies that the beloved Prophet Muhammad is among the prophets عليهم السلام who conveyed Allah Almighty's revelation to humankind.

Salat (Prayer)

Performing five daily prayers from dawn to dusk facing the Kaaba. Salah was performed in some form or the other throughout history by all Prophets عليهم السلام and their followers as an essential part of Almighty Allah's religion. However, Islam considers it crucial. So, a Muslim is required to pray five times a day within specific periods as taught by the Holy Prophet Muhammad ﷺ.

Zakat (Charity)

The word Zakaah means purification and growth. In Islam, an important principle is giving to the poor. This amount donated is called zakaah. Giving a fixed portion of one's wealth as decreed by the sharia to help those in need. Zakaat is only due on Muslims that have the minimum required amount which varies with the type of wealth. Zakaah is a major source to cleanse your heart from greed, selfishness and the love of temporary world.

Sawm (Fasting)

Allah Almighty has instructed Muslims to observe the fast dawn to sunset during the holy month of Ramadan. The Islamic way of fasting involves abstinence from eating, drinking, smoking and sexual intercourse, etc. The is observed throughout the daylight hours of the lunar month of Ramadan. Also, fasting is not a retreat from life, it is a supplement to the Muslims' ordinary activities.

Hajj (Pilgrimage)

The annual pilgrimage to Mecca is a once-in-a-lifetime obligation. That means undertaking a pilgrimage to Mecca at least once in a lifetime is mandatory for every Muslim - if physically and financially able. Millions of Muslims journey to the Sanctified city of Makkah each year from all corners of the globe. This provides a unique opportunity for people of various nations to meet one another as guests of Allah. Moreover, a person that has completed hajj comes out with a fresh outlook on life, with a purified soul and blessings from Allah.

Quran and Hadith

The foundations of Islam rest on two primary sources: the Quran, the verbatim word of Allah as revealed to the Prophet Muhammad ﷺ, and the Hadith, a collection of the sayings and actions of the Prophet Muhammad ﷺ.

Quran

The Glorious Quran presents all the Prophets of Allah Almighty as belonging to one single brotherhood. All the prophets' عليهم السلام had a similar mission and conveyed the same basic message.

The source of their message was Allah. Similarly, the source of the Quran is Allah Himself. Moreover, the Holy Quran was revealed to humanity at large and not to any specific nation. So, all humanity can benefit from its timeless and ultimate wisdom.

Hadith and Sunnah

Hadiths are the sayings of the Holy Prophet Muhammad ﷺ. Sunnah is the way the Holy Prophet ﷺ led his life. These are example from which Muslims can receive guidance in their everyday life. Both of these, Hadith and Sunnah, help Muslims to lead a life of purity, truth and righteousness.

So, the texts of Quran and Sunnah provide guidance on every aspect of life, from spiritual worship to daily human interactions, and they are studied by Muslims to live a life in accordance with Allah's will.

Islamic Practices and Festivals

Daily life for a Muslim involves practices that remind them of their connection to Allah Almighty. In addition to the five basic pillars of Islam, Muslims follow dietary laws (like abstaining from pork and alcohol), adhere to modest dress, and follow ethical and moral guidelines in business and personal dealings.

Furthermore, regular recitation of the Holy Quran (Tilawat) and remembrance of Allah (dhikr) are integral parts of a Muslim's spiritual practice.

Muslims also celebrate special occasions like Eid ul Fitr which comes after Ramadan and Eid ul Adha in which Muslims offer sacrifice of cattle, sheep, goat, camel, etc. for Allah Almighty. These are the two main festivals in Islam. Eid Milad un Nabi is the birthday of the prophet ﷺ and widespread celebrations are held in the Prophet's ﷺ honor.

Islam facts

- Islam Religion is the second-largest in the world after Christianity.

- The Quran is written in Arabic, and while it has been translated into many languages, Arabic remains the liturgical language of Islam.

- Muslims consider Mecca, Medina, and Jerusalem as the three holiest cities.

- Islam has a rich cultural heritage, with contributions to art, science, literature, and architecture. [Source:https://www.dawateislami.net/discover-islam/en/islam ]

**Buddhism**

One of the central views in Buddhism is a nondual worldview, in which subject and object are the same, and the sense of doer-ship is illusionary. On this account, the meaning of life is to become enlightened as to the nature and oneness of the universe. According to the scriptures, the Buddha taught that in life there exists dukkha, which is in essence sorrow/suffering, that is caused by desire and it can be brought to cessation by following the Noble Eightfold Path. This teaching is called the Catvāry

Āryasatyāni (Pali: Cattāri Ariyasaccāni), or the "Four Noble Truths":

## Jainism

Jainism teaches that every human is responsible for his or her actions. The Jain view of karma is that every action, every word, every thought produces, besides its visible, an invisible, transcendental effect on the soul. The ethical system of Jainism promotes self-discipline above all else. By following the ascetic teachings of the Tirthankara or Jina, the 24 enlightened spiritual masters, a human can reach a point of enlightenment, where he or she attains infinite knowledge and is delivered from the cycle of reincarnation beyond the yoke of karma. That state is called Siddhashila. Although Jainism does not teach the existence of God(s), the ascetic teachings of the Tirthankara are highly developed regarding right faith, right knowledge, and right conduct. The meaning of life consists in achievement of complete enlightenment and bliss in Siddhashila by practicing them.

Jains also believe that all living beings have an eternal soul, jīva, and that all souls are equal because they all possess the potential of being liberated. So, Jainism includes strict adherence to ahimsa (or ahinsā), a form of nonviolence that goes far beyond vegetarianism. Food obtained with unnecessary cruelty is refused. Hence the universal ethic of reciprocity in Jainism: "Just as pain is not agreeable to you, it is so with others. Knowing this principle of equality treat other with respect and compassion" (Saman Suttam 150).

## Sikhism

Sikhism sees life as an opportunity to understand God the Creator as well as to discover the divinity which lies in each individual. God is omnipresent (sarav viāpak) in all creation and visible everywhere to the spiritually awakened. Guru Nanak Dev stresses that God must be seen from "the inward eye," or the "heart," of a human being: devotees must meditate to progress towards enlightenment. In this context of the omnipresence of God, humans are to love one another, and they are not enemies to one another.

According to Sikhism, every creature has a soul. In death, the soul passes from one body to another until final liberation. The journey of the soul is governed by the karma of the deeds and actions we perform during our lives, and depending on the goodness or wrongdoings committed by a person in their life they will either be rewarded or punished in their next life. As the spirit of God is found in all life and matter, a soul can be passed onto other life forms, such as plants and insects - not just human bodies. A person who has evolved to achieve spiritual perfection in his lifetimes attains salvation – union with God and liberation from rebirth in the material world.

East Asian religions

In Taoism, the Taijitu symbolizes the unity of opposites between ying and yang, described in the theory of the Taiji.

Confucianism

Confucianism places the meaning of life in the context of human relationships. People's character is formed in the given relationships to their parents, siblings, spouse, friends and social roles. There is need for discipline and education to learn the ways of harmony and success within these social contexts. The purpose of life, then, is to fulfill one's role in society, by showing honesty, propriety, politeness, filial piety, loyalty, humaneness, benevolence, etc. in accordance with the order in the cosmos manifested by Tian (Heaven).

Confucianism deemphasizes afterlife. Even after humans pass away, they are connected with their descendants in this world through rituals deeply rooted in the virtue of filial piety that closely links different generations. The emphasis is on normal living in this world, according to the contemporary scholar of Confucianism Wei-Ming Tu, "We can realize the ultimate meaning of life in ordinary human existence."[4]

Daoism

The Daoist cosmogony emphasizes the need for all humans and all sentient beings to return to the primordial or to rejoin with the Oneness of the Universe by way of self-correction and self-realization. It is the objective for all adherents to understand and be in tune with the Dao (Way) of nature's ebb and flow.

Within the theology of Daoism, originally all humans were beings called yuanling ("original spirits") from Taiji and Tao, and the meaning in life for the adherents is to realize the temporal nature of their existence, and all adherents are expected to practice, hone and conduct their mortal lives by way of Xiuzhen (practice of the truth) and Xiushen (betterment of the self), as a preparation for spiritual transcendence here and hereafter.

"Religion has played an important role in the life of human beings from ancient times. Unable to understand or explain the complexities of nature, early humanity sought answers through their religious beliefs. Over the years, many different religions have emerged with their core beliefs, values, practices and rituals. However, among social scientists, there has been a considerable debate about the conceptualization and measurement of religiosity. While some scholars have conceptualized religiosity as a multi-dimensional construct, others have argued that religiosity represents a single construct. Arguments have also been presented whether the treatment of religiosity as a single dimensional construct or a multidimensional construct should be based on the objective of the research. Despite this debate, there is some degree of agreement that religiosity comprises three integral components: affiliation, activity (attendance or participation in religious activities) and corresponding beliefs. Also, this agreement does not imply that there is consensus about the measurement of religiosity. Hill and Hood have compiled a long list of scales to measure religiosity and related constructs. Moreover, studies attempting to establish measurement invariance of a scale of religiosity could not be located. For the purpose of the present research, we conceptualize religiosity to be a single dimensional construct. Similar to the argument presented by Schwartz and Huisman, it is desirable to consider religiosity as a single dimensional construct because this research is focusing on evaluating measurement invariance of a scale to measure religiosity and the samples are drawn from heterogeneous populations." (Source: Mathur, A. J Target Meas Anal Mark (2012) 20: 84. https://doi.org/10.1057/jt.2012.6)

"A religion is a set of spiritual beliefs about two key aspects of life: concern with the ultimate meaning of human existence; and identification with a supernatural power beyond the limits of the human and natural worlds. The many different religions have different beliefs about these two aspects of life. However, religions generally have the following characteristics in common: A belief in supernatural beings, or gods; A code of morality believed to be sanctioned by the gods; Ceremonial and ritual acts which focus on sacred objects and symbols; Communication, notably through prayer, with the supernatural; Particular religious feelings, such as a sense of mystery, awe, adoration and reverence, that tend to be aroused in the presence of sacred objects or symbols, and during ceremonies and rituals associated with the supernatural; A particular world view, or a general understanding of the world and the individual's place in the universe, that shapes the religion's overall organization and style of life; and A social group expressing the above features with and to which the individual identifies and contributes." (Source: Adapted from Bell, R. and Hall, R. (1991) Impacts: Contemporary Issues and Global Problems, Jacaranda Press, Brisbane.)

Our country consists of various cultures and religions. Those cultures and religions born from the Holy Scripts. Our society is the mixture of cultures and religions living in next door and neighborhood visible to each other's eyes. Share each other's pleasant times and sorrows. It is natural, at times, that differences arise but those differences are not made arousing because the essence of living together gains greater support and strength. That is how our country is formed and lives. Intermittent quarrels also happen on one pretext or the other. Living together does not allow them to persist because of power of reconciliation and mutuality. Environment of living thus fostered is long lasting. Being belonging to different cultures and religions within that togetherness or collective living, each one of them practice their Faith and Belief. They consider it sinful to criticize one other's Faith and Belief that is what they learn from their Holy Scripts. They may be of different Faiths but convey essence of mutual appreciation and harmony.

Experience over the past seventy five years also shows that what is said here is open to provocations and disharmony. This operates through a different kind of modus operandi which is created by certain vested interests seizing opportunities found favorable to them. They represent by and large the political and religious class. They are actively involved but invisible. They control the operation silently through remote control. They want to live with and enjoy the British Legacy "Divide and Rule". We use divide and rule to refer to a policy which is intended to keep someone in a position of power by causing disagreements between people who might otherwise unite against them. Even a religio-political theorist of the Pakistan movement and a zealous supporter of the two nation theory' (F.K. Khan Durrani. The Meaning of Pakistan. Lahore, S.H. Muhammad

Ashraf. 19~p.29) argued: "The plain undisputable fact is that communal riots between the two peoples are not a feature of Indian history. It is towards the close of the 19th century that we come to bear of Hindu Muslim riots for the first time. Even then they remained few and far between. It was after 1923 that they began to become a regular feature of Indian life. And quite convincingly he blamed the British rule for creating animosity between the two denominations."

"The seeds of 'Divide and rule' were sown by British Imperial Rule, but blossomed in full after India gained Independence in 1947. While laying down the foundation of some democratic institutions and policies, the Imperial rulers set the example of how policies of great scope can be used for serving the vested interests of political leaders/political parties in power. The Indian politicians have inherited from British rulers three powerful democratic weapons i.e. Electoral policy, Census operations, and Reservation Policy. The present day politicians have learnt very well from British rulers, how to use these systems for pacifying the masses and prolonging their hold on political authority longer. They are following the footsteps of their predecessor i.e. British Imperialist rulers and are creating their own separate empires." [Source: Latasinha's Weblog - Social and political Values and Systems in India.]

In India, we are increasingly witnessing the harmful effects of hateful, derogatory, communal and divisive rhetoric made by our political leaders, their parties and politically inspired independent organizations. In theory, the democratic framework exists in our country but in practice, the politicians are strengthening the British Empire policy as evident from the continued use of the same weapons today as could be seen in our daily democratic life. The weapons stated before which were there during the British Empire seem to have been further sharpened rather than blunting them after the country became independent.

The weapons used then are the same being used by the politicians, namely, Electoral policy, Census operations and Reservation policy. These continue to be the topics of the day in our democracy. Additionally, the religions have found and made their place in the democratic system which are also voicing in all the four corners of the country. The dynastic rule both at the national and state level that stretched over fifty eight years after the independence, of which, twenty eight years included wholly the dynasticism. This is being pursued vigorously even today. Then, where is the democratic voice in the country?

Author knows he is erroneously dealing this subject matter in this book but has no option having regard to the fact that the citizen's lives and religions that come within the domain of the God are integral part of our constitution which is one and the same for all the citizens of the country. The presence of God in every aspect of the citizens and institutional lives is being pushed backward which is the sign of disharmony in harmony. There is a need for the future generations to reset this trend and uphold the moral and ethical values bestowed by the God upon the humans. Lest, dehumanization process in the democratic life will set in, the end results of which are unpredictable? First safeguard the moral and ethical values both of the citizens and of the democratic framework embedded in the constitution that alone has the guiding virtue towards couching our democracy; no system works without first respecting and upholding the given values by the God to the humans. This is the Rule of the Mother Earth for the humans as the laws are for the citizens. The latter has no value unless we first accord highest respect for the former.

It is time for all of us to stop responding to dangerous political rhetoric. The next time a politician asks a woman to not go out, we should ask the politician to make our streets safer, the next time a leader asks Hindus and Muslims to remain at a distance from one another, we should ask our leader to remember that we are a secular nation and the next time a leader propagates that it's anti-national to be learning English and computers, we should remind him of the dismal state of our economy. Political rhetoric is dangerous, but only because we feed into it." This is precisely the approach we should adopt .The political and religious leaders will always be haunting a hunting ground and every one of us should realize that if and when any of such leader's intentions are indicative of his divide and rule postures, such person should be given such a blunt answer, such as the one above and should be publicly shamed to stop him right there. It is our pursuit of life to live together, smile together and share together and any one interfering in such ideals must be branded as the betrayer of his Faith. Such people are generally 'Paid' people forced to do by someone sitting at home or elsewhere watching what has happened or what is happening and what could be done to further instigate it if not showing the motives concealed in the eyes. The political and religious leaders also should realize that if the fire of hatred and insult is to play freely among the dominations, the fire would return to their homes and engulf it because it is nature's fury to jump in one form or the other against such persons doing greatest harm to the wellbeing of the peaceful society.

To promote harmony and the spirit of common brotherhood amongst all the people of India transcending religious, linguistic and regional or sectional diversities; to renounce practices derogatory to the dignity of women is one of the fundamental duties of every citizen to be maintained and ensured. These duties, set out in Part IV–A of the Constitution concern individuals and the nation. Citizens are morally obligated by the Constitution to perform these duties. However, like the Directive Principles, these are non-justiciable, without any legal sanction in case of their violation or non-compliance. It may be so but there are a number of provisions in the existing criminal laws to ensure that the activities which encourage enmity between different groups of people on grounds of religion, race, place of birth, residence, language, etc. are adequately punished. Writings, speeches, gestures, activities, exercise, drills, etc. aimed at creating a feeling of insecurity or ill-will among the members of other communities, etc. have been prohibited under Section 153A of the Indian Penal Code (IPC). Sections 123(3) and 123(3A) of the Representation of People Act, 1951 declares that soliciting of vote on the ground of religion and the promotion or attempt to promote feelings of enmity or hatred between different classes of citizens of India on the grounds of religion, race, caste, community or language is a corrupt practice. A person indulging in a corrupt practice can be disqualified for being a Member of Parliament or a State Legislature under Section 8A of the Representation of People Act, 1951.

Are our learned politicians and religious leaders not aware of these provisions in the constitution and in other laws made under the constitution? They know but don't intend to practice in life rather they think it more beneficial for self-growth to promote hatred and disharmony among the citizens' on one pretext or the other. As noted earlier, the vision of independence incorporated in the constitution has, however, faded away, reminding one that as our nation gains more years of independence, our sight has also become increasingly clouded. Today, we are shocked to witness the news we read, the stories we hear and the dangerous political rhetoric that is now clear propaganda for modern day divide-and-rule policies by our political leaders. So also the practice followed in religious matters. The religious and caste cult is openly and brazenly talked about in political speeches including in election campaigns. Law enforcing agencies are silently watching what all is happening. This may be because of unnoticeable pressures upon them from some source who consider those making such speeches are respectable leaders and stand above the rule of law. Wintson S. Churchill said "The letter of the law must not in supreme emergency obstruct those who are charged with its protection and enforcement. It would not be right or rational that the aggressor power should gain one set of advantages by tearing up all laws, and another set by sheltering behind the innate respect for law of its opponents. Humanity, rather than legality, must be our guide" (Churchill, Winston S., The Gathering strom (Bostom, Mass: Houghton Mifflin Co., 1948) P.547.).

These respected leaders are knowingly showing their ignorance to disregard the moral obligations and fundamental duties they expect to be observed by every citizen which also forms part of their speech depending upon the occasion. For them, the moral obligations and fundamental duties seem to be occasion based for, what is against the moral obligation and fundamental duties becomes moral and not obligatory to comply on one occasion and vice versa on another occasion. They claim to be the leaders of the people promising them to do their best for the wellbeing and welfare of those people. This is the state of mind of our leaders today. Then, who should protect the moral obligation and fundamental duties enshrined in the constitution for the human benefit?

# SECTION [5] ATHEIST VS AGNOSTIC

Atheist vs. Agnostic: What's The Difference? - August 15, 2022 "In the context of religious and spiritual belief—or non-belief—there are two terms that often cause confusion: *atheist* and *agnostic*. But these terms do not mean the same thing. Read on to learn the distinction.

Agnostic vs. Atheist

There is a key distinction between these terms. An atheist doesn't believe in the existence of a god or divine being. The word atheist originates with the Greek atheos, which is built from the roots a- ("without") and theos ("a god"). Atheism is the doctrine or belief that there is no god.

In contrast, the word agnostic refers to a person who neither believes nor disbelieves in a god or religious doctrine. Agnostics assert that it's impossible to know how the universe was created and whether or not divine beings exist.

The word agnostic was coined by biologist T.H. Huxley and comes from the Greek ágnōstos, which means "unknown or unknowable." The doctrine is known as agnosticism.

Both atheist and agnostic can also be used as adjectives. The adjective atheistic is also used. And the word agnostic can also be used in a more general way outside the context of religion to describe stances that do not adhere to either side of an opinion, argument, etc.

Theist vs. Deist

To complicate matters, atheists and agnostics are often confused with theists and deists. A theist is the opposite of an atheist. Theists believe in the existence of a god or gods."

These doctrines are based on humans' understanding with underlying difference that one believes in god while the other does not. The doctrines however, include the word 'god', the belief or non-belief being a matter of choice of the humans as stated in the respective doctrines. The existence and belief in god are two different matters but the sole matter that god exists is not denied but belief stands apart. [Source: https://www.dictionary.com/e/atheism-agnosticism/

# SECTION [6]
# WHO CREATED THE GOD

From the views and expressions of the Saints, Sages and Holy Scripts of major Religions noted in the preceding Sections, one could naturally invest in the faith that God does exist and, by virtue of that, Mother Earth exists. Questions have been raised by the learned scholars in the world that 'Who Created God? There is no scope for us to question the Question or dispute about what is raised in Question. There is, however, scope for the humans to ponder over the Question based on what the Great Saints, Sages and Holy Scripts also say on the subject matter. Their thoughts and knowledge in this regard passed through the past civilizations who would have confronted with the Question and what they answered or expressed is critical for us, the humans, that being the only Source to seek the answer to the Question. On the face of it, though the Question seems to be illusory but we cannot ignore the fact that the Question had been raised. What is, however, important for us the humans is whether we should believe the Question or believe in them who pointedly answered the Question from their deep and scholarly approach to the Question and placed before the humans whether or not it was worthwhile to have asked the Question? Author wishes to proceed towards this aspect to know from the scholars who lived in the past as also from those who are living in the present to match the old thoughts with modern thoughts to understand what kind of difference lies in between them. Before that, read the Quote: *"TELL ME AND I FORGET, TEACH ME AND I MAY REMEMBER, INVOLVE ME AND I LEARN." – BENJAMIN FRANKLIN.* That is what inspires the author to involve himself into this cosmic area beyond the control of the humans to comprehend, yet one's involvement in search of it guides one to learn about it.

Wikipedia notes in this respect as under:
**Problem of the creator of God**

From Wikipedia, the free encyclopedia

"In philosophy, the **problem of the creator of God** is the controversy regarding the hypothetical cause responsible for the existence of God, on the assumption God exists. It contests the proposition that the universe cannot exist without a creator by asserting that the creator of the Universe must have the same restrictions. This, in turn, may lead to a problem of infinite regress wherein each new presumed creator of a creator is itself presumed to have its own creator. A common challenge to theistic propositions of a creator deity as a necessary first-cause explanation for the universe is the question: "Who created God?"[1] Some faith traditions have such an element as part of their doctrine. Jainism posits that the universe is eternal and has always existed. Isma'ilism rejects the idea of God as the *first cause*, due to the doctrine of God's incomparability and source of any existence including abstract objects.[2]

Perspectives

[edit]

Osho writes:

No, don't ask that. That's what all the religions say – don't ask who created God. But this is strange – why not? If the question is valid about existence, why does it become invalid when it is applied to God? And once you ask who created God, you are falling into a regress absurdum.[3]

John Humphreys writes:

... If someone were able to provide the explanation, we would be forced to embark upon what philosophers call an infinite regress. Having established who created God, we would then have to answer the question of who created God's creator.[4]

Alan Lurie writes:

In response to one of my blogs about God's purpose in the creation of the universe, one person wrote, "All you've done is diverting the question. If God created the Universe, who created God? That is a dilemma that religious folks desperately try to avoid." The question, "Who created God?", has been pondered by theologians for millennia, and the answer is both surprisingly obvious and philosophically subtle ... whatever one thinks about the beginnings of the Universe, there is "something" at the very origin that was not created. This is an inescapable given, a cosmic truth.[5] [Emphasis added by the author]

Joseph Smith stated in the King Follett discourse:

God himself was once as we are now, and is an exalted man, and sits enthroned in yonder heavens! That is the great secret. If the veil were rent today, and the great God who holds this world in its orbit, and who upholds all worlds and all things by His power, was to make himself visible—I say, if you were to see him today, you would see him like a man in form—like yourselves in all the person, image, and very form as a man ... it is necessary we should understand the character and being of God and how He came to be so; for I am going to tell you how God came to be God. We have imagined and supposed that God was God from all eternity. I will refute that idea, and take away the veil ... It is the first principle of the gospel to know for a certainty the character of God, and to know that we may converse with Him as one man converses with another, and that He was once a man like us; yea, that God himself, the Father of us all, dwelt on an earth, the same as Jesus Christ Himself did ... Is it logic to say that a spirit is immortal and yet has a beginning? Because if a spirit has a beginning, it will have an end. ... All the fools and learned and wise men from the beginning of creation who say that man had a beginning prove that he must have an end. If that were so, the doctrine of annihilation would be true. But if I am right, I might with boldness proclaim from the house tops that God never did have power to create the spirit of man at all. God himself could not create himself. Intelligence exists upon a self-existent principle; it is a spirit from age to age, and there is no creation about it. Moreover, all the spirits that God ever sent into the world are susceptible to enlargement.

Responses

[edit]

Defenders of religion have countered that, by definition, God is the first cause, and thus that the question is improper:

We ask, "If all things have a creator, then who created God?" Actually, only created things have a creator, so it's improper to lump God with his creation. God has revealed himself to us in the Bible as having always existed.[6]

Ray Comfort, author and evangelist, writes:

No person or thing created God. He created "time," and because we dwell in the dimension of time, *reason* demands that all things have a beginning and an end. God, however, dwells outside of the dimension of time. He moves through time as we flip through a history book...He dwells in "eternity," having no beginning or end.[7]

Tzvi Freeman writes on the official Chabad website:

Ibn Sina, the preeminent Arabic philosopher, answered this question a thousand years ago, when he described G-d as non-contingent, absolute existence. If so, to ask "Why is there G-d?" is the equivalent of asking, "Why is there is-ness?"[8]

Atheists counter that there is no reason to assume the universe was created. The question becomes irrelevant if the universe is presumed to have circular time instead of linear time, undergoing an infinite series of big bangs and big crunches on its own.[9]

John Lennox, professor of Mathematics at Oxford writes:[10]

Now Dawkins candidly tells us that he does not like people telling him that they also do not believe in the God in which he does not believe. But we cannot afford to base our arguments on his dislikes. For, whether he likes it or not, he openly invites the charge. After all, it is he who is arguing that God is a delusion. In order to weigh his argument we need first of all to know what he means by God. And his main argument is focused on a created God. Well, several billion of us would share his disbelief in such a god. He needn't have bothered. Most of us have long since been convinced of what he is trying to tell us. Certainly, no Christian would ever dream of suggesting that God was created. Nor, indeed, would Jews or Muslims. His argument, by his own admission, has nothing to say about an eternal God. It is entirely beside the point. Dawkins should shelve it on the shelf marked 'Celestial Teapots' where it belongs. For the God who created and upholds the universe was not created – he is eternal. He was not 'made' and therefore subject to the laws that science discovered; it was he who made the universe with its laws. Indeed, that fact constitutes the fundamental distinction between God and the universe. The universe came to be, God did not."

## Indian Philosophy Website - Swami Vivekananda on God, Cosmos, and the Human Spirit - December 24, 2023

"Swami Vivekananda, one of India's most revered spiritual leaders, brought forth a revolutionary view of God, the cosmos, and the human spirit. His philosophy, deeply rooted in Vedantic ideals, offers a unique perspective on the interconnectedness of the universe, the divine and human existence. For Vivekananda, the ultimate reality—Brahman—is the foundation of all things, transcending time, space, and causality. Through his teachings, he presents a monistic approach to life, where the divine is not just a distant force but is intimately woven into the fabric of everything, including each human being. In this blog, we will delve into Swami Vivekananda's profound insights on God, the cosmos, and the human spirit, exploring how his ideas foster a vision of spiritual unity that remains relevant even today.

**The Nature of Reality: Monism and Brahman**

Swami Vivekananda's philosophy is deeply influenced by the ancient Vedantic tradition, particularly Advaita Vedanta, which advocates a monistic view of reality. According to this view, there is only one fundamental substance that underlies everything in the universe—Brahman. Brahman is the ultimate reality, eternal and beyond human comprehension. It is neither created nor destroyed, existing beyond the constraints of time, space, and causality. For Vivekananda, the apparent diversity of the world—be it in nature, humans, or gods—arises from this single, unified source.

In his lectures and writings, Vivekananda repeatedly emphasized the oneness of all existence. The world, as we perceive it, is an illusion or "Maya," which veils the underlying unity of Brahman. This monistic view denies the duality between the divine and the material world, suggesting that everything in existence, from the highest spiritual experiences to the most mundane aspects of life, is an expression of Brahman. This perspective is rooted in the ancient Upanishadic teachings, where Brahman is described as both immanent (present in all things) and transcendent (beyond the limitations of the material world).

**God: Impersonal and Personal**

One of the most profound aspects of Vivekananda's philosophy is his interpretation of God. He presents God as both impersonal and personal, a nuanced view that sets his teachings apart from traditional religious notions. Vivekananda explained that God is ultimately impersonal—Brahman, the formless, omnipresent, and omniscient essence that underlies all creation. This formless aspect of God transcends all human concepts and cannot be fully grasped by the limited human mind.

However, Vivekananda also acknowledged the need for a personal conception of God for the spiritual development of individuals. For the ordinary person, the abstract, impersonal Brahman may seem too distant and incomprehensible. Thus, he advocated the worship of God in a personal form—whether as Vishnu, Shiva, or any other deity that resonates with the devotee. Through this personal aspect, the devotee can establish a relationship with the divine, gradually moving towards a higher understanding of the ultimate reality.

Vivekananda believed that both the personal and impersonal aspects of God are essential for the spiritual journey. The personal God provides a way for individuals to connect with the divine on a more intimate level, while the impersonal Brahman offers a deeper understanding of the true nature of existence. Ultimately, both perspectives are reflections of the same divine reality, and one is not superior to the other. The goal of spiritual practice is to realize this unity and transcend the illusion of separation.

## The Cosmos: Interconnected and Divine

According to Swami Vivekananda, the cosmos is not a random collection of material forces but is imbued with divine presence. Everything in the universe, from the stars to the smallest particles, is an expression of Brahman. He saw the cosmos as a living, dynamic entity, constantly evolving, yet always governed by divine laws. For him, the universe is not separate from God but is an extension of God's own nature.

Vivekananda's view of the cosmos also emphasizes the idea of spiritual unity. All living beings, from humans to animals, share a common essence, which is none other than Brahman. This interconnectedness of all beings is what gives rise to compassion, empathy, and a sense of universal brotherhood. In his teachings, he urged people to see beyond the apparent differences of race, religion, and nationality, recognizing the underlying divinity in all forms of life.

This holistic view of the cosmos also extends to the laws of nature. Vivekananda was deeply influenced by science and believed that the laws governing the universe—whether physical, psychological, or spiritual—are reflections of the divine order. He often remarked that true knowledge involves understanding both the outer world of science and the inner world of the spirit. To him, the study of the natural world was a way of delving deeper into the nature of the divine, as the laws of nature are nothing but the expression of Brahman in the material world.

## The Human Spirit: Divine Potential Within

At the core of Vivekananda's teachings is the belief that every human being is divine in nature. He rejected the notion of inherent human weakness and instead proclaimed the potential of the human spirit to realize its divine essence. According to Vivekananda, the human person is not separate from God but is an embodiment of the divine, with the ultimate goal of life being the realization of this divinity.

He explained that the soul, or Atman, is eternal and unchanging, and it is the same as Brahman. This means that every individual is, at their core, an expression of the ultimate reality. The primary task of human life, therefore, is to recognize this divine nature within and realize one's unity with Brahman. Vivekananda saw this realization as the ultimate goal of human existence, one that can be achieved through self-discipline, meditation, and the practice of devotion.

For Vivekananda, the path to realizing the divine within was not limited to any one tradition or set of practices. He advocated a synthesis of paths, including Bhakti (devotion), Jnana (knowledge), and Karma (selfless action). By combining these approaches, a person could gradually uncover the divine potential within, transcending the ego and realizing their true nature as Brahman. This spiritual awakening was, for Vivekananda, not only the highest goal but the key to transforming the world, as individuals who realized their divine nature would act with compassion, wisdom, and love for all beings.

## Spiritual Unity: Connecting God, Cosmos, and Humanity

At the heart of Vivekananda's philosophy is the concept of spiritual unity—an interconnectedness that binds God, the cosmos, and the human spirit. For him, the realization of this unity was the ultimate spiritual goal, transcending the illusion of separation that we perceive in the material world. Through meditation, selfless action, and devotion, individuals can come to understand that they are not separate from the divine but are integral parts of the cosmic whole.

This vision of spiritual unity has profound implications for how we view ourselves and the world around us. If we truly understand that we are one with the cosmos and the divine, our actions will naturally reflect this awareness. We will begin to treat others with kindness and respect, recognizing their inherent divinity. The boundaries between individuals, societies, and nations begin to dissolve as we realize that we are all part of the same spiritual fabric. This, for Vivekananda, was the key to social transformation and world peace.

## Conclusion

Swami Vivekananda's teachings on God, the cosmos, and the human spirit offer a profound vision of the universe as an interconnected, divine whole. His monistic philosophy, which sees Brahman as the ultimate reality, challenges the dualistic thinking that often separates the divine from the material world. By recognizing the divinity within ourselves and in all things, Vivekananda urges us to transcend the ego and live in harmony with the universe. His emphasis on spiritual unity provides a timeless message for humanity, one that calls for compassion, wisdom, and a deep sense of oneness with all of creation."

## SOUL AND SPIRIT [Source: https://universal-spirituality.net/humanity/soul-and-spirit/

"This Article gives insights into the nature of soul and spirit and their interaction on both the human and divine levels.

The subject of the soul is of vast importance, but difficult to explain, for there is nothing on earth that it can be compared with. Therefore, to understand the nature of the soul, humans must have reached a level of a spiritual development from which come soul perceptions. Only soul can understand soul, and the soul that seeks to comprehend its own nature must be a live soul, with its faculties developed to at least a small degree.

The human soul is a creature of God the Father, not an emanation from Him, or a part of His soul – the Over-Soul. Like the other parts of each person, such as the intellect, the spirit body, and the material body, it had no existence before its creation. It has not always existed, but had its beginning, and only God knows whether it will ever cease to exist. However, any soul that partakes of the Love essence of the Father will become divine with which comes immortality. Such soul can never lose the Divine Love essence and ever become less than immortal, and never again can the decree, "dying thou shalt die," be pronounced upon it.

At some point each human soul was created by the Father and made the highest and most perfect of God's creation. It was the only one of all His creations that was made in His image, and the only part of each human that is in God's image. This is true in the sense that the soul is the individual person, and all the person's attributes and qualities, such as intellect, spirit body, material body, as well as appetites and passions, are merely appendages or means of manifestation given to that soul while it is passing through its earthly existence and into the spirit world.

As great and wonderful as the soul is, it was created in the mere image and likeness of God, and not of His substance or essence, and thus may cease to exist without any part of the divine nature or substance of the Father being in any way affected. So the teaching that the human soul is of and by itself divine or has divine qualities is erroneous. Like the lower created beings, it is a creation, not an emanation, of its Creator.

While originally made perfect, the soul can never become anything different or greater than a human, unless it receives the divine essence and qualities of the Father. This wasn't given to man at creation, but at that time God offered humans the privilege and opportunity for receiving the divine substance and nature, and thereby become divine. The perfectly created man and woman could become divine angels, if they so willed and pursued the way provided by the Father for obtaining and possessing that divinity.

The human souls, destined to live for a time in material bodies and experience mortal lives, were created long before the appearance of man on earth. Prior to this, each soul existed in the spirit world as a substantial conscious entity, although without visible form and individuality. Yet, it had a distinct personality, thus being different from every other soul. Its presence could be sensed by every other soul that came in contact with it, and yet it was invisible to the spirit vision of the other soul. This is still the case. The spirit world is filled with souls awaiting incarnation. The spirits know of and sense the presence of these souls, yet cannot see them. These souls only become visible when they take on the human form and have a spirit body.

This is also true of God. Spirits can sense the presence of the Father, but cannot see Him even with their spiritual eyes. Only when their souls are developed by the divine essence of His Love, can they perceive Him with their soul perception. To its possessor, the vision of the soul perception is just as real or objective as is the vision of the mortal sight to the mortal.

The question may be asked, "were all souls that have been incarnated, or that are yet awaiting incarnation, created at the same time, or is that creation still going on?" The spirit world contains many souls awaiting their temporary homes and the assumption of individuality in the human form. However, as to whether that creation has ended, or whether at some time the human reproduction for the embodying of these souls will cease, has not been revealed by the Father.

As has been stated, the soul is the "human" before incarnation, during their mortal existence, and ever after in the spirit world. All the human parts, such as the mind, body and spirit are mere attributes, which may be lost or discarded as the soul progresses in its development toward its destiny of either the perfect human or the divine angel. In the latter progression, the human, or carnal, mind becomes, as it were, non-existent. It becomes replaced by the mind of the transformed soul, which is in substance and quality, to a degree, the mind of God.

Many theologians, philosophers and metaphysicians teach that the soul, spirit and mind are substantially one and the same, and that anyone of them may be said to be the man or the ego. It is also believed that in the spirit world, one or the other of these entities continue and their degree of development determines the state of the individual after death. This concept, however, is erroneous, for these parts each have a separate existence and functioning, whether man be a mortal or spirit. The mind in its qualities and operations is well known to man because of its manifestations. Being the more material part of man, it has been the subject of more research and study than the soul or the spirit.

While humans have, over the centuries, speculated upon and attempted to define the soul and its attributes, because it cannot be comprehended by the intellect, the question of what is the soul has never been satisfactorily answered. However, some of the searchers, with inspiration, saw glimpses of the soul.

The soul is separate and made of real substance, though invisible to mortals. It is the discerner and portrayer of the person's moral and spiritual condition, never dying, so far as is known, and the real ego of the man. In it are the love principle, affections, appetites and passions, and possibilities of receiving that which will either elevate man to the state of the divine angel or the perfect man, or lower him to the condition that fits him for the hells of darkness and suffering.

The soul is subject to the human will, which is the greatest endowment bestowed upon him by his Maker at his creation. Based on the working of the will, qualities of love and affection or wrong appetites and passions will manifest either for good or evil. The soul may be dormant and stagnate, or it may be active and progress. Its integral energies may be ruled by the will for good or evil.

The soul's home is the spirit body, whether or not that body is encased in a mortal body. It is never without the spirit body, the appearance and composition of which is determined by the soul's state. The soul condition determines the destiny of the individual as they continue living in the spirit world. This, however, is not a final destiny, because the soul's condition is never fixed, and as it changes, the person's destiny changes. The progress of the soul will continue until it becomes the perfect man in the sixth sphere and is then satisfied and seeks no higher progress.

In common language as well as in theological and philosophical terms, mortals who have passed to spirit life are said to be spirits, and in a certain sense this is true. However, as such, they are not nebulous, unformed and invisible existences – they have a substance which is more real and enduring than that of a mortal. Their form and features are visible and subject to touch and other spiritual senses.

When people speak of soul, spirit, and body, a more accurate way would be to say, soul, spirit body, and material body.

There is a spirit, but it is altogether different from both the spirit body and the soul. It is not part of the spirit body, but is an attribute of the soul, without which it could not exist. The spirit has no body, substance or form and is not visible to even the spirit vision – only the effect of its working can be seen or understood. Yet it is real and powerful, and when exists, never ceasing in its operations. The spirit is simply the active energy of the soul. The soul has its energy, which may be either dormant or active. If dormant, the spirit is not in existence; if active, the spirit is present, and manifests itself in action. So the spirit and soul are not identical. Rather, the spirit is only present when the energy of the soul is active.

It is true that God is spirit, for spirit is a part of His great soul qualities, which manifest His presence in the universe. However, it is incorrect to say that spirit is God unless meaning that a part is the whole. In the divine economy, God is altogether spirit, but spirit is only the messenger of God, by which He manifests the energies of His Great Soul.

And so it is with man. Spirit is the instrumentality by which the human soul makes known its energies, powers and presence. Man is soul created in the image of the God, the Divine Soul or Over-soul, and all manifestations, such as spirit and spirit body are mere evidences of the existence of the soul – the real human individual."

The preceding Article throws some light on the God and the Soul relatable to the humans and other living beings on Mother Earth. Author believes based on the said Article that there is a mistaken notion about the God and the Creator of God. Earnestly considered, the Question should have been instead of WHO IS THE CREATOR OF GOD, WHO IS THE CREATOR OF THE SOULS' that fits into the age old perceived concept of the humans that GOD IS ONE AND THE SOULS ARE DIFFERENT. The soul, as noted in the said Article, is Spirit or an Image of God and exists in the humans and other living beings are the Spirits and not the God. That way, one could conceive that the Creator of all the Souls [Spirit] is God and, as such, there cannot be any Creator of God. The spirit is present in the minuscule insects and all other living beings on Mother Earth including the humans. These are different souls in different forms as willed by the God having born on Mother Earth according to their evaluated deeds by the God in their previous lives which is the determining Factor known only to the God. The Creation of the millions of creatures, different from each other, besides the humans are the creatures created by God according, as stated before, the degree of the deeds of each one of them adjudged by the God.

Neither the humans nor the creatures can survive on Mother Earth without the presence of soul in them. The day the soul leaves the body whether of the humans or of the creatures, the humans and the creatures are the dead bodies. It is also noted in the Article stated before that those humans and creatures which lived with love and affection, the godly qualities, are emancipated from the rebirth as such on Mother Earth and assume the shape of angels. God has shown to the humans how they could move to a higher level of spirit only when they discard the Ego and follow the path of love, affection and moral values while on Mother Earth through process of upholding the moral values coupled with continuous Dhyana or Meditation as practised and left behind by the Great Saints and Sages whose proof worthiness of having succeeded crossing over Ego and realizing the Inner Spirit that showed them the reflection and image of Cosmic existence wherein one could see the image of the God. All the saints and sages were humans on Mother Earth before they attained the glimpse of Cosmic Image. Every particle in their body, way of living with egoless and adhering to the moral values with inherent presence of love and affection towards one and all including the humans and other living beings lifted them beyond the soul existed in them. They have become today worthy of worshipping as we worship the God and the Holy Scripts on Mother Earth. The humans are today seeking from them and searching for the path they followed. The humans of this kind are few and far in the present days, the consequences of which is the increasing conflicts and confrontation among the humans, one claiming superiority over the other through artificial dressing up their belief in the ALMIGHTY.

The humans today want to show themselves as if they know every aspect of the Great Saints and Sages other than following the imprint they left behind for the humans for upholding humanity and humanness. In today's world, these words are visible to the humans only in the dictionaries which they memorize and present to the world as the followers of the Great Saints and Sages of their Faith. Such attitude on the part of humans at best is described as Memorizing. Let us read the following Article in this regard:

## The Essence of Wisdom: Unraveling the Meaning of a Sage Person

**24 December, 2023** – [Source: https://www.neuralword.com/en/philosophy-religion/philosophy/the-essence-of-wisdom-unraveling-the-meaning-of-a-sage-person

"Wisdom is a concept deeply ingrained in human culture, yet its true essence remains elusive to many. Throughout history, societies have revered and sought guidance from sage individuals who possess a profound understanding of life. In this blog post, we aim to demystify the meaning of a sage person and explore the qualities that make them wise.

### What does it mean to be a Sage Person?

A sage person, commonly referred to as a wise person or sage, is someone who has cultivated exceptional wisdom and insight through years of experience, introspection, and deep reflection. Sages are known for their ability to offer valuable guidance, solve complex problems, and navigate life's challenges with grace and clarity.

### Qualities of a Sage Person

The path to becoming a sage is a lifelong journey, and it encompasses various qualities and attributes. Here are some notable characteristics often associated with sage individuals:

- **Deep knowledge**: Sages possess an extensive understanding of various subjects, including philosophy, psychology, spirituality, and more. Their knowledge goes beyond mere facts and delves into profound insights and connections.

- **Humility: Despite** their vast wisdom, sages often exhibit great humility. They recognize the limitations of their knowledge and continuously seek to learn and grow.

- **Empathy: Sages** have a remarkable ability to empathize with others. They can understand and share the feelings and experiences of those around them, offering compassionate guidance and support.

- **Integrity:** Honesty, authenticity, and integrity are fundamental values for sages. They consistently uphold moral and ethical principles in their actions and interactions.

- **Adaptability**: Wise individuals understand the ever-changing nature of life and are adaptable in their thinking and approach. They embrace new perspectives and are open to reevaluating their beliefs and ideas.

- **Objectivity**: Sages have the ability to detach themselves from personal biases and prejudices.

They can see situations from multiple angles and provide objective insights and advice.

- **Cultivating Wisdom**

While some individuals may seem naturally inclined toward wisdom, it is a trait that can be nurtured and developed. Here are a few practices and approaches that can contribute to the cultivation of wisdom:

**Reflection:** Taking the time for introspection and self-reflection allows one to gain insights into their own thoughts, emotions, and actions. Regular reflective practices, such as journaling or meditation, provide an opportunity for growth and self-discovery.

**Learning from others:** Engaging in meaningful conversations and seeking guidance from individuals with diverse perspectives can broaden one's understanding and wisdom.

**Seeking knowledge:** Continuous learning through reading books, attending lectures, or pursuing formal education enables the acquisition of knowledge, which serves as a foundation for wisdom.

**Embracing uncertainty:** Wise individuals recognize that life is full of uncertainties. Embracing these uncertainties with curiosity and an open mind allows for personal growth and the development of wisdom.

**Practicing mindfulness:** Being fully present in the moment and observing our thoughts and emotions without judgment helps cultivate clarity and deeper understanding.

**The Importance of Sages in Society**

Sage individuals play a vital role in society by offering guidance, wisdom, and perspective. Their insights can help navigate complex societal, political, and personal challenges. Sages also contribute to the preservation and transmission of cultural knowledge, ensuring that wisdom is passed down through generations.

By recognizing and valuing the wisdom of sage individuals, society benefits from their ability to shed light on important issues, promote understanding, and foster personal and collective growth.

Next time you encounter a wise person, take a moment to appreciate their profound understanding of life and the invaluable guidance they offer."

Are those persons who claim superiority over the others aware of the above qualities? Let us not 'Fool Ourselves' thinking that others who are listening them are greater fools. Time the politicians and the religious leaders realize that all the political parties and all the religions are equal under our Constitution. The Constitution is amendable but cannot be questionable. To test whether the Constitution withstood the times and the country has moved and moving forward towards the wellbeing and welfare of the citizens, a debate on the Constitution is not the solution but respect for it. It is legitimate to question the party in power if it departed from any corner of the Constitution which power, however lies within the jurisdiction of the Hon'ble Supreme Court of India. This Hon'ble Court is the interpreter of every word in the Constitution and the interpretation so handed over becomes the law of land. Sadly, the politicians and the religious leaders want to ride over such rulings of the

Hon'ble Supreme Court and place their expressions before the people who are misguided for; an ordinary citizen is not capable of understanding the inner strength of the rulings and are, therefore, made to believe the politicians and religious leaders than the interpretations made by the Hon'ble Court. This authority is vested solely in the Hon'ble Supreme Court, not even the parliamentarians have the power ignore or overrule it except through amendments, the validity of which is also subject to interpretation of the Hon'ble Supreme Court.

There thus exists today a polluted atmosphere in the understanding of the Constitution, each political party and the religions contesting each other's interpretation as if the interpretation so advocated by each of them stands to the test of the constitutionality. This kind of obsession on the functionality of the constitution is welcoming new worms in the prevailing environment creating a wedge between them as also reaching the doors of the citizens.

Author is of the view that, as a result, we are in sorry state of functioning of the democratic framework. The politicians speak much about what they have done or doing for the country more through their advertisements in the print and electronic media which did not exist in the sixties and seventies, the ruling leaders being true to their words and did make impressive advancement in the development of the country that stands as the foundation for the further growth. The religious leaders becoming merely more emphatic towards their religion that is undermining the essence and existence of other religions. One feels it is easy to swim and cross and swollen river than living in the politics and religion combinational atmosphere that is mesmerizing the citizens driving them gradually far from the constitutional mandates.

One may ask what all said in the foregoing paragraphs has to do with the title of this book. Author is conscious about this. Author has submitted in the foregoing sections about the morality, moral values, affection, compassion, love and kindness that have a greater strength than the modern weapons and systems which have the effect of overriding the moral values when used other than for the security and protection of the country. What the author is begging for here is the indispensable need for bringing back the citizens more and more towards the moral values more so, the politicians and the religious leaders rather than hiding moral values in the guise of heightening speeches one is made to listen that are bereft of the moral and human values, the humanity, the humanness that safeguard the living lives of the humans and other living beings on Mother Earth than chorus of everything about the humans and other living beings with emptiness of the values and the virtues most needed for the survival and sustainability of the humans and other living beings. There exists God in all these Qualities and hence their relevance in this book devoted to God.

**"ANY MAN IS LIABLE TO ERR; ONLY A FOOL PERSISTS IN ERROR" - MARCUS TULLIUS CICERO**

**"THE GREATEST QUALITIES OF LOVE, KINDNESS, COMPASSION AND FORGIVENESS ARE THE WEAPONS MORE STRONGER THAN ANY OTHER WEAPONS IN THE WHOLE**

**UNIVERSE REVEALED BY LORD SHIVA TO KING BALI AFTER THE CHURNING THE OCEAN OF MILK IN RESPONSE TO THE QUESTION KING BALI ASKED LORD SHIVA AS TO WHICH ARE THE STRONGEST WEAPONS IN THE WHOLE UNIVERSE."**

The development and growth of the country in every aspect of life of the humans and other living beings solely rest on how honest we are in our words and deeds, the citadels of wellbeing and welfare of the every being on Mother Earth. Rest is rhetoric about the wellbeing and welfare of the citizens of the country.

**"IF YOU TELL THE TRUTH, YOU DON'T HAVE TO REMEMBER ANYTHING". - MARK TWAIN**

# SECTION [7] WHAT HOLY SCRIPTS SAY

To reach and achieve that path, one has to go according to the process contemplated in the Holy Scripts for; those Saints went through that process to know about the God - ONE IN ALL AND ALL IN ONE, their aim thus being realization of god that fulfilled once they succeeded in their path and process. They never interested about who is the Creator of Creator which, according to them, is superfluous effort in so far as the human is concerned. That is the Spiritual Limit beyond which nothing could be either sought for or pursued as the truth seems to have been understood by them.

The present civilization is interested rather seeking to know who the Creator of the Creator is. This was not relevant for anyone in the past civilizations as aforesaid and raising this question now, either out of keenness or to write on the black board to know if there is someone who could answer the question, not realizing the fact that when the question itself is wrong, there cannot be any answer by anyone to such question. The students in the schools and colleges answer the questions put by the teacher, lecturer or professor on the assumption that they know the answer themselves and are in a position to answer the question correctly as they know. That is not so in the case of the question – who is the Creator of the Creator? Author is not in that state of mind that he could say someone would answer this question. Author considers, if someone is there, that is the Creator. In a way asking the Creator such question by itself does not befit to the Creator.

In line with the Hindu belief in reincarnation, the universe we live in is not the first or indeed the last universe. For Hindus the universe was created by Brahma, the creator who made the universe out of himself. After Brahma created the world, it is the power of Vishnu which preserves the world and human beings. Hindu Website.com [https://www.hinduwebsite.com/hinduism/brahma.asp#gsc.tab=0] notes]:

## "Gods of Hinduism - Brahma, the Creator [by Jayaram V]

Brahma is the source, the seed and the creator of all beings in this world. He is also the revealer of sacred knowledge including the Vedas. At the time of creation, he emerged as the first differentiated consciousness (the first ego) from the primal waters (universal consciousness). He is called svayambhu because in reality none created him. As Isvara, he created himself…………….

Although, Brahma is described as the creator god (srishti karta), he is not the primary creator or the source of all. Rather he himself manifests at the beginning of each cycle of creation from Isvara or the Manifested Brahman, who is considered the primary creator of all. Brahma, therefore, is considered one of the Triple Gods (Trimurthis), the other two being Shiva and Vishnu. Each day of Brahma constitutes one cycle of creation (Kalpa) and his duration is said to be 100 years in

Brahma time. Some Puranas suggest that there may be hundreds of Brahmas in a multiverse…………….."

"………….According to Hindu mythology, Brahma emerged from the cosmic egg (Hiranyagarbha) as a golden lotus flower. He then created the universe and all living beings within it. This myth illustrates Brahma's power and importance as the creator of all things.

In the myth, Hindu god Brahma is often depicted with four faces, each facing a different direction. This represents his ability to see and control all aspects of creation, from every corner of the universe. Brahma is also often shown holding a book or a lotus flower, symbolizing his role as the source of knowledge and enlightenment………….." [Source: https://historycooperative.org/brahma-god/ ]

**The Religion of Islam [Islam Religion.com] states about 'WHO IS THE CREATOR', an Article authored by Dr. Jaafar Sheik Idris – Published on 08 January, 2007 - Last modified on 04 October, 2009 as follows:**

"A very popular question among atheists is, 'Granted that the existence of temporal things necessitates the existence of an eternal cause, why should that cause be the God of religion? Why can't matter be eternal and be therefore in no need of an eternal creator?' I shall argue, on an Islamic basis but at the same time also on a rational basis, that the attribute of eternity entails other attributes, which matter does not and cannot have, and cannot, in view of this, play the role of the original and ultimate cause of temporal things. Muslim theologians say that eternity of existence logically implies everlastingness. This is true because, if something is eternal then it does not depend for its existence on anything outside itself. If this is so then it can never pass away, because only those things pass away that lose some of the external conditions on which they depend for their existence. If the ultimate cause of temporal things is eternal and everlasting, it must of necessity be self-sufficient, [in Arabic] *qayyoom* and *ghanee.*

Can there be more than one such creator? The Quran tells us that this is impossible:

***"God never had a child, nor have there been any gods beside him. [Had there been any], each of them would have appropriated to himself what he created, and some would have overcome others..." (Quran 23:91)***

This Quranic argument was paraphrased by some Muslims theologians in a way somewhat like the following:

The assumption that there are gods beside the one true God leads to false consequences and must therefore be false. If there is more than one god, then:

(a) if every detail of everything in the world was the result of the action of one of the gods, it cannot at the same time be the result of the action of another god. But if,

(b) some things in the world were created by some gods and others by other gods, then each god would rule independently over what he created, which means that nothing in his world can even in principle, be influenced by anything outside it. But this contradicts the observed unity and interdependence of the world. And if that is impossible, then

(c) some gods will overcome others, but if that happens then the ones who are vanquished cannot be true gods. There can, therefore, be no more than one creator.

How does this creator create? Since He is self-sufficient, He cannot be said to depend on anything outside Himself in any actions, and cannot therefore be said to produce His effects the way natural causes do. But if He is not a natural cause, He must be a volitional agent. And since intention implies knowledge, and knowledge and intention imply life, he must be a living being. Since He is an eternal and everlasting being, all His attributes must reflect this quality; thus He must be not only knowing, but all-knowing, not only powerful, but all-powerful, etc.

Since no matter in any form can answer to these attributes, and since all these attributes are implied by the two attributes of eternity and everlastingness, no form of matter can be either eternal or everlasting, and thus no matter of any form can play the role of that ultimate cause. This much of the attributes that an eternal and everlasting creator must have is enough, I suppose, to show that it cannot be matter.

But this conclusion can be further confirmed by what modern science tells us about the nature of matter.

Why should He be the God of Islam?

Some might say, 'Granted that this god is a personal and living God, and that He has the attributes which you mentioned, why should He be the God of Islam and not, say the Christian or Jewish God?' The God of Islam is the God of all true prophets of God from Adam down to Moses, Jesus and Muhammad. But it is a basic claim of the religion with which Muhammad came that previous religions (including Christianity and Judaism) have not been kept in their pristine form which those prophets advocated, but have been tampered with and distorted. The only religion whose book has taken upon itself to be preserved from any such distortions is the religion of the last of God's prophets, namely Muhammad, may the mercy and blessings of God be upon him. This is not to say that everything in those religions is false or bad. No! There is much in them that is good and true; it is only those elements in them that contradict Islam which must be false or bad. But even if they were to be purged of everything that is not in consonance with Islam, they would still be less perfect than Islam is, especially in their conceptions of God, therefore unsuitable for being universal religions.

Having said this, let me give one example of a non-Islamic religious belief which the Quran considers to be a stupendous blasphemy against God, namely that He has children. At the time of the Prophet, some Arabs believed that the angels were the daughters of God, while some Christians believed that Jesus was the son of God, and some Jews believed that Ezra was the son of God. Just as the Quran gave arguments for the impossibility of there being any gods besides the one true God, it also gave elaborate arguments to show the impossibility of Him having a child, whether male or female. If the Creator is one and self-sufficient, then He is also unique, ahad:

*"...Nothing is like Him..." (Quran 42:11)*

But if so then:

*"He neither begets nor is He begotten." (Quran 112:3)*

*"...How can He have a child if He has no wife, and if He created everything?..." (Quran 6:101)*

The Quran is here saying that the claim that God has children contradicts the facts (acknowledged by those who make this claim) that He is the Creator of everything, that He is self-sufficient, and that He has no spouse. Now if He is the creator of everything, this necessarily includes the one who is claimed to be His child. But if this is created by Him, it cannot be His child; it has to be one of His creations. One does not create one's child; one begets it. If it is insisted that the child is actually begotten and not created by God, this will entail the following false consequences:

The begotten child must be of the same nature as its father, in which case God will not be unique or one.

God will not be the creator of everything.

God will have to have a spouse, who must of course be of the same nature as He is, otherwise they cannot beget anything.

But in that case the number of beings who are of the same nature as God will be raised to three.

If the child is begotten then it cannot be eternal, i.e. it cannot be of the same nature as the father.

It must therefore be temporal; but in that case it has to have a creator. But if the God who is its father cannot at the same time be its creator, then there must be its creator, then there must be another creator besides that God the father; but in that case, this other creator will be the one true creator because it was through his power that the first one was able to beget its son. This will raise the number of gods to four.

No wonder than that the Quran said about those who claimed that God has a child:

*"You have indeed come with something most monstrous, of which the skies almost burst, the earth split asunder, and the mountains fall down in utter ruin. All this because of their attributing a child to God." (Quran 19:89-91)*

## CHURCH LEADERS Website - Who Created God? The Eternal Mystery of the Origin of God - February 23, 2024, among others, notes as follows:

"………………………………Addressing the Question: "Who Created God?"

When posed with the question "Who created God?" Christian theology offers a perspective that transcends human understanding of causality and creation. The question itself is based on the assumption that everything must have a cause or an origin within the confines of time. However, if God is eternal and exists outside of time, the concept of creation does not apply to Him.

### God's Self-Existence

One of the key attributes ascribed to God in Christian theology is self-existence, or aseity. This means that God's existence is not contingent upon anything else. He is the necessary being that brings all other beings into existence. The Apostle Paul, speaking to the philosophers in Athens, declared, "The God who made the world and everything in it is the Lord of heaven and earth and does not live in temples built by hands. And He is not served by human hands, as if He needed anything, because He himself gives all men life and breath and everything else" (**Acts 17:24-25**). This highlights the concept that God is self-sufficient, requiring nothing outside Himself to exist………………."

"Buddhism has no creator god to explain the origin of the universe. Instead, it teaches that everything depends on everything else: present events are caused by past events and become the cause of future events……" [Source: BBC - The Buddhist universe - *Last updated 2009-11-23*]

"Jainism, an ancient religion from India, offers a unique perspective that challenges conventional theistic views. It redefines godhood not as a creator but as an ultimate state of being that any soul can potentially achieve. ……." [Source: Philosophy. Institute - September 4, 2023 - Prince Kumar - Jainism's Unique Concept of God - September 4, 2023

"Guru Nanak describes the attributes of God in the prayer, Japji: "There is but one God. His name is True and Everlasting. He is the Creator, Fearless and without Enmity, the Timeless Form, Unborn and Self-existing." [Source: Sikhism – Sikh Missionary Society: Publications: Introduction to Sikhism.}

Author wanted to know from the Google Website whether there is any religion in the world that says there is a Creator of Creator God. Answer he got from one of the Articles reads as follows:

"Existence of God, in religion, the proposition that there is a supreme supernatural or preternatural being that is the creator or sustainer or ruler of the universe and all things in it, including human beings. In many religions God is also conceived as perfect and unfathomable by humans, as all-powerful and all-knowing (omnipotent and omniscient), and as the source and ultimate ground of morality............" [Source: Britannica - existence of God- Written and fact-checked by The Editors of Encyclopaedia Britannica - Last Updated: Oct 11, 2024].

The foregoing statements make one to accept the fact that there is 'no creator of the Creator God'.

The Golden Rule: A Universal Ethic [Source: https://discover.hubpages.com/religion-philosophy/Every-Religion-Has-A-Golden-Rule

| RELIGION | GOLDEN RULE | SOURCE |
|---|---|---|
| Christianity | All things whatsoever ye would that men should do to you, do ye so to them; | Matthew 7:12 ; Luke 6:31 |

| RELIGION | GOLDEN RULE | SOURCE |
| --- | --- | --- |
| | for this is the law and the prophets | |
| Confucianism | Do not do to others what you would not like yourself. Then there will be no resentment against you, either in the family or in the state. | Analects 12:2 |
| Buddhism | Hurt not others in ways that you yourself would find hurtful. | Udana-Varga 5,1 |
| Hinduism | One should not behave | Mahabharata 5,1517 |

| RELIGION | GOLDEN RULE | SOURCE |
| --- | --- | --- |
| | towards others in a way which is disagreeable to oneself. This is the essence of morality. All other activities are due to selfish desire. | |
| Islam | No one of you is a believer until he desires for his brother that which he desires for himself. | Sunnah |
| Judaism | What is hateful to you, do not do to your fellowman. | Talmud, Shabbat 3id |

| RELIGION | GOLDEN RULE | SOURCE |
|---|---|---|
|  | This is the entire Law; all the rest is commentary. |  |
| Taoism | Regard your neighbor's gain as your gain, and your neighbor's loss as your own loss. | Tai Shang Kan Yin P'ien |
| Zoroastrianism | That nature alone is good which refrains from doing another whatsoever is not good for itself. | Dadisten-I-dinik, 94,5 |
| Jainism | A man should wander about treating all | Sutrakritanga 1.11.33 |

| RELIGION | GOLDEN RULE | SOURCE |
|---|---|---|
| | creatures as he himself would be treated. | |
| Confucianism | Try your best to treat others as you would wish to be treated yourself, and you will find that this is the shortest way to benevolence. | Me |

# SECTION [8] WHAT RISHIS AND SAGES SAY

[Rishi vs sage: what is the difference? When used as nouns, rishi means a Vedic poet and seer who composed Rigvedic hymns, who alone or with others invoke the deities with poetry of a sacred character, whereas sage means a wise person or spiritual teacher.] - [Source Google Website]

**Hinduism:**

**"The Story of the Seven Rishis: Creators of Humanity"**

I. Introduction to the Seven Rishis

The Seven Rishis, also known as the Saptarishi, hold a paramount place in Hindu mythology and spirituality. These ancient sages are revered for their immense wisdom and spiritual prowess. They are considered the guiding forces in the evolution of mankind, embodying the ideal qualities of righteousness, knowledge, and devotion.

In Hindu tradition, rishis are seers who have attained a high level of spiritual insight and understanding. The Seven Rishis are not just revered figures; they are regarded as the archetypes of wisdom, serving as the bridge between the divine and humanity.

II. The Origin of the Seven Rishis

The story of the Seven Rishis begins in the cosmic context of creation. According to Hindu cosmology, at the beginning of each cycle of creation, the universe is developed from the primordial elements by divine will. The Seven Rishis were created by Brahma, the creator god, to assist in the preservation of dharma (cosmic law and order) on Earth.

The connection of the rishis to the divine emphasizes their role as conduits of spiritual knowledge, drawing upon the primordial elements of nature—earth, water, fire, air, and ether. They symbolize the integration of these elements in the pursuit of higher consciousness.

III. The Names and Attributes of the Seven Rishis - The Seven Rishis are:

**Vasishtha:** Known for his wisdom and the author of several hymns in the Rigveda. He is regarded as a teacher of kings and possesses immense spiritual power.

**Vishwamitra:** Initially a king, he became a great sage known for his rigorous penance and the creation of the Gayatri mantra. He is often seen as a symbol of the struggle for enlightenment.

**Atri:** Recognized for his deep knowledge and as a progenitor of several important lineages. He is associated with the Atri Upanishad and is revered for his devotion and commitment to truth.

**Bharadwaja:** A sage known for his contributions to Ayurveda and military sciences. He is often depicted as a learned scholar and a practitioner of various forms of knowledge.

**Gautama:** Famous for his philosophical inquiries and as a figure in various stories, including that of his wife Ahalya, who was turned to stone and later redeemed.

**Jamadagni:** Known for his fierce devotion and as the father of Parashurama, he symbolizes the ideal of a warrior-sage.

**Kashyapa:** Considered the father of many creatures, he represents the unity of life and is associated with numerous mythological narratives.

IV. The Seven Rishis and the Creation of Humanity

The Seven Rishis played a crucial role in the creation and evolution of humanity. They are said to have contributed to the formation of the first human beings, imparting knowledge, rituals, and the essence of dharma. Their teachings laid the foundation for ethical conduct, social order, and spiritual growth.

The significance of the rishis' contributions to dharma cannot be overstated. They taught humanity the importance of living in harmony with nature, following righteous paths, and seeking spiritual enlightenment. Their guidance was instrumental in shaping the moral fabric of society.

V. The Rishis and the Vedas

The connection between the Seven Rishis and the Vedas is profound. The rishis are traditionally considered the seers of the Vedic texts, having received divine revelations that form the basis of these sacred scriptures. Each rishi is associated with specific hymns and mantras found in the Rigveda and other Vedic texts.

Their wisdom has significantly influenced Hindu philosophy and spirituality, providing insights into the nature of reality, the self, and the universe. The teachings of the rishis encourage individuals to seek knowledge, practice meditation, and strive for self-realization.

## VI. Legends and Tales Involving the Seven Rishis

Numerous legends and tales involving the Seven Rishis are found in ancient Hindu texts. These stories often highlight their virtues, trials, and tribulations, imparting moral lessons to humanity. Some notable tales include:

The story of Vasishtha and Vishwamitra rivalry, which illustrates the themes of ego, humility, and the pursuit of knowledge.

Atri's encounter with the divine and his quest for the truth of existence.

The tale of Gautama and Ahalya, showcasing themes of redemption and forgiveness.

These narratives serve as moral fables, teaching values such as compassion, honesty, and the importance of spiritual practice.

## VII. The Relevance of the Seven Rishis in Modern Hinduism

In contemporary Hinduism, the Seven Rishis continue to have a profound impact on spiritual practices and beliefs. They are often invoked in rituals and prayers, symbolizing the pursuit of wisdom and guidance in the modern world.

Symbolically, the rishis represent the quest for knowledge, the importance of living a righteous life, and the connection between the material and spiritual realms. Their teachings inspire individuals to engage in self-study, meditation, and ethical living.

VIII. Conclusion

The Seven Rishis hold a significant place in Hindu mythology as the creators and nurturers of humanity. Their wisdom and teachings have shaped the course of human existence, providing guidance on the path of righteousness and spiritual fulfillment.

As we reflect on their enduring legacy, it is clear that the Seven Rishis are not just historical figures but essential symbols of the quest for knowledge and enlightenment in Hindu culture. Their stories continue to inspire generations, reminding us of the profound connection between humanity and the divine." [Source: Hindu Mythology

Post published: September 25, 2024 - Post category: Creation}

**Islam**

**The Rishi Sufi Order of Kashmir, Established In The 15th Century By Shaikh Nūru'd-Dīn (Nund Rishi), Blends Hindu And Islamic Ascetic Traditions. Revered For His Poetry And Environmental Awareness, Nund Rishi Championed Hindu-Muslim Unity, With His Teachings Influencing Generations Of Saints And Mystics In The Valley.**

**Main Points:**

1. *Origins of the Rishi Order: Rooted in Hindu ascetic and Buddhist traditions, the order was later infused with Islamic principles by Shaikh Nūru'd-Dīn.*

2. *Shaikh Nūru'd-Dīn's Life: Known as Nund Rishi, he renounced Shaikh Nūru'd-Dīn's Life: Known as Nund Rishi, he renounced worldly life at 30, spreading his teachings through poetry called Shruks.*

3. *Hindu-Muslim Unity: Nund Rishi emphasized interfaith harmony, drawing inspiration from Hindu poet Lal Ded.*

4. *Environmental Legacy: His verse "Ann Poshi Teli Yeli Yeli Wan Poshi" underscores the interdependence of nature and sustenance.*

5. *Shrine at Charar-e-Sharif: His tomb, a symbol of communal respect, attracts visitors of all faiths and hosts annual Urs celebrations.*

[Source: Rishi Sufi Order in Kashmir: Roots, Legacy, and Impact *by Sahil Razvi,*

*New Age Islam* - 26 November 2024]

# SECTION [9] WHICH PATH THE GREAT SAINTS OF DIFFERENT RELIGIONS IN THE WORLD FOLLOWED TO REALIZE THE INNER SPIRIT [GOD]?

ENLIGHTENMENT BLOGTHE JOURNEY TO ENLIGHTENMENT: HOW THE WORLD'S GREAT RELIGIONS TEACH THE PATH TO INNER PEACE AND SPIRITUAL AWAKENING [Source: https://backpackbuddha.com/blogs/enlightenment/the-journey-to-enlightenment-how-the-worlds-great-religions-teach-the-path-to-inner-peace-and-spiritual-awakening posted on the MythLok Website.

Enlightenment is a concept that has been explored and sought after by many different cultures and religious traditions throughout history. From Buddhism and Hinduism, to Christianity and Islam, the world's great religions all offer a path towards a deeper understanding of oneself and the world around us. They teach us to look beyond our everyday concerns and find inner peace, wisdom and inner happiness.

How Do The World's Great Religions Teach the Path to Enlightenment?

*It is worth noting that the idea of enlightenment, its meaning and its path of attainment may vary within the different sects or denominations within the same religion, it's not a one-size-fits-all concept.

## In Buddhism

Enlightenment is known as "Nirvana" and is described as the state of being free from suffering and the cycle of rebirth. The Buddhist path to enlightenment involves following the Eightfold Path, which includes practices such as right understanding, right intention, right speech, right action, right livelihood, right effort, right mindfulness, and right concentration. By following the Eightfold Path, Buddhists aim to develop wisdom, compassion, and inner peace and ultimately to transcend the ego and realize the interconnectedness of all things.

## In Hinduism

Enlightenment is known as "Moksha" and is described as the state of liberation from the cycle of reincarnation and union with the ultimate reality. The Hindu path to enlightenment involves following the Four Purusharthas which are: Dharma (duty), Artha (material wealth), Kama (pleasures), and Moksha (spiritual liberation). The path also includes yoga, meditation, devotion, study of scripture and service to others. It's understood that the ultimate goal of these practices is to transcend the ego and realize one's true nature as part of the ultimate reality or Brahman.

## In Jainism

The path to enlightenment is known as "Nirvana" or "Kaivalya" and is described as the state of being free from the cycle of reincarnation. Jainism's path is based on the Three Jewels: Right Faith, Right Knowledge and Right Conduct. It emphasizes on non-violence, non-attachment and self-control as essential steps towards spiritual advancement. The ultimate goal is to attain spiritual liberation by purifying the soul and ultimately attaining a state of perfect knowledge, vision, conduct and power.

### In Sikhism

Enlightenment is known as "Mukti" and is described as the state of union with the ultimate reality. Sikhs believe that the ultimate goal of human life is to merge with the ultimate reality, or God. This is achieved by following the teachings of the Gurus, performing selfless service, and engaging in the practice of meditation and prayer. The focus is on living a virtuous life, based on the principles of love, devotion and self-surrender, and ultimately to transcend the ego and realize one's unity with God.

### In Christianity

Enlightenment is referred to as "Salvation" or "Union with God" and is described as the state of being saved from sin and eternal death, and gaining eternal life in heaven. The Christian path to enlightenment involves a personal relationship with God through faith in Jesus Christ and repentance for past sins. Christians believe that by following the teachings of Jesus, living a virtuous life, and through the sacraments of the church, they can achieve salvation and eternal life with God.

### In Islam

Enlightenment is referred to as "Tawheed" or "Oneness" and is described as the state of knowing and experiencing the unity of God. The Islamic path to enlightenment involves the submission to the will of God and adherence to the Five Pillars of Islam: the declaration of faith, prayer, fasting, giving to charity, and pilgrimage to Mecca. Muslims believe that by following the teachings of the Quran and the example of the Prophet Muhammad, they can achieve a deep understanding of the unity of God and ultimately reach a state of spiritual enlightenment.

**In Judaism**

Enlightenment is referred to as "Devekut" and is described as the state of spiritual attachment to God. The Jewish path to enlightenment involves the study of the Torah, performing mitzvot, and engaging in prayer and meditation. Through these practices, Jews believe they can achieve a deeper understanding of God, and ultimately reach a state of spiritual enlightenment and connection to God.

**Conclusion**

In summary, each of the world's great religions emphasizes different practices and teachings, but they all strive to help followers reach enlightenment, which is often described as a state of wisdom, inner peace, and spiritual connection to the ultimate reality. The path to enlightenment may involve studying spiritual teachings, engaging in meditative and contemplative practices, living an ethical and compassionate life, and developing a personal relationship with the divine. And even though each religion emphasizes different paths and methods, they all ultimately aim to transcend the ego and experience a deeper understanding and connection to the ultimate reality.

**Final Remarks**

Additionally, it's important to remember that enlightenment is not a destination, but rather a lifelong journey of personal growth and self-discovery. It's not something that can be attained overnight, but rather something that takes time and effort to achieve. Each person's journey to enlightenment is unique and personal, and it's important for individuals to find the path and practices that resonate with them the most.

It's also important to mention that some believe that enlightenment is not something that can be taught, it can only be realized through self-discovery and self-realization. And that any guide, teaching or religious doctrine can only point the way but can't guarantee enlightenment.

In conclusion, achieving enlightenment is a central goal in many of the world's great religions and each tradition has its own unique path and teachings for reaching this state. The path to enlightenment may involve studying spiritual teachings, living an ethical and compassionate life, engaging in meditative and contemplative practices, and developing a personal relationship with the divine. However, it's important to remember that the journey to enlightenment is a personal one and it requires time, effort and a willingness to let go of the ego and to transcend it."

# SECTION [10] PRESENT DAY PRACTICE

**The Practice in Present Days**

The religions born in India and practiced and continue to be practiced in the present days offer to the humans a treasure trove and magnifying knowledge to help the humans to know more about themselves than comparing with others and criticizing as well as condemning each other. These religions are Jewels the humans to wear according to one's Faith and be conscious of Oneness that resides in everyone but each one of us has been trying to distance ourselves to know that what Resides within us. All the religions in the world, according to the understanding of the author, understand that they cannot move an inch forward without there being something invisible within us though we say that the god resides within us – a shining Spirit, the knowledge of which in every human is common but making best endeavours to know that Spirit and be integral part of its Qualities and Characterstics is different one. When we see a great Architectural work or a Painting, we get merged in them and question ourselves how that could have been done and whether there were humans who made them thinking that such Architectural or Painting fete could be possible to be created only by god. This is known as our outward appearance and with such image, we continue to remain content within ourselves which is something someone thinking the discontentment as the contentment.

Question that confronts us as to why we are not able to know the One that resides within ONESELF. Answer to the question could be that we have become so much materialistic that we want to live our life in materialism which places us far away even to think that some kind of Spirit resides within us. In pursuing the materialistic world, we become more attached to the rituals than to search for the right path to find peace of mind. All that we are doing today is doing something for the sake self-satisfaction whether it is traditional or religious nature. Our religions as of now taught us doing the need and obligation to do those things that satisfies the religious as well as individual's sentiments. Neither the religion nor its followers have occasion or time to think beyond this binding boundary that we have created ourselves. We have learnt the art of dummying rather knowing the practical essentials of life that include, besides the rituals, also to know ourselves about more within us. Online Free Dictionary defines 'rituals' as follows:

"1.

a. A ceremony in which the actions and wording follow a prescribed form and order.

b. The body of ceremonies or rites used in a place of worship or by an organization: according to Catholic ritual.

2. A book of rites or ceremonial forms.

3. A set of actions that are conducted routinely in the same manner: My household chores have become a morning ritual."

This happens when our individualism [Ego] captures like the spider captures some living object within its net thereby we become used to remain under its captivity.

Ego is materialistic. What is the meaning of 'materialistic'? Online Free Dictionary defines this word as follows:

1. Philosophy: The doctrine that physical matter is the only reality and that everything including thought, feeling, mind, and will, can be explained in terms of matter and physical phenomena.

2. The theory or attitude that physical wellbeing and worldly possessions constitute the greatest good and highest value in life.

3. Concern for possessions or material wealth and physical comfort, especially to the exclusion of spiritual or intellectual pursuits.'

Who Am I?" What Is My Purpose In Life? Why I Am Here? – Great philosophers and spiritual leaders pondered over these questions and gave variegated answers. Some other such great persons pointed these questions to Spirit for seeking an answer through meditation and devotion.. Many others advocate to the followers and devotees that the purpose of meditation should be to seek answers to such questions. These questions can be answered only by those Great Saints and Sages who realized the inner Spirit and merged with it. By this, they obtained the entire COSMIC COMPREHENSION otherwise said as known only to God.

. Asking such questions to seek answers from the Spirit, the Spiritual Existence in the human body, by that very human in his physical form existing on the earth, is something like trying to know the predetermined not knowable, therefore, he would come to know himself or herself of who he or she was, what was his or her purpose in life, why he or she was here and what he or she had done in his or her life, just before his or her departure from the earth, all of which has happened by what Spirit contemplated for him or her when he or she was born. Human's duty is be in action which is life. This is the Ultimate. Every human should express his or her gratitude to the Spirit at the time of departure from the earth. That is what a human being could do having come to earth in human form and having done his or her duty on the earth, whether righteous or unrighteous answerable by him or her.

Author does not know who is God because he has not seen Him in his eighty eight years of life but has been hearing a lot about God all around in different languages, in different moods, in different methods, in different attitudes, in different writings, in different speeches, articles written in different magazines, newspapers and so on, as presented in different electronic medias, as manifested in different Temples, Mosques, Churches, as told by the parents, as told by the highly learned and so on. The cruellest world as called by Swami Chinmayananda in his booklet 'Hasten Slowly' according to whom the greatness of a man or woman does not lie in reaching to Himalayas because there doesn't exist worldly livings and experiences other than the living nature all around but in living in this cruel world and learning how to live in such world, according to him, the person's patience and impatience are put to great amount of test and stress and, in that situation, how to sustain oneself living and doing his or her duties. The former ceaselessly makes efforts to reach the worthiness of the sages through the process of honest and devotional Karma.

To him, the great pain of a person is recalling the past and revolving around it in mind remembering what he or she was, how happy he or she was, the best times he or she had, how he or she enjoyed his or her life in this very world not knowing that past has gone and what had to happen has happened. Also to him or her, sitting over the past repeatedly on one account or the other when one stands at a critical time in the present is like carrying the corpse on one's shoulder. This agitates the mind and agonises the self even to the extent that the person may need psychological treatment attention. There is nothing of that sort in reality. All the past happenings appear before him or her as shadows of images making him or her fearsome. Because, reality is different, the one that in which the person lives, that is present. Also to him or her, the present is the one that gives everyone to seek for flourishing and betterment of own and lives of others who are integral part of the living environment.

Author doesn't know neurological or psychological aspects of pleasure and pain in humans. However, in terms of the living lives on Mother Earth, the humans as well as the other living beings are captured both by the pleasure and pain. [Exist but unnoticeable in the other living beings]. The relationship between the two could be better understood from the Quote: **"PLEASURE IS REGARDED AS PAIN BECAUSE OF IT'S BEING MIXED UP WITH PAIN; AND PLEASURE (ACCOMPANIED BY PAIN) IS CALLED PAIN IN**

THE SAME MANNER AS HONEY MIXED WITH POISON IS CALLED POISON." – NYAYA BHASYA (NYAYA SUTRAS WRITTEN BY AKSAPADA GAUTAMA IN THE 2ND CENTURY CE.). Article given below provides the broad framework of Pleasure and Pain that helps the human how to adjust themselves in both the situations:

**Stoicism on Pleasure and Pain: Finding Balance and Control - By Mark / [Source: https://stoicismu.com/stoicism-on-pleasure-and-pain/ ]**

"In our modern world, the pursuit of pleasure and the avoidance of pain often dominate our choices.

Yet, Stoicism, an ancient philosophy rooted in wisdom and virtue, offers a different approach to managing pleasure and pain. [Added by author: Online Dictionary defines Stoicism as a person who can endure pain or hardship without showing their feelings or complaining.]

Cultivate a balanced mindset that remains steady in the face of both.

In this article, we'll explore how Stoic philosophy helps individuals navigate pleasure and pain, maintaining inner peace regardless of external circumstances.

The Stoic View on Pleasure and Pain

In Stoicism, both pleasure and pain are considered indifferent.

This doesn't mean they don't matter or affect us, but rather that they are not inherently good or bad.

According to the Stoics, what truly matters is how we respond to them.

Marcus Aurelius, a prominent Stoic philosopher, wrote:

**"If you are distressed by anything external, the pain is not due to the thing itself, but to your estimate of it; and this you have the power to revoke at any moment."**

For the Stoics, both pleasure and pain are part of life, but they shouldn't control our actions or dictate our happiness.

True contentment, according to Stoicism, comes from living virtuously—focusing on wisdom, courage, justice, and self-discipline.

Pleasure: A Stoic Approach

While pleasure may seem desirable, the Stoics warned against becoming attached to it.

The pursuit of pleasure can lead to excess, dependency, and ultimately dissatisfaction.

Stoicism encourages moderation, teaching that we should enjoy pleasure when it naturally arises but not chase after it or let it dominate our lives.

**Actionable Tip:**

Practice mindful detachment when experiencing pleasure.

Enjoy good food, entertainment, or other pleasures, but remind yourself that your happiness does not depend on them.

Ask, "Would I still be content if this pleasure were taken away"

Pain: Stoic **Resilience**

Pain, whether physical or emotional, is an unavoidable part of life.

Stoicism teaches us not to fear pain but to view it as an opportunity for growth and self-improvement.

Epictetus, another influential Stoic, emphasized that while we can't control external events that cause pain, we can control our reactions to them.

The Stoic approach to pain is about cultivating endurance and resilience—understanding that pain is temporary and can be faced with courage.

**Actionable Tip:**

When experiencing pain or hardship, focus on what is within your control—your thoughts and attitudes.

Remind yourself that while the pain is real, your reaction is what truly shapes the experience.

Use the mantra: "This too shall pass."

**The Middle Path: Moderation and Self-Control**

The Stoics advocated for living in accordance with nature, which means neither seeking excessive pleasure nor avoiding all discomfort.

The key is moderation.

Indulging too much in pleasure leads to dependency and fearing pain too much leads to a life of avoidance.

The Stoic approach is to remain balanced—enjoying life's pleasures in moderation and facing pain with strength.

**Actionable Tip:**

Practice voluntary discomfort, a Stoic exercise where you intentionally experience minor discomforts (like skipping a meal or taking a cold shower) to build resilience.

This helps train your mind to be less dependent on comfort and less fearful of pain.

**Stoic Exercises for Managing Pleasure and Pain**

Stoicism offers practical exercises to help manage pleasure and pain with a calm and rational mind.

Below are a few techniques you can start incorporating into your daily life:

**Negative Visualization:**

Imagine losing the things that bring you pleasure.

This Stoic practice helps you appreciate what you have while reminding you not to depend on it for happiness.

**Momentary Detachment:**

When you feel intense pleasure or pain, mentally step back and observe the sensation without judgment.

This creates emotional distance and prevents overreaction.

**Journaling:**

Reflect on moments where pleasure or pain influenced your actions.

Write about how you could respond with more balance next time. This builds self-awareness.

## Overcoming Hedonic Adaptation

Hedonic adaptation is the human tendency to return to a baseline level of happiness after experiencing pleasure or pain.

Stoicism helps counter this by encouraging gratitude for what we have and focusing on living virtuously rather than chasing external rewards.

## Actionable Tip:

Practice daily gratitude by listing three things you're thankful for each day.

This helps you appreciate life's pleasures without becoming dependent on them and strengthens your Stoic mindset in the face of challenges.

## The Role of Virtue in Navigating Pleasure and Pain

Ultimately, the Stoics believed that true happiness is found in virtue, not in pleasure or the absence of pain.

Stoicism teaches that living a life guided by wisdom, justice, courage, and self-discipline is far more valuable than indulging in short-term pleasures or avoiding discomfort.

When we align our lives with virtue, pleasure and pain become secondary—they are experiences we can navigate with equanimity and grace.

## Actionable Tip:

Each day, reflect on your actions and ask, "Did I act with virtue today?"

Focusing on virtue over external pleasure or pain will help you lead a more fulfilling and Stoic life.

Embrace Stoic Balance in Pleasure and Pain

Stoicism offers a powerful framework for managing pleasure and pain in a balanced and thoughtful way.

By understanding that neither is inherently good or bad, and by focusing on virtue and inner control, we can navigate life's ups and downs with greater resilience and peace of mind.

Incorporating Stoic practices into your daily life will help you enjoy pleasure without becoming attached to it, and face pain with courage and composure.

# SECTION [11] ASTROLOGICAL & RELIGIOUS APPROACH

**Astrological Approach**

Giving to others gives great pleasure than receiving from others for, giving imbibes a culture of goodness and sacrifice of whatever nature and in whatever manner and that goodness and sacrifice serves as the protecting shield which is blessed with good wishes of those to whom the person has given or sacrificed something, putting aside his or her selfishness. Giving should not be made judgmental; it should be spontaneous flowing from one's inner voice. Nor, one should look at the future. Future is always frightening being unknown. To know this unknown, we run to astrologers with eagerness to find what lies ahead. For astrologers, it is a profession and they would have been, with all respect to them, highly knowledgeable by virtue of having studied and understood the basic tenets of astrology. In essence, when one feels compelled to visit an astrologer, he or she may do so, seek his or her guidance and blessings and do the rituals the way he suggests. All this is based on his or her understanding of the subject matter of astrology which is limited and not limitless.

Limitless is beyond one's comprehension including that of the astrologer. What is intended in writing this book is to acquaint the readers, most of whom would have gone through or are going through critical times. All that lies in the unknown future should be embraced as it comes and enjoy it with positivity in mind. Question is how to live in such times as human being having born on the earth. Earth empowers human beings all it has and leaves to the human beings how he or she wished to avail that empowerment, for good or bad, all that rests with the human beings. It is not to be construed as something the author is advocating with respect to humans or their religion or their caste or creed or their way of living and life style. Not that. Everyone is free to do what he or she wants in the living environment. Time tested path laid down by the great rishis and sages have the strong strength to practice and move on in one's life. They are not there today but their imprints exist for one who wants to search the imprints and walk in his or her life according to them.

**Religious Approach**

**Visit to Worship-Prayer Places**

We visit places of worship according to one's belief that there is God in one form or the other according to our faith. We perform religious rituals according to the practice of the faith followed. We also visit the places of our worship daily or at some regular intervals or festivities or holy occasions or whenever we are passing through critical times in life, to seek the blessings of God in whatever form God is found there. That is for our satisfaction and fulfilment of our belief. The basis of Faith lies in oneself. To understand that or for seeking the blessings of God in places of our worship, how honest and devoted we are (Shraddhaa), the foundation of any prayer wherever we are. Word 'Shraddhaa' which is prevalent in Hinduism or the corresponding words as may be prevalent in other Faiths invokes a sense of Utmost sincerity, honesty and devotion (Bhakti).

Mere knowledge has no meaning when one stands in front of God. Introducing Bhaj Govindum composed by Sri Adi Shankara and sung by M.S. Subbalakshmi; Dr. S. Radhakrishnan [a noted Scholar and the former President of India] noted that "Ray of Knowledge and Bhakti are one and the same. When Knowledge lodges securely in mind, it becomes Wisdom. When Wisdom is integrated with Life and shoots out into action, it becomes Bhakti. Knowledge when matures is Bhakti. If the Knowledge does not transform into Bhakti, such Knowledge is useless. To believe Bhakti and Knowledge are different from each other is ignorance." Knowledge is theoretical while Bhakti is practical. Bhakti is to translate the knowledge in actuality when the knowledge attains fruitfulness. What one wants to achieve in one's life through his or her bestowed knowledge is possible only when that knowledge is encompassed with the devotional commitment that is a sincere and honest effort to earn that which one wants to achieve in life and, that devotion and commitment is Bhakti. Sincerity and honesty are the integral part of Bhakti and Bhakti is to centralize the entire energy in concentration and it is that concentration that enables one to create something visible to the eyes for one's own benefit and for the benefit of the humanity or the community.

It is not to suggest here that what is being presently practiced according to one's own faith is not correct. It has been correct and would continue to be correct having mass appeal. What the author has emboldened to talk about the practice is to supplement the one practised is not intended to differentiate or belittle that practice but to enlarge and expand its meaning and intent to include therein the Greatest Qualities of Life manifested in God described above to enable the devotees also to practice them to the extent one is able to with earnest feeling for greater goodness of one and all.

One realizes the real meaning of life and worthiness of living on earth when one endeavours to imbibe those Qualities. Going to places of worship or pilgrimages is in itself spiritual in all its essence. That is, relating to, consisting of, or having the nature of the spirit; not material; supernatural: spiritual power: concerned with, or affecting the soul: spiritual guidance; spiritual growth. The spiritual offerings combined with material offerings create a wonderful experience in oneself that takes one to the existence of the Spirit within oneself. All the human spiritual efforts are to trace that pulse of Spirit pervading within the body. Once that is felt, a thin line of link moves that feeling towards the mind (Ego) and helps slowly and slowly silence the agitating mind responsible for creating various kinds of negative attitudes and agitations disturbing the equilibrium of the human behaviour within as well as outside of oneself.

The spirituality or being spiritual plays an important and effective role to reset the wandering mind (ego) and to soften its reactionary acts and movements. One can experience this through humblest and honest offerings (Bhakti) to establish a kind of relationship with the Spirit residing within oneself. The intensity of response depends upon the intensity of gratitude one develops toward the existence of the Spirit. Let us not mistake that spirituality is religion. They are different. While spirituality searches for the Unknown or God within, the religion is a way of life to be regulated by humans according to the Holy Scripts of one's own faith which aims at searching for the Spirit. This is to enforce discipline in life for, without discipline, the mind and body miss the prescribed route to be followed in life. This is the foundation for evolvement into a state of mind where one sees everyone as one while practicing one's way of life that is, religion. To interpret religion in another way is missing the direction of the life practiced and handed over to humans by our ancestors.

What we are doing today is more of showmanship than normality [as supposed to be the standard practice according to one's Faith]. The first is the picturesque while the second is the practical as prescribed. It may be relevant to elucidate it based on the authoritative writers.

We seem to be misplaced in our thinking that what is laid down in one's Faith is rigid and difficult in the present days of complexities of way of life that detaches us from the essence of human – the Bhakti, Shraddha or Devotion. These three words connote identical spirit of understanding but we have misunderstood them thinking them as a rigorous route. It is not so. These three essentials are not confined from the point of one's Faith alone. Those essentials embrace one's very way of life.

How?

These essentials form the foundation in any personal and professional processes. One does something in one or the other capacity, the process of life one yearns to earn and live with dignity of life. Any practice or profession irrespective of its level in life and its possession by one cannot fulfil its object of success without the presence of the essentials aforesaid which sum up in one word 'Concentration'. Could one lead a life in any profession or practice so chosen without the basic centric of thought i.e. concentration. When it is said that 'WORK IS WORSHIP', why it is said so? What work has to do with worship? For that, one knows what about his or her or work but don't know why 'worship' is made part of it. What is worship besides one's Faith's point of view, also from the point of view of 'Work'? This proverb is not born or proposed today. It had been there and will continue to be there for ever in human life. But the human understands one and doesn't understand the other thinking its colour is more suited to religiosity. Author differs with this and begs to be excused.

All the religions and faiths follow that proverb to secure peace of mind both during the prayers as well as in the practical life. Author urges the readers to read the following Article posted on the Google Website

[https://www.teachingbanyan.com/proverbs/work-is-worship-proverb/] written by Akash:

**Work is Worship – Proverb Meaning and Expansion of idea -** / Proverbs / By Akash

## Meaning

"The proverb 'Work is Worship' establishes a relationship between God and your actions. You could be of any faith – Hindu, Muslim or Christian, your actions in everyday life, what you do, what you speak, etc. are worthy of worship, if they bring glory to God and to humanity as well. In other words – if you work devotedly and stay obedient and don't harm anyone, then you can do without literally worshipping God.

Perhaps, God is more pleased by your actions than the time you spend worshipping him. Your actions are more significant than the worship when it comes to glorifying God.

## Expansion of idea

The expansion of 'work is worship' combines the idea of work performed in offices or other places, with the worship performed in places of religion.

Professionals go to the office; farmers and laborers work in fields – everyone works in their respective places. Likewise, for worship, we go to temples, churches, or mosques. The phrase combines these two activities.

Work, as we all know is something that we do for a living, to sustain the needs of our loved ones. The word 'worship' has come from 'worth-ship' which means that whatever we do; we must add the worthiness to it. Whatever you do, if it is worthy of doing and done with sincerity then it is equivalent to worship.

Therefore, the phrase, 'work is worship' teaches us to keep the right attitude towards our work. If we are able to do that, yet doesn't worship, then also, we need not to worry because 'work is worship'.

## Short Stories on 'Work is Worship'

A story is the best way to understand the true worth of a proverb. Keeping this in mind, I am giving below a couple of stories on 'work is worship', that will give you a deeper understanding of the proverb.

## Short Story 1

There lived a lazy farmer who didn't want to go to the fields and sat in a temple the whole day, thinking that he can seek out a living with what the people offer. So whatever the grain, food people offer to God, the farmer took it and cooked it as dinner. He was living the life of his dreams – not working at all, resting all day, yet getting enough food to survive.

It so happened, that, once the village was struck by drought followed by famine. There was hardly any food left with the villagers, thankfully they all were surviving on grains they had saved in years. But, one man was left without even an ounce of grain, and it was the poor lazy farmer. Because of the famine, there were no offerings made to the temple and so the farmer faced hunger every day. He cursed himself every moment for not working and instead of sitting in the temple and praying. Had he worked and not only worshipped for months; probably he wouldn't be starving today. At last, the farmer learnt the lesson that 'work is actual worship'.

## Short Story 2

There lived two friends in a remote Indian village. One was a poor yet hardworking blacksmith while other was a lazy priest in a small village temple. The priest often jokingly says to the blacksmith that however hard he works, God will favor only the priest as he worships regularly.

The blacksmith was so engrossed in his everyday work that he never got time to visit the temple. The two of them meet only during late night hours or in a village meeting or so. Time passed by and after years of hard work and persistence, the blacksmith became the richest man in the village. He decided to donate a decent amount of money to the village temple and was called for a small felicitation ceremony.

There he met his old friend, the priest, who by this time has realized the true worth of working hard. When the blacksmith was asked about the secret of his success, he just uttered three words 'Work is Worship'. Indeed!! Thought the priest.

**Examples**

A well-written sentence as an example to explain a proverb is worth more than a complete paragraph in this regard. I have given below some fresh examples on the proverb 'work is worship' that will help you understand the true meaning of the proverb.

"A soldier who guards our borders for months at a time, without even visiting a temple or mosque; still, is more dear to God than we, who worship every day. Indeed work is worship".

"Rony asked his doctor mother to visit the Church together on Sunday, but she told him that she has a very important surgery to attend on Sunday morning. Rony went alone filled with all sorts of atheistic views about her mother. There in the sermon, he heard words 'work is worship'. His views about his mother were completely changed."

The God doesn't want you to worship him every day he just wants you to do whatever you do with passion and a kind heart for everyone else. Your actions are as good as worship, if they are sincere, honest, and done with good intentions. Work is indeed worship."

"If you worship five times a day, still your actions are foul and malignant, then the worship will get you no reward from God at all. In fact, you would be punished."

"A man who does his work, honestly and diligently, needs not to fear God, because he is worshipping God through his work."

**"DEVOTION TO DUTY IS THE HIGHEST FORM OF WORSHIP OF GOD." — SWAMI VIVEKANANDA**

**"WORK IS LOVE MADE VISIBLE." — KAHLIL GIBRAN**

# SECTION [12] SELF, EGO & PERSONA

In all acts in our life, increasing attachment is to the mind (ego) that makes up our behavioural pattern in the society or in our work culture or in our relationships or in our outlook or in our biasness, or in our respects for others, in our readiness to listen to others and so on. This has become a way of our life. Why is it so? Gap between one's mind (ego) and the Spirit one has built up in oneself subordinating the Spirit to the ego. Ego in itself has no form and it postures its presence through human physical existence making that existence to believe as one and to feel the materialistic world as more important for living than anything else. This is where we get trapped in real life birthing increasing miseries, selfishness, insensibility, failures, depression leading sometimes to suicide, exuberance and excitement resulting in disastrous consequences and so on. Attitudes of this kind preoccupy with a sense of egoism prepared to take high risks and rashness unmindful of the harm these would cause to oneself and others. The persons of this nature don't think beyond their self-image and venture upon discarding the reality staring at the eyes. They disregard the signals of the inner voice against such adventurism. They scorn at any one advising them not to do such act. The cause for this is again the dominance of egoism bereft of reasoning and rationality. Mishaps, accidents, tragedies for families and kith and kin strike in most of these cases.

**RADHA SOAMI SATSANG BEAS – SCIENCE OF THE SOUL WEBSITE posted an article 'Spiritual Link' [Spiritual Link - May 2017 - The Obstacle of Ego** which worthwhile reading in the present context:

When Maharaj Sawan Singh was asked "What is ego?" he replied:

Ego is the feeling or consciousness of one's separate existence from God. We strive to make everything ours. This causes strife and struggle, competition and quarrels. Then attachment, love and affection for the objects we call 'our own' enchain us to them and cloud our sense of discrimination, and we find ourselves caught in the cobweb of jealousy, greed, anger, hatred and all the evils born of ignorance.

*The Call of the Great Master*

In Greek mythology, there is the story of Arachne, an expert weaver, who challenged the goddess Athena to see who the better weaver was. The result was that Athena turned Arachne into a spider and she and her descendants are forever attached to the webs that they weave.

Unknowingly, we also are attached to the web of karmas that we have woven throughout millions of past lives. In the book *One Being One* we read:

Thoughts, moods, desires, attractions, aversions, images, and all the rest of it, pass through our minds like a confused and never-ending movie, with many scenes unfinished and unresolved. And each, however fleeting, grabs the attention of our self.... "We pronounce it 'I,' as if it were the whole of us, despite the fact that the very next moment when external circumstances change, another 'I' has ousted it and taken over control."

Ego, it seems, is fundamental to our self-concept and identity. For this reason, it is so difficult to subdue and conquer it. Ego is so much more than arrogance or pride. The ego's many attributes are always lurking in the background, diligently ready to block our awareness of the truth within. It is only through a deep feeling of love that one can get a glimpse of life guided by a consciousness devoid of ego. Only when we are filled with love of the Lord is true loss of ego achieved. Only true saints and mystics can give us the method by which this love can be achieved and egoless consciousness attained, but few are willing to listen to them and act on their advice.

Saints teach us that everything belongs to the Lord and that everything in this world is given to us by the Lord. When we labour under the illusion that we own or control anything, it is really our ego and pride that are controlling us. Over time, the saints show us that meekness and humility are essential to overcoming pride. Maharaj Sawan Singh says in *Philosophy of the Masters*, Vol. III:

What is false pride or vainglory? To be proud of a virtue we do not possess, or we possess merely as a gift from someone else, is false pride.... Another person is proud of his beautiful hair, fair face, soft hand or healthy body and walks about the streets like a bloated bag. Such pride is false: pride such as this is due to that all powerful Creator and nature which made him or to the Spirit granted by the Lord.

Only when we find a true Master or teacher will we be able to escape this profound obstacle of ego which fills our mind with such a false sense of identity. By following the teachings of a true Master we can eliminate our ego, see our true self, and find our origin where true peace and happiness prevail. [Volume 13 · Issue 5]

# SECTION [13] NEGATIVITY, POSITIVITY & MEDITATION

**Negativity & Positivity**

Negativity, according to author's limited knowledge, occurs because of the circumstances. How one permits the negativity or what makes the negativity to enter into the mind and body. Body is the reflection of the mood of the mind – negative or positive. This is important to understand first. Negativity is born out of denial mode. This is not willing to accept the better part of life or refusal to listen a sane and sensible suggestion or advice, not willing to acknowledge the gratefulness to someone who helped in certain situations, accumulating ideas unhelpful to the individual, floating in some thoughts believing them practical but not able to materialize them, always sitting in fixation on some or the other matter that doesn't exist or has become part of past, always brooding over the doubts on ability or capacity to do, feeling a sense of loss of faith, belief, confidence and control in oneself. All these characters get settled in the mind start moving in the senses in the body leading to physical reactions and a sense of rejection of life. These characters are either forced upon in a given circumstance or caused due to inhuman and abusive treatment at some place or the other which severely hurts the person's sentiments. Let us understand that the negativity with the signs of the kind mentioned ordinarily does not come of its own. It is the result of a kind of treatment meted out in one's life within or outside the family and compels to loosing belief, faith, confidence, control, the foundations of the normal functional body and mind. That one who is thus subjected to finds him or her expressionless building up pressurising negative thoughts and communication within, there being none, as believed by him or her, to whom he or she could open up that helps ease the mental pressure. That further leads to loneliness most harmful to one's health and life.

'When every thought absorbs your attention completely, when you are so identified with the voice in your head and the emotions that accompany it that you lose yourself in every thought and every emotion, then you are totally identified with form and therefore in the grip of **ego**'. 'Ego is a conglomeration of recurring thought forms and conditioned mental-emotional patterns that are invested with a sense of I, a sense of self.'[WikiDiff]

'The mind is the totality of psychological phenomena and capacities, encompassing consciousness, thought, perception, feeling, mood, motivation, behavior, memory, and learning.[1] The term is sometimes used in a more narrow sense to refer only to higher or more abstract cognitive functions associated with reasoning and awareness.[2] Minds were traditionally conceived as immaterial substances or independent entities and contrasted with matter and body. In the contemporary discourse, they are more commonly seen as features of other entities and are often understood as capacities of material brains.[3] The precise definition of mind is disputed and while it is generally accepted that some non-human animals also have mind, there is no agreement on where exactly the boundary lies.[4]

Despite these disputes, there is wide agreement that mind plays a central role in most aspects of human life as the seat of consciousness, emotions, thoughts, and sense of personal identity.[5] Various fields of inquiry study the mind; the main ones include psychology, cognitive science, neuroscience, and philosophy.'[6] [Wikipedia]

Question is whether giving weight and attaching importance, may be because of failure to get what one wants or failure to achieve adds to the agony. Success comes through failures, what Great men realized and ultimately achieved their goal and earned fame in the world. Let us look at them rather than sitting with soreness. Read their life and achievements to regain self-confidence and sense of positivity. <u>It is said that "To fail is not to succeed, and success is the absence of failure. ... Firstly, failure starts where success ends, and it defines the limits of success. But secondly, success often follows failure, since it frequently occurs after other options have been tried and failed". It is also said that "Failure won't kill you but your fear to fail just may keep you from success. ... Failure simply means there is something to be learned or another direction to be taken. Here's why failure is GOOD: Failure is a redirection." Successful people who failed and became renowned in the world: Thomas Edison, Elvis Presley, Michael Jordan, Vincent van Gogh, Stephen King, Fred Astaire, Abraham Lincoln, JK Rowling and Albert Einstein</u>.

There is also another way, simple, to conquer the negativity and depression. Mind is like a floating boat in the water regardless which direction it takes and which shore of the sea it reaches. If one happens to be in that boat, one's fear is one would sink, that is giving up the hope. It is not so. Boat has to reach shore that is the functional character of sea, the only thing one does not know is which shore it would reach. Since one may not be knowing the navigating the boat, that makes one further fearsome which is not called for because the boat is bound to reach some shore and, that is assured by the sea. "For the ocean is big and my boat is small. Find the courage: Alanis Morissette". "Boat is nothing without water and man without his dreams! Mehmet Murat ildan." Most of us believe and act according to what comes from one's mind. As noted, mind doesn't have any form. Its form is ego embedded in the humans. Mind is also not independent. It draws its behavioural features or acts from the conscious, to perform. Mind always lives in wandering and wavering mood. Entire exercise is to crystallize and centralize that mood. One may ask how it could be humanly possible. It would be possible and that possibility has been proved by the great spiritual leaders and saints in our country and in the world. Author knows that we are not those great spiritual leaders or saints. Being ordinary human beings engaged in life activities – actions at work place and home- to earn and survive oneself.

What we have to appreciate that we have the footprints of the Sages and Saints and of our own ancestors. Our ancestors followed the path shown by those Sages and Saints. We need to understand this in right perspective. Though we may not be sages and saints, the fact, however, cannot be denied that they left their footprints for the benefit of the future generations. Our ancestors followed them and lived their lives with contentment.

When that could have happened, why we should say that we are not those sages and saints. The Prophets born in every civilization put forth the path for the succeeding generations to follow that have greatest benefit of self-content which is the highest gift a human can aspire for. The path shown by the Prophets of every religion became part and parcel of the life being very much existing in the Holy Scripts they left behind as well as in the inscriptions found in the worshipping places. Everyone in any religion is aware of this fact and those who belong to that religion continue to practice them in daily life. Then, how can we say we are not those great saints and sages and, therefore, cannot be able to follow their footprints? One should not think in terms of what those sages and staints were wearing and of their appearance. That was what was necessary during the times they were there.

That should not be criteria that we are not sages and saints. The criteria should be imbibing the greatest values of life embedded in the Holy Scripts as well as at the places of the Worship. Any human in any ordinary way of life can enrich himself or herself with the path of life as shown in the footprints. These are more valuable than any golden ornaments for; these ornaments make us to spend sleepless nights because of the fear of loosing them for one or the other reason. That is the attachment we have towards such ornaments because we consider the ornaments are more valuable to the individual.

That is not so in the case of the footprints for; no one can erase or takeaway them although those have the value higher than ornaments. We consider the ornaments in physical possession terms. The footprints of the sages and saints in the Holy Scripts may, one could say, have no value from the point of view of physical possession unlike ornaments. That is where we are self-misleading.

The ornaments are available in the market all the time for purchase. Peace and firmness of the mind are not available in the market and are to be self-created. The ornaments represent materialistic possession but the footprints represent the spiritual possession. Unless this is there in the human being, the human being always remain in the state of fearsomeness which makes him or her restless because of the wavering mind. The mind, as noted before, can be in negativity or positivity depending upon the prevailing circumstances and psychological fear. When this happens, the humans become the captive of negativity in the mind. It becomes more frightening about lthe safeguarding and security of the ornaments. Whereas, the footprints aim at creating confidence, courage and fearlessness. What is troubling the humans is not possession of the ornaments but the fear of loosing them which happens for reason of dominance of negativity.

The posivity does not invite any such fear because it is firm in itself and secures mental firmness and measures to safeguard that keeps the fearseomeness away from the mental outlook. That is the beauty of those footprints that stand settled in every religion to enable every human belonging to particular Faith submissively follow them for the betterment of own life and the lives of other humans. The footprints remain valid for ever whereas the ornaments being materialistic are consumables bound to part with possession according to one's needs and necessaties. The footprints remain within the humans both during the good and bad times in life. This is the crux of humanity upheld by the great saints and sages that remain valid for ever.

So, one need not be conscious and concerned about the the validity of the dress code then existed and now existing but be conscious and concerned about one's belief, faith and commitment in the footprints and practice them with full sincerity that assures tranquility of the mind, the basis for survival with positivity and hopefulness in one's life that convert one's efforts into worshipping the god. Let us do, whatever we want for survival, with honest commitment to the achieve what we aspire for in our life with the help of the guiding light of the footprints which is also worship of God as worshipped in the temples, mosques, churches etc. This should not be misunderstood that one need not go to temples, mosques and churches etc. which should be done respectfully, Author has noted before that combination of prayer with offerings would have wonderful pleasure to the so doer. However, the offering to the needy humans will please the God more than offering to Himself.

**Definition and Significance of Dhyana [Meditation]**

"Dhyan is a state of pure consciousness, which transcends the inner and outer senses. The climax of Dhyana is samadhi. In Indian tradition, it is used for inner soul growth. Western psychologists link it with mental concentration and consider it a special state of mind. But this is only the early phase of Dhyan. The techniques and nature of Dhyana might vary but even the modern scientific research validates and highlights its benefits.

The term 'Dhyana' comes from 'dhyai' dhatu used in 'lat' pratyaya. Its meaning is contemplation or the natural tendency and direction of senses. Patanjal Yogashastra links it with ekagrata or concentration. According to Sri Aurobindo, Dhyana is that state in which the inner mind tries to see the reality behind things. Ekagrata means focusing the consciousness on one point or object and keeping it steady in one state. In yoga, ekagrata is achieved when the mind is deeply engrossed in a special condition like quietude, or action or aspiration or resolve. This is called meditation. It is a form of Dhyana. Dhyana, when constant, is called dharana. In dharana, for the first time, the power of consciousness is directed towards the inner being. When the mind, fixated with only one object, sees only that object and nothing else, it is the state of Dhyana. And when meditating upon the object the mind becomes completely still and merges into that object, the yogis call this condition paramdhyan. In yoga, the process of keeping chitta centered on any external or internal object for a long time is called avadhan. In dharana, the flow of this process or action remains constant in the desired direction. In its normal condition it is not continuous. The action of making this very flow of chitta continuous and unbroken is called Dhyana. It is a special state of chitta. Dharana and Dhyana may be compared to the flow of water and ghee (milk fat). When Dhyana is centered on the desired objective, it activates the power of resolve. Dhyana helps to strengthen resolve, and the resolve regulates Dhyana. The two are mutually complementary.

For the humans who are more engrossed in professional and worldly life, it is possible to practice Dhyana as integral of the normal life.. How? Give ten minutes every day, to start with, at whatever time and wherever one is and try to find that golden time from out of one's busiest life. Gradually try to increase the duration up to twenty minutes.. It all depends of each individual's constraints and choice. This is so because, we don't believe that the success or failure of the busiest life itself is dependent on how much calm and quiet one is – that is something that guides and leads one to self-satisfaction and, when one is self-satisfied, he or she acquires the capacity and capabilities to convince and satisfy others for whom the work or activity is undertaken. It subsumes the confidence and self-conviction and occupies a position that can answer anything and everything asked. This generates in oneself satisfaction and contentment and a feeling that one has done his or her best for achieving the success equivalent to responsibility vested and the remuneration received.

Next is what to do during those ten minutes. "Dhyana". "Dhyāna means "contemplation, reflection". It also refers to "imaginative vision". Dhyana is abstract meditation and not the meditation as ordinarily understood. Abstract meditation, according to "Abs-Tract Organization - Medium" means "to retreat, to introspect, to practice solitude and equanimity, in order to find meditation in its simplest and purist form." When one meditates, he or she abstracting the self. The stage after that meditation itself is Dhyana. But, both of them are concentration only.

The difference is – Meditation is an Objective Concentration; Dhyana means Subjective Concentration." If one has to practice meditation, one has to concentrate on her or him. First, one must feel freely ready or available to do during that duration of time. Sit at home or anywhere else where one enjoys freedom to do – one can sit on a mat, a chair, a sofa, on bed at place earmarked for daily prayers or any other place with folded legs and hands. When one wants to sit on the floor, one should sit on a mat. There has to be disconnection between earth and Dhayana otherwise, the earth draws the energy that is being built through Dhayana. There need not be any photo of God or candle or idol or anything of that kind. Just sit with eyes closed. Allow the mind to wander wherever it wants. Never try to stop it. Just watch within. Mind may take one to Himalayas, Heaven, loved ones, and relationships, to America, to London, to Antarctica and so on.

Let it move around the world. Never be attentive to that. Sit in a straight position with eyes closed. If one tries to stop movement of the mind, one gets touched to earthly happenings or the object. That is what is intended to be avoided when one sits with closed eyes. During Dhyana, one can develop an 'imaginative vision" of any kind one finds appealing to self. Suggested time, as far as possible, could be any time between 7 pm and 10 pm before dinner. Go on practicing it daily. After about three months or so, if one had been sincerely and faithfully practicing, one feels a chilling effect in the body. Once that chilling effect happens in the body that signals reverting of the mind from wandering, gradually and settling or say, the process of quietening the mind begins. Quietening the mind is the emergence of signs of concentration in mind. The concentration enhances gradually with the intensity of one's sincerity and faith while practising. This exercise should form integral part of life like food and sleep. Never give it up. Feel what wonders the concentration bestows upon the doer. One may be doing gym daily at home or outside but that exercise helps one to build physical strength while Dhyana builds spiritual strength. Spiritual strength is stronger than physical strength; physical strength is scared of injury while Dhyana is mainly concerned with minimizing the mental injury caused by physical injury.

All great saints and sages and those learned and realized strive and practice for attaining Quietitude. They do that in their own way. A Karmic can also attain Quietitude practising the method mentioned. Beginning of concentration in one's mind gives impetus to achieve excellence in whatever one wants to do living in busy life. Few Quotes with sources: "I am not what happened to me. I am what I chose to become." (Carl Jung), "Love people for who they are and not for who you want them to be" (Alex Elle) and "The serenity implied by Quietitude does not in any way exclude the external activities and involvement. In fact the attainment of this enlightened subjective depth and fullness empowers one to pursue activities to a far greater magnitude while remaining anchored to the action less subject within what more? It has its unique sublimating influence on everything around be it a place, a person or an event." (Swami Bhoomananda Tirtha).

Quietitude means calm, calmness, hush, peace, peacefulness, placidity, quiet, quietness, repose, restfulness, sereneness, serenity, still, stillness, tranquillity. Once Quietitude is settled, the mind remains under self-control. Quietitude opens up through regular practice invincible link between the mind and the Spirit. How the doer would know it. Doer while practising with faith and humbleness daily, finds vibrations in the body like the folded hands moving upward of their own towards the forehead or the legs showing the signs of lifting up, also signs of expansion of the body, not in physical form but in spiritual form. On feeling this kind of experience or the signals, one should start shifting focus slowly towards the Spirit that resides deep in the Heart, invisible to human eyes even when the Heart is opened for surgery. Spirit means 'God' while 'Soul' is the 'eternal self'.. The continuous practice takes self to Heightened Consciousness, that is, heightened consciousness used as a term for a permanent calm, calmness, hush, peace, peacefulness, placidity, quiet, quietness, response, restfulness, sereneness, serenity, still, stillness, tranquility.

Quietude is not to be viewed merely from spiritual angle, The spiritual angle as explained before is an effort to attain and capture in order to practice it in daily life by the humans engaged in any kind of profession in life for; the Quietitude enhances the absolutism of the profession or practice enabling the humans to unknowingly know that their effort is imprinting the concentrative characters in the work done and, such work encompassed with in the Quietude is as good as one tries to attain through Yoga and Meditation in solitary place or lonely locations which, the most of the humans think is the only way to possess. That is not so. Quietitude can be attained living in the wordly movements for which the intent, sincerity and commitment form the foundations. Never do anything for the sake of doing or for the sake others saying. As noted before, greatness of human lies in performing his or her Karma [Duty] as undertaken while remaining in busier system of daily life is of more meritorious than going to isolated or lonely place and trying to achieve this. The Bhagavad Gita offers guidance on life's purpose and self-realization through Karma, Dharma, and Moksha. It emphasizes selfless action, adherence to duty, and the pursuit of liberation from the cycle of birth and death.

Quietitude is not to be misunderstood as practicing quietness all through the day whether one is walking, standing, talking, crossing, working, in meetings, presentation and so on. These are part of routine life. One has to do what is expected of from one's duty in whatever capacity according to the official code and prevailing circumstances. Duty is also God. Quietitude resides within even while doing the duties and various kinds of necessities in the working place. Those who are able to establish Quietitude within are always heard within and not outside. That is, whatever may be the duty or activity one is performing is able to draw the concentration and orderliness of doing for doing so and such concentration and orderliness makes one to achieve excellence and appreciation. Because, one is to understand that if he or she were to be in a state of mind not accomplished with Quietitude, the behavioural pattern of the state of mind is unpredictable, there being no centric force to control it and that leads, many times, to fear, loss of confidence, nervousness, memory loss, a psychological signal that one has not been able to do what was expected of him or her. Quietitude acts as strength to intellectual capacity and physical efforts.

One should not concern oneself of its relevance in the present days. Its relevance was valid in the past and continues to be in the present and for ever. This is what the past generations understood. That understanding did not stop there because the humans didn't exist only then but exist presently and continue to exist in future. Quietitude bestows immense courage, confidence and conviction which are as essential as food for the humans for achieving the life aspiring for. These days physical exercise attending the gyms is considered as must for the humans. Most of the people accordingly made it a practice in their daily life. Mere physical exercise presents the outside status of the person which is open to injuries for one or other reason. Such injury, when happens, makes the person to suffer physically and mentally. The physical injury is curable through the medical process. The mental injury, though the psychologist claim could cure it, the process is prolonging unsure of the complete restoration to the original status. The practising of Quietitude has inbuilt strength to stand up to the physical injury, more than the process followed by the psychologists. It self-exists in one who practises it also as part of the daily life process. We seem to believe today the physical exercise is more important for one's sustainability of the body and outside appearance. Such thinking is like an empty drum. The spiritual strength has more sustainable capacity for curing the physical injuries and regulating the life more confidently. So, its relevance is as much the same as the physical exercise today as well free of cost.

Above approach through the spiritual force of concentration gathered and fixed in the mind binds the mind to always look towards positivity. Thus, the negativity gets itself dissolved in the mind. Dhyana further adds strength to maintain and practice the positivity in life. Life in such a state of mind is hardly concerned with the abstracts and diversions and enables the doer to place the positive energy and the concentrated effort in workplace or home or elsewhere to achieve excellence and outstanding results and achievements in life. Take it to heart and carry forward practice to touch the heart of those who are undergoing negativity and depression. They will be greatly obliged for having brought them back to their normal life and to look for a better and brighter future. Spiritual practice such as Dhyana succeeds in overthrowing the negativity including depression and establishing positivity. Spiritual practice is self-generated through spiritual means and efforts while other kinds of treatments are mechanically tested.

Swami Vivekananda said "The easiest way to get hold of the mind is to sit quiet and let it drift where it will for a while. Hold fast to the idea, "I am the witness watching my mind drifting. The mind is not I." Then see it think as if it were a thing entirely apart from yourself. Identify yourself with God, never with matter or with the mind. Picture the mind as a calm lake stretched before you and the thoughts that come and go as bubbles rising and breaking on its surface. Make no effort to control the thoughts, but watch them and follow them in imagination as they float away. This will gradually lessen the circles. For the mind ranges over wide circles of thought and those circles widen out into ever increasing circles, as in a pond when we throw a stone into it. We want to reverse the process and starting with a huge circle make it narrower until at last we can fix the mind on one point and make it stay there. Hold to the idea, "I am not the mind, I see that I am thinking, I am watching my mind act', and each day the identification of yourself with thought and feeling will grow less, until at last you can entirely separate yourself from the mind and actually know it to be apart from yourself. When this is done, the mind is your servant to control as you will. The first stage of being a yogi is to go beyond the senses. When the mind is conquered, he has reached the highest stage."

God is unknown to the eyes of all beings on earth. Spirit is the embodiment of God and the soul is personal to human and other living beings, the only Absolute Truth, not visible but resides invisibly in the Spirit. For all beings on earth, death is the only Truth that happens when Soul leaves the body on the earth as destined by the Spirit. What humans experience pleasure and pain on earth is in material and spiritual forms, in most cases, in material form. It is also true that humans, most of whom, believe in God and lead a life of materialism and spiritualism, the extent the circumstances permit. All other beings on earth live in their own natural ways not knowing materialism and spiritualism; they do experience pleasure and pain which is understood by their own way of communication among each other in expressionless term, also noticeable by humans. The elements of pleasure and pain are the parts of the materialistic way of living of humans because of physical sensitiveness the mind and body present.

It is not to suggest here that one should give up materialistic living and live like a Sanyasi. It is not that. Practising Dhayna is more relevant and important for those living in worldly affairs than a Sanyasi. Because, one could learn how controlled materialistic world one can lead. One should also learn how to prevail over the mind through the practice of Dhyana to secure Quietitude that helps the humans develop much needed concentration, confidence and excellence using the same mind which gets converted into Quietitude, to live a happy and healthy life and do one's duties with all earnestness, humility and humanness. Quietitude also helps controlling and self-treatment of Blood Pressure, Sugar (to prevent Diabetes), positive breathing system very vital for the functioning of the body and mind, increasing positivity that also helps control growth of chronic diseases. Above all, quietened mind makes human to live in peace or do in peace whatever one wants or supposed to do as part of profession, duty, activity, business etc.

In a human or other conscious being, the element, part, substance, or process that reasons, thinks, feels, wills, perceives, judges, etc.: the processes of the human mind. ... Reason, sanity, or sound mental condition: to lose one's mind, a way of thinking and feeling; disposition; temper: a liberal mind. Ego is the part of the mind that mediates between the conscious and the unconscious and is responsible for reality testing and a sense of personal identity. It represents the person, the mind in itself not having any form, acts both in positive and negative ways depending upon the leads it gets from the intellect (conscious) [intelligence is the general mental ability to reason, solve problems and learn, while consciousness is awareness and awareness of what is inside and outside]. Intellect becomes wisdom when it securely lodges in the mind, according to Dr. S. Radhakrishnan, noted before. If that does not happen, it thinks independent of Spirit thus breaking its connect with that Source of Life, rather it becomes indifferent to that Source, the Conscience that is capable of discriminating what is good and what is bad of what a person intends to do or not to do. Being forced by the leads of the conscious, the mind conveys to the senses that triggers into ultimate commissioning of an act. An act whether it is good or bad is understandable by a person only when he or she is able to establish and maintain a discernable connection between himself or herself with the spiritual route to feel the pulse of the God manifested in Spirit which further links to Conscience that cautions the person what he or she intends to do is good or bad. What ultimately a human does or acts, he alone become answerable to that and also undergo the pleasure or painful process in life. That linkage is the ever shining expression of spirituality honestly and sincerely understood and followed. When there is a conflict between the Conscience and Conscious, Conscience must prevail.

# SECTION [14] SOUL

**Hinduism**

What one can understand is that the mind is the source origination of positive or negative bias. When mind is in search for fulfillment of the 'desires' under the direction of Buddhi [Intellect], it has no capacity to test the positivity or the negativity of the direction but blindly goes in search. There is 'Conscience' adjacent to the Spirit and Conscience within humans. ['Conscience', according to Online Dictionary means 'what we mean by conscience. One very common view of conscience is that it is a distinct mental faculty, an intuitive moral sense that determines the rightness and wrongness of actions.] The mind of humans when it starts thinking does not distinguish what is right or wrong. The one that it thinks right, it takes the positive bias while the one that it thinks wrong, it takes the negative bias. Those humans who practiced and developed the capacity to control the mind wandering in pursuit of desires through the practice of Dhyana [Meditation] or Yoga. The word "yoga" itself is a Sanskrit noun derived from the root word "yuj" which means "to attach, join, harness, yoke". The most literal translation into English is "yoke". In the U.S. it's often defined as "the unification of mind and body".

While this is not entirely inaccurate, the traditional Hindu meaning goes a bit deeper. The traditional definition is the union of individual consciousness and the divine, or Atman. Loosely translated, Atman is a person's true self or soul. The meaning is complex.']

[Lingua Link DC] and Dhyana [Meditation] both of which capture the 'concentration' as the centric point. Through this process, they were enlightened and followed the path towards GOD, which suggests their absolute Faith in the existence of GOD and derive His Qualitative Descriptions as contained in the Holy Book of every religion. The path they followed imbibed in them the Qualities of God which they not only practiced but also propagated the same among the humans for the survival of the mankind whereupon the religion rests and the concept of God continues to exists and to dive in deep depth continual efforts to understand about the god through religions and scientific research as one could find the Google Website. The human believes in god but at the same questions himself or herself whether god exists. This is contradictory conceptions and its reconciliation lies one's within.

The humans who get tagged with the mind with negative bias for various reasons that occur in one's life that leads to loss of sensibility, creates depression, loneliness, abject approach to the life and reasons of similar natures while those who by constant and continual practice of Dhyana or Yoga make best efforts to not to come within the clutches of Ego. That is, they bypass the Ego whereby they move towards understanding the Atman within the humans.

Ego lands itself in complexities for reasons of its individualized or isolated approach ignoring the existence of the 'Conscience' also within the human adjacent to Spirit, the critical function of which is to weigh the weight of rightness or wrongness in a given situation or circumstance. Those who are able to put aside the Egoism and to make the Ego to seek access to the Conscience to know whether what it intended to do or not to do are right or wrong. 'Conscience is the feeling you get when you evaluate if you've done something "correct" or "wrong". It is with the help of our conscience, developed at an individual (personal) level, that we understand the moral principles we hold. This motivates us to act on them and therefore helps us assess our character and behavior. Ultimately, it helps us judge ourselves against those principles, in terms of how well we follow them.'[Science ABC]. Author personally believes that the 'Conscience' draws its judgemental capacity from Spirit. What is Conscience according to the meaning assigned under the major Religions is also explained below.

"In Hindu philosophy, the conscience is closely tied to the concept of Dharma, which refers to righteous living, moral law, and duty. Dharma guides individuals on how to live their lives in accordance with ethical principles and societal norms. A clear and guiltless conscience is seen as a result of adhering to one's Dharma." [Source: https://www.hindu-blog.com/2024/09/a-guiltless-conscience-is-what-brings.html

**Islam**

"……The Islamic concept of Taqwa is closely related to conscience. In the Qur'an verses 2:197 & 22:37 Taqwa refers to "right conduct" or "piety", "guarding of oneself" or "guarding against evil".[20] Qur'an verse 47:17 says that God is the ultimate source of the believer's Taqwa which is not simply the product of individual will but requires inspiration from God.[21] In Qur'an verses 91:7–8, God the Almighty talks about how He has perfected the soul, the conscience and has taught it the wrong (fujūr) and right (Taqwa). Hence, the awareness of vice and virtue is inherent in the soul, allowing it to be tested fairly in the life of this world and tried, held accountable on the day of judgment for responsibilities to God and all humans.[2........." [Source: Conscience – Wikipedia]

**Buddhism**

Do Buddhists believe in a soul? We answer your questions on Buddhism and meditation.- Lion's Roar - 2 August 2017

"The short answer is no. In fact, this is the defining premise of Buddhism and one of the main things that differentiates it from other religions. In ancient Hinduism, the soul was called the *atman* and the basic Buddhist view was described as *anatman*—no soul.

A soul is considered to be something at our core that is single, independent, and unchanging. This isn't just a religious belief; deep down, we all believe we have a soul. When I feel hurt, I must believe there is a separate "me" that is being hurt. In that sense, soul, self, and ego all refer to the same thing—our belief in a single, independent, and unchanging "me," whether mundane or transcendent.

The Buddha said that all phenomena—including us—are conditioned, and all conditioned phenomena are impermanent. Far from being single, independent, and unchanging, we are made up of many parts, a product of causes and conditions, and constantly changing.

Yet Buddhism does say we have an essential nature that transcends conditioned or material existence. In the Mahayana, this is called *buddhanature*, the open expanse of awakeness in which all good qualities reside.

Is this just another version of a soul? Well, it is if you think of it that way—if you try to identify yourself with it. But in reality, buddhanature is said to be empty of all concepts of self and identity, as well as birth, death, time, space, etc. To be *anatman*, if you will." [Source: https://www.lionsroar.com/do-buddhists-believe-in-a-soul/ ]

### Jainism

"The soul - Last updated 2009-09-10 - an overview of Jain beliefs about the soul.

Jain beliefs about the soul

Jain ideas about the soul differ from those of many other religions.

The Jain word that comes closest to soul is *jiva*, which means a conscious, living being. For Jains body and soul are different things: the body is just an inanimate container - the conscious being is the jiva.

After each bodily death, the jiva is reborn into a different body to live another life, until it achieves liberation. When a jiva is *embodied* (i.e. in a body), it exists throughout that body and isn't found in any particular bit of it.

Jains believe:

the soul exists forever

each soul is always independent

the soul is responsible for what it does

the soul experiences the consequences of its actions

the soul can become liberated from the cycle of birth and death

not all souls can be liberated - some souls are inherently incapable of achieving this

the soul can evolve towards that liberation by following principles of behaviour

Individuality

Each jiva is an individual quite independent of other jivas. This is different from one of the Hindu Vedanta schools of belief where each soul is part of a single ultimate reality.

Jains believe that there are an infinite number of souls in the universe - every living thing, no matter how primitive, is a jiva - and at any given time many of these jivas are not embodied.

Souls have not fallen from perfection

For Jains, each jiva has been associated with matter, and involved in the cycle of birth and death since the beginning of time. They did not in some way fall from perfection to become involved in this cycle.

Some jivas, through their own efforts, have become liberated and escaped from the cycle.

Liberated souls

Some jivas have achieved liberation from the cycle of samsara or reincarnation and are not reborn. They are called *siddhas*.

Liberated jivas don't have physical bodies; they possess infinite knowledge, infinite vision, infinite power, and infinite bliss - in effect they have become perfect beings.

This makes liberated jivas the beings most like gods in Jain belief, but they are very different from the conventional idea of gods:

they do not create or destroy

it's not possible to have any sort of relationship with them

they do not intervene in the universe

they did not set down the laws of the universe

they do not make any demands on human beings

they don't reward human beings in any way, or forgive their sins, or give them grace

human beings don't owe their existence to them

humans can only use them as an inspiration

So when Jains worship 'gods' they do so to set before themselves the example of perfection that they want to follow in their own lives.

Non-liberated souls

Every jiva has the possibility of achieving liberation, and thus of becoming a god, and each soul is involved in a process of evolving towards that state.

Categories of non-liberated soul

**Ekendriya** - beings with one sense

Jains include many things as jivas that non-Jains regard as either inanimate or plants. They classify these as immobile beings, with only one sense - the sense of touch:

**Earth-bodied**: clay, sand, metal etc

**Water-bodied**: fog, rain, ice etc

**Fire-bodied**: fire, lightning etc.

**Air-bodied**: wind, gas etc.

**Plant-bodied**: trees, flowers, vegetables etc

**Beindriya** - beings with two senses

These are very simple organisms that are thought to have two senses - touch and taste. This category includes things like worms and termites.

**Treindriya** - beings with three senses

These have the senses of touch, taste and smell. This category includes insects like ants, beetles and moths.

**Chaurindriya** - beings with four senses

These have the senses of touch, taste, smell and sight. This category includes wasps, locusts and scorpions.

**Panchendriya** - beings with five senses

These have the senses of touch, taste, smell, sight and hearing. There are four classes of these beings:

Infernal beings: souls living in hell. This form of jiva experiences the greatest suffering.

**Higher animals**: This includes all non-human animals above insects.

Human beings: This is the only form of jiva which is able to obtain liberation directly.

Heavenly beings: This form of jiva is the happiest."[Source: https://www.bbc.co.uk/religion/religions/jainism/beliefs/soul.shtml#:~:text=Jain%20ideas%20about%20the%20soul%20differ%20from%20those,container%20-%20the%20conscious%20being%20is%20the%20jiva

**Sikhism**

"Sikhs believe in the moral order of the universe and know that God is both just and generous. He resides in the individual. The God within guides the human being through an inner voice. This is generally termed as conscience, within the individual. There is a perpetual struggle between good and evil. The conscience denounces evil and supports the good. We feel happy when we follow its command and unhappy, if we disobey it." [Source: https://sikhheritageeducation.com/introduction-to-sikhism-by-g-s-mansukhani-what-is-conscience/ ]

**Christianity**

**What Does the Bible Say about the Soul? -So, what is the soul? Is it more than just the non-corporeal part of a person? The Bible seems to teach that it is. The soul is an integrated living being, comprising both physical and non-physical parts. - Ed Jarrett - Contributing Writer - Updated Dec 14, 2022**

"What is the soul? This question has been asked and answered many times over the years. And the answers to this question vary considerably. The nature of the soul is challenging to define fully, and I make no claims to having anything like a complete understanding of the topic. But this article will take a brief survey of the Bible and see what it has to say.

The Soul in Greek Thought

It may seem strange to discuss the Greek conception of the soul in a paper about what the Bible teaches. But it is important to understand some of the influence that

Greek thought has had on the Christian perspective of the soul.

For the early Greek philosophers, the soul was quite distinct from the body, forming a dualism. The soul was immortal but imprisoned within a mortal body.

Many of their schools of thought held that the souls are housed in a series of physical bodies until they become virtuous enough to finally escape the cycle. This is similar to the reincarnation of eastern religions, and it may be that the Greeks were somewhat influenced.

While Christianity rightly rejects the idea of reincarnation, the duality of soul and body is a concept that is shared with many Christian thinkers. A look into what the scriptures say will help determine if that view is valid or not.

The Soul in the Old Testament

The Hebrew word nepeš is the word translated as "soul" in the Old Testament. It is found 754 times in the Old

Testament and is also translated into a variety of other English words, including being, life, me, you, heart, people, and creature.

Most of us are familiar with the account of God's forming of Adam in Genesis chapter 2. God formed him from the dust, breathed into him the breath of life, and he became a living soul (nepeš) or being. But this is not the first usage of nepeš in the creation account.

In Genesis 1:20, God created the living creatures (nepeš) that inhabited the seas. And in Genesis 1:24, God created living creatures (nepeš) on the land according to their kinds. And finally, in Genesis 1:30, God gave the green plants to everything that had the breath (nepeš) of life in it.

Some other places where nepeš is used are shown below:

"Adam named every living creature (nepeš)" (Genesis 2:19). "God will demand an accounting for the life (nepeš) of a human" (Genesis 9:5).

"Abram took his wife, Lot, their possessions, and all of the people (nepeš) they had acquired in Harran and went to Canaan" (Genesis 12:5). "The angels told Lot and his family to flee for their lives (nepeš)" (Genesis 19:17).

"Shechem's heart (nepeš) was drawn to Diana" (Genesis 34:3). "For a serious injury, you are to take life (nepeš) for life (nepeš)" (Exodus 21-23).

"If any member (nepeš) of the community sins unintentionally" (Leviticus 4:27). "Priests must not go near a dead body (nepeš)" (Leviticus 21:11).

"Love the LORD your God with all your heart and with all your soul (nepeš) and with all your strength" (Deuteronomy 6:5).

As you can see from this brief list, the Old Testament concept of the soul is not what we often think about. In the Old Testament, every living creature is a soul (nepeš), not just humans.

And nepeš is used to refer to the whole person, not just some non-corporeal part of the person. A nepeš can die, and it can be acquired by another person as a slave. All those usages are contrary to how most of us think of the soul.

The one passage listed above that could be used to support a soul distinct from the body is Deuteronomy 6:5.

But considering other uses of nepeš, you have to wonder if the Deuteronomy passage is listing discrete parts of a person or if it is referring to the whole person and all that they are.

The Soul in the New Testament

In the New Testament, the Greek word psyche is the word translated as soul. This word is found in the New Testament 102 times and is also translated as life, heart, mind, you, and man, among many others, with life being the most common word.

Psyche is frequently used to refer to the whole person. But at other times, it is distinct from the body.

The following list will give you a sampling of how this word is used in the New Testament:

"Do not worry about your life (psychē), what you will eat or drink; or about your body, what you will wear" (Matthew 6:25).

"Do not be afraid of those who kill the body but cannot kill the soul (psychē). Rather, be afraid of the One who can destroy both soul (psychē) and body in hell" (Matthew 10:28).

"For even the Son of Man did not come to be served, but to serve, and to give his life (psychē) as a ransom for many" (Mark 10:45).

"Just as the Father knows me and I know the Father — and I lay down my life (psychē) for the sheep" (John 10:15).

"Men who have risked their lives (psychē) for the name of our Lord Jesus Christ" (Acts 15:26).

The passage in Matthew 6:25, at first glance, seems to separate psychē and body. But if that is really the case in this passage, you would have to consider what value food and drink have to a non-corporeal entity.

This would seem to be more a matter of parallelism where psychē and body are just two different ways of saying the same thing.

Matthew 10:28 is clearer in its distinction between the psychē and the body. Satan can destroy the body but cannot harm the psychē.

1 Thessalonians 5:23 also supports a distinction between the body and the psychē, although it adds a third component, the spirit.

But if we consider the psychē as an immortal non-corporeal part of us, then the passages that refer to laying down our psychē or risking our psychē become more challenging.

And when Jesus laid down his psychē for us, he was certainly referring to his physical life rather than giving up his immortal self.

Most of the time, it seems like psychē is used in a very similar fashion to nepeš, referring to the whole person. The physical and spiritual components of life are tightly bound together. At least until separated by physical death.

The Soul and the Body

It should be clear from the way that nepeš and psychē are used in the Bible that a clear distinction between body and soul, our corporeal and non-corporeal parts, is not supported. That distinction is one that has been adopted into Christianity from.

Greek thought.

In the scriptures, I am a soul rather than a soul living in a body. While some passages support some form of distinction between the two, the bulk of the Scripture does not make that distinction. So much so that at death, it is the soul that is said to die.

The great creatures of the sea and the beasts living on the land are also identified as souls. A soul is a living, breathing, and probably thinking being. It is not unique to humans. What is unique to us is that death is not the end for us.

The Soul after Death

So, what happens when the physical part of me ceases to function? When I die?

What happens to the non-corporeal part of me, that part we often identify as the soul?

I have written more about that here [Author of this book adds: It is a separate Article. Not reproduced]. But in short, we are, for a time, unclothed. Absent from our bodies but present with the Lord. And looking forward to the resurrection at the end of the age when we will again be united with a body and be complete.

What Does This Mean?

So, what is the soul? Is it more than just the non-corporeal part of a person? The Bible seems to teach that it is. The soul is an integrated living being comprising both physical and non-physical parts. And that is true of both humans and animals.

While a distinction might be drawn between the corporeal and non-corporeal parts of a person, it is like drawing a distinction between a person's arm and leg.

They are not the same thing, but they are both necessary for a complete person. Even so, both the physical and non-physical portions of me are necessary for a complete person, a soul.

A soul will be temporarily unclothed in death. But, at least for believers, that unclothed state is temporary. At the resurrection at the end of the age, it will be reclothed with a new body, one that will last for eternity.

# SECTION [15]
# CONSCIENCE AND CONSCIOUSNESS

## The difference between consciousness and conscience - June 14, 2023|Chapter 18, Text 62, Nourish your devotion, Understanding Gita concepts

"Consciousness is the fundamental energy of the soul. The Sanskrit word for it is chetana. If we compare the soul to a flashlight, consciousness is the beam of light. Consciousness arising from the soul enters the mind, spreads across the body, and then expands outward, enabling us to be aware of our surroundings, analyze those inputs, and act appropriately. Consciousness is the energy that utilizes the mind and body as instruments for awareness, analysis and action.

Without consciousness, we can't function — as happens when we are unconscious or in a coma. During such times, the beam of light is obscured — that is, the consciousness coming from the soul no longer surfaces to the level of the physical body, which is why we observe no signs of consciousness in the person.

Within our consciousness is the specific faculty for moral awareness, which is called conscience, known in Sanskrit as Vivek-buddhi. Conscience is the source of our sense of right and wrong. While all living beings are driven in their choices by their biological instincts, our choices as human beings are guided by one additional factor: conscious moral awareness or conscience.

Both consciousness and conscience can become conditioned and contaminated. Just as a polluted consciousness can distort our awareness, a polluted conscience can distort our moral compass. While everyone possesses some sense of right and wrong, not everyone's sense of right and wrong always aligns with what is objectively right and wrong. For instance, suppose someone grew up in a family where meat-eating is the norm. If they choose to become vegan, they may feel guilty that they are betraying their family or tradition. Though they are doing something good — ceasing violence against animals perpetrated to satisfy their palate — why do they feel bad about doing something good? Because of their culturally conditioned conscience, which is misled and misleading?

Therefore, while our conscience is important as a guide for discerning right and wrong, it is equally important to recognize that conscience is not the ultimate authority. We need to align our conscience with wisdom derived from time-tested sources like scripture. When conscience becomes thus purified, it becomes a channel for the voice of the divinity within us, the Supersoul. A divinely aligned conscience is a potent guide to take us toward our highest good, as indicated in the Bhagavad-gita (18.62).

Summary:

Consciousness is the foundational faculty for all awareness; conscience is the specific faculty for moral awareness."

[Source: https://gitadaily.com/the-difference-between-consciousness-and-conscience/

# Conscience or Consciousness: Understanding Their Differences and Roles in Human Mind - By Josh / 14 October 2024.

"In our quest to understand the human mind, we often encounter the terms "conscience" and "consciousness". These concepts, while seemingly similar, play distinct roles in our mental world. Conscience acts as our moral compass, guiding us through right and wrong, while consciousness is the state of being aware of ourselves and our surroundings.

Exploring the nuances between conscience and consciousness not only enriches our understanding of ourselves but also enhances our appreciation of the complex nature of human cognition. As we investigate deeper, we uncover how these two facets intertwine, influencing our decisions and perceptions.

By distinguishing between them, we can better navigate our thoughts and actions, leading to a more profound grasp of what it truly means to be human. Join us as we unravel the intricacies of these fascinating elements of our psyche.

Key Takeaways

Distinct Definitions: Conscience serves as a moral compass, guiding ethical decisions, while consciousness refers to awareness of self and surroundings, forming the basis of personal identity.

Historical Evolution: The terms "conscience" and "consciousness" have evolved, with significant influences from philosophical and linguistic shifts, particularly during the 17th and 18th centuries.

Role in Cognition: Conscience and consciousness contribute uniquely to human cognition, with conscience influencing moral judgment and consciousness driving self-awareness and perception.

Scientific Insights: Both neuroscience and cognitive psychology offer valuable insights into these concepts, highlighting their distinct functions and impacts on decision-making processes.

Common Confusions: Despite their different meanings, "conscience" and "consciousness" are often confused due to their similar spelling and historic interchange in media and culture.

Influence on Daily Life: Conscience influences ethical decision-making and personal growth through self-reflection, while consciousness enhances interaction with the world and personal identity development.

Understanding Conscience and Consciousness

Let's clarify the distinct elements of conscience and consciousness, as each plays a unique role in human cognition. Our exploration focuses on the key differences and their impact on human behaviour.

**Defining Conscience**

Conscience is our internal guide determining the morality of our actions. It involves moral awareness and a sense of obligation towards righteousness. Typically involving feelings of guilt, conscience influences choices based on moral standards. Culturally, it's represented by figures like Jiminy Cricket in Pinocchio, embodying the character's moral advisor.

Conscience evolves through philosophical and theological interpretations, reflecting collective moral values. Our natural instincts, such as survival, drive its development. It remains pivotal in evaluating the ethical implications of our actions, serving as a crucial component in the decision-making process.

**Defining Consciousness**

Consciousness, contrastingly, relates to our awareness of ourselves and our environment. It refers to the state of being awake and aware. Consciousness is the foundation of self-perception and interpretation of surroundings. This awareness forms the basis for personal identity and subjective experiences, differentiating us from unconscious entities.

Understanding consciousness involves examining perception, thoughts, and responses to stimuli. It integrates data from our sensory inputs, providing a cohesive experience of reality. Through enhanced consciousness, we cultivate a richer awareness of our existence and interconnectedness with the world.

By exploring these concepts separately, we enhance our appreciation of the intricate dynamics shaping human thought and action.

**Historical Perspectives**

In the 17th century, the meanings of "conscience" and "consciousness" evolved significantly. Initially, the Latin conscientia and French conscience were predominantly about morality. But, these terms began to adopt a purely psychological interpretation during this period.

**Philosophical Views**

Philosophical shifts were pivotal to the evolution of these terms. René Descartes, a significant figure in this change, used the term conscientia to align more with what we now understand as consciousness. This marked a departure from traditional moral implications. The absence of a clear linguistic distinction in Latin and French created ambiguity between conscientia and conscience. While "conscience" retained its moral focus, "consciousness" emerged to identify the evolving concept separate from morality.

Psychological Approaches

Psychological approaches began distinguishing between moral conscience and self-awareness. The English language adopted "consciousness" in the 17th century to reflect this difference. Meanwhile, in Germany, "Bewusstsein" emerged in the early 18th century to denote awareness, whereas "Gewissen" continued to refer to moral conscience. This differentiation enabled a more precise understanding of the human psyche, allowing thinkers to explore consciousness as awareness of self and environment, distinct from moral judgment.

Key Differences Between Conscience and Consciousness

Exploring the distinctions between conscience and consciousness helps us understand the complexity of the human mind. Conscience, driven by moral principles, contrasts with consciousness, which governs our awareness.

Moral Awareness vs. Self-Awareness

Conscience reflects moral awareness, guiding our sense of right and wrong. It acts as an internal moral compass, steering our actions based on ethical values. Conscience influences feelings such as guilt and pride, shaping our character and defining our moral judgments. In contrast, consciousness represents self-awareness. It refers to our ability to perceive, process, and respond to our thoughts and environment. Consciousness allows us to experience and interact with the world, forming the basis of personal identity.

Decision Making and Self-Regulation

Conscience plays a crucial role in decision-making, influencing us to align actions with moral codes. It's essential for self-regulation as it helps evaluate actions as good or evil, influencing choices through a sense of obligation or virtue. On the other hand, consciousness is vital for self-regulation through awareness and perception. It enables us to understand our internal states and external environments, affecting how we process information and make decisions. Together, conscience and consciousness shape human behaviour, although through distinct mechanisms and awareness levels.

Scientific Research

Our understanding of conscience and consciousness is enriched by scientific research, which delves into their distinct aspects. Neuroscience and cognitive psychology both provide key insights into these concepts.

Neuroscientific Insights

From a neuroscientific perspective, conscience is part of a complex system influencing decision-making processes. Although less explored than consciousness, conscience integrates instinctual factors like survival to guide moral judgment. The neurophysiology of conscience involves neural networks that evaluate ethical behaviour. These networks process social norms and personal beliefs, weighing them in our moral framework.

Cognitive Psychology Findings

Cognitive psychology offers additional insights into how conscience functions. It posits that conscience is linked to moral self-awareness and self-assessment, reflecting on our actions as right or wrong. This evaluative process involves integrating various information sources and aligning them with internal moral principles. Psychological studies suggest that through socialisation, conscience evolves and helps us navigate complex moral landscapes, informing decisions with an inherent sense of moral duty.

The Role in Everyday Life

Conscience significantly influences our daily decisions, acting as a moral compass. It guides us through complex situations by distinguishing right from wrong, invoking feelings such as guilt or satisfaction.

Ethical Decision Making

Conscience frames the choices we make by assessing their ethical implications. It evaluates actions against our internal moral benchmarks. When facing dilemmas, such as whether to disclose a mistake at work, our conscience prompts us to consider honesty over immediate benefits. This guiding voice aligns our actions with ethical standards, often reflecting collective societal values.

Self-Reflection and Growth

Conscience also fosters self-reflection and personal growth. By prompting us to revisit past actions, it encourages introspection and self-assessment. Experiencing remorse after a heated argument with a friend nudges us to examine our behaviour and aspire for improvement. This ongoing process shapes character development, as we align closer with our ethical ideals, eventually enhancing our moral and personal identity.

Common Misconceptions

Confusing "conscience" and "consciousness" is quite common. Their spelling similarities contribute to frequent misunderstandings in language learning and everyday conversations, even among native English speakers.

Confusion in Terminology

Both terms originate from Latin roots, furthering their mix-up. Conscience refers to a moral compass, guiding our perception of right and wrong. In contrast, consciousness deals with awareness and perception of our environment and self. Such confusion becomes evident when considering learning platforms or courses like IELTS [International English Language Testing System (IELTS0] and TOEFL, [Test of English as a Foreign Language (TOEFL)] where clarity in understanding language nuances can be essential for success.

Media and Cultural Influences

Media often blurs the line between conscience and consciousness, affecting public perception. Movies, literature, and cultural narratives use these terms interchangeably, leading to further misunderstandings. Recognising the distinct meanings of these terms can enhance comprehension, especially for those in Business English or Language Immersion programmes where precise language usage is necessary.

Conclusion

Understanding the distinct yet interconnected roles of conscience and consciousness enriches our grasp of human cognition. By recognising conscience as our moral compass and consciousness as our self-awareness, we gain insight into how these elements shape our decisions and identity. This knowledge not only enhances personal growth but also aids in effective communication by clarifying commonly confused terms. As we continue to explore these concepts, we deepen our appreciation for the complexities of the human mind and its remarkable capacity for introspection and ethical reasoning."

[Source: [https://thebritishlanguageschool.com/conscience-or-consciousness/]

**Ana Nogales, Ph.D.,** is a clinical psychologist and well-known media personality, columnist, and speaker. A family therapy specialist, she is the author of *Parents Who Cheat: How Children and Adults Are Affected When Their Parents Are Unfaithfu*l, as well as *Latina Power! Using 7 Strengths You Already Have to Create the Success You Deserve* and *Dr. Ana Nogales' Book of*

*Love, Sex and Relationships*. Dr. Nogales is also the Clinical Director of the non-profit organization that she founded, Casa de la Familia, established for victims of rape, sexual assault, child sexual and physical abuse, human trafficking, and domestic violence.

"She wrote an Article in Psychology Today posted on website which emphatically encourages the youths to live their life to the fullest rather than develop frustration in life detrimental to one's own life. Excerpts from the Article which the author considers highly motivating:

- Life is an invitation to learn. We can learn something from every moment, good or bad.

- Life is not static; it's in constant movement, much like the waves of the ocean. Each wave that comes brings with it new experiences, and each one is different. Just as the bad waves can sometimes show no mercy, the good ones come along and refresh us. Nothing lasts forever.

- Life is a gift; some people depart too soon and don't have the fortune to know life. Those who have it should enjoy it.

- Our lives are not only our own. They also belong to those who surround us. We should take care of ourselves because we are important to others—even though we sometimes forget it.

- Each new day is a new experience. If we don't live it, we won't know what we're missing.

- We are the designers of our life. It is our challenge to find beauty, even—and especially—when the opposite occurs. Finding beauty in the world is possible and brings countless rewards.

- We all live through experiences that leave scars. However, there is always someone to give us a hand during those difficult times. The important thing is to accept that help.

- Making an effort to deal with problems can make us aware of how strong we really are. Life's challenges don't exist only to upset us—they exist so that we understand ourselves better and get to know who we really are.

- To live is to discover something about ourselves of which we were not aware.

- To live is to look at ourselves in the mirror and discover a message of love in our own eyes.

- To live is to allow ourselves to fall in love—with someone, with something, or with life itself.

- Viewing death as a source of meaning can be comforting for many—but rather than using this as an argument in favour of suicide, it's critical to leverage such a perspective in order to make the most of life while it lasts.

- Death is waiting for each of us anyway; why call on it before our time?"

Ana Nogales has enwrapped the meaning of real life which engrosses every human. This spirit needs to be inculcated in the way of living of every human that embraces the Soul that offers more positivity to human thinking and enables to discard the negativity effects. Understanding of the essence of life as envisaged in the Article empowers all those self-caged into negativity and depression to wake up to the reality of life to enjoy as enjoyed by other humans on the earth. Author earnestly believes that his efforts on elimination of negativity in thoughts and depression, among the humans, would be able to succeed in overcoming them. Author considers it a greatest satisfaction and gratitude to those engaged in bringing succour to the affected ones to throw out the negativity and to practice the positivity.

Absence of God-fearing culture has become order of the day. This is evident from the types of mishaps and crimes are happening. (God-fearing used to describe religious people who try to obey the rules of their religion and to live in a way that is considered morally right). These are frightening and horrendous. The religious rules and the state laws have little or no concern for those committing such acts. Late APJ Abdul Kalam, former President once said "........ in India we only read about death, sickness, terrorism, crime. Why are we so NEGATIVE? ........" Negativity has replaced the positivity in our thoughts and deeds.

So also are our actions and behavioural patterns. It could be said that it is one of the reasons why the sense of God-fearing is disappearing both among the literate and illiterate people who commit crimes. That is the reason that we hardly hesitate to do things that are religiously not permitted. This negativity is so strong that the person reacts wildly at the smallest disagreement or provocation. This is the sign of egoism at the peak. That means the positivity is sinking and negativity is rising.

Why is it so? Because the humans, particularly the politicians and the religious leaders, are not sincere to themselves, more so in our country whose speeches are melodious to the people, the reason being the majority of population of the country is rural oriented? For them, when they talk to the people, the group of people, in the assembly of people, in the public gatherings of the people on important occasions, they are not sincere but exhibit sincerity as a gesture while what they do in their real lives and what the people who heard them at different times, is not the same what they talked to the people. This is creating a yawning gap of belief among the people who are constrained to think that the people who are not sincere to themselves, how they could be sincere to the people. This is echoing in every corner of the world because they don't practice what they preach to the people. It results in loss of faith among the sustainers of democracy and reverse questions are posed by the people to such people. They haven't learnt to be true themselves first before talking about the same to others. Thus a visible gap exists between talk and walking the talk.

**WHEN A PERSON WANTS TO GO TO A PLACE, IF HE OR SHE SEES IT THROUGH EYES, IT LOOKS FAR OFF BUT WHEN HE OR SHE STARTS WALKING TO THAT PLACE, IT BECOMES NEARBY. SO, IT IS BETTER TO WALK THE TALK RATHER THAN TALK THE WALK. THUS GOES THE SAYING "IN THE END, IT'S NOT TALK BUT THE WALK THAT MATTERS" – UNKNOWN.**

# SECTION [16]
# ORIGIN OF UNIVERSE

**Vedicfeed.com in an Article 'Origin of the Universe according to Rigveda' - By Drishith - March 10, 2022 posted on its Website notes: [Excerpts]**

Nasadiya Sukta with translation

*Then even nothingness was not, nor existence, There was no air then, nor the heavens beyond it. What covered it? Where was it? In whose keeping Was there then cosmic water, in depths unfathomed?*

The Veda says that neither non-existence nor existence existed in the beginning. This is possible if there is no time. Veda says there was no time before the creation. Modern science also agrees with this hypothesis. According to Stephen W. Hawking, there was no time before the big bang and time began at the moment of the Big Bang.

The second line talks about the absence of the sky and atmosphere. The third line puts on the question, what covered these "Timeless" things? Where and Who/What is responsible for this?

The fourth line puts another question regarding cosmic water. (*Some scholars claim that this fourth line regarding a question about "Cosmic Water" is later additions to Vedas during estimated 900 BCE*)

**Then there was neither death nor immortality nor was there then the torch of night and day. The One breathed windlessly and self-sustaining. There was that One then, and there was no other.**

Veda says there is neither death nor immortality before the creation and there was no night, no day. This means there was no biological life, no light or darkness, no Sun/Moon/Stars or any other planets. The third line talks about the causeless cause. The cause is the cause of its own existence. It requires no air (external impulse) to exist. It exists on svadha, self-impulse.

The fourth line corresponds to the Vedic concept of a single cause: There was only that one, no other. That one exists on its own, and the existence of cause cannot be said to be an existence since there is time.

*At first there was only darkness wrapped in darkness. All this was only unillumined water. That One which came to be, enclosed in nothing, arose at last, born of the power of heat.*

This line talks about the absence of light, and space. The darkness existed refers to darkness due to the absence of light. The darkness that covers it refers to the mysticism that remains in a dark void spaceless timeless entity. In the absolute void that existed before time was that, which caused one entity to be formed from heat (or energy, tapas). Present physics theories of Big Bang also says the energy causes the one quark to form the whole universe.

*In the beginning desire descended on it that was the primal seed, born of the mind. The sages who have searched their hearts with wisdom know that which kin to that which is not is.*

According to modern science, creation of the universe is a spontaneous process from nothing, by separation of positive and negative energies. The zero-energy process is said to be "spontaneous". This "spontaneity" is what is termed "desire" in the verse. The "seed" may stand for a quark too. The seed is referred to poetically as the "mind" of the universe. It is that which acts. The third line tells that sages know what is connected to "the not existing" to the timeless cause seems as non-existing. This paradox, however, has been solved by sages, searching their hearts for wisdom.

*And they have stretched their cord across the void (or Rays), and know what was above, and what below. Seminal powers made fertile mighty forces. Below was strength, and over it was impulse.*

The word "Rashmi" can mean both void and rays. The sages went transverse through the quest of creation, and they knew that powers of seed made forces, self-power was below all, an effort was the above of all. Through self-power, the God (One) creates the seed, the seed creates through effort. (Seed can also be Hiranyagarbha, a Cosmic Egg)

*But, after all, who knows, and who can say Whence it all came, and how creation happened? The gods and the seekers are later than creation, So who knows truly whence it has arisen?*

The Veda repeats the questions of atheists and ignorant people and shows that who is the only One who can tell regarding all this, and that is timeless. The verse also uses a word Arvak that means both before and after. The third line can thus mean simultaneously "Since God is after the creation" or "Gods are before creation". The first meaning of the third line makes the third and fourth lines a question put by the atheists. The second meaning of the same word says the answer: "God is before the creation", so that who is the only one that knows truly whence all this has come to be.

*Whence all creation had its origin, Maybe he holds the reins, or maybe he doesn't, He, who surveys it all from highest heaven, Maybe he knows it all, or maybe even he doesn't.*

All creation has its origin, without a cause there is no creation. Veda says the "Cause" may or may not even know the "Cause of the creation". The cause is omnipotent through zero-knowledge. A common intellect of ours cannot figure out the "cause" of the creation of the universe. But, Vedic Sages (Rishis) knew it all and transferred the knowledge by composing beautiful literary works like Vedas**."**

**"DESTROY YOUR ILLUSIONS SO YOU CAN SEE REALITY. DESTROY YOUR FEARS SO YOU CAN TAKE RISKS. DESTROY YOUR EGO SO YOU CAN SEE LIFE." MAXIME LAGACÉ**

# CHARACTERISTICS OF THE FOUR YUGAS IN HINDUISM – BY ABHILASH RAJENDRAN – POSTED ON HINDU BLOG

The Hindu Puranas frequently discuss the four yugas — Krita, Treta, Dwapara, and Kali—which unfold in a cyclical sequence, each characterized by distinct features. A concise summary of the yuga-dharmas, describing the essential traits of each Yuga, is found in the Parasarasmriti (100 CE). Here

In Krita Yuga (also known as Satya Yuga), austerity (tapas) held paramount importance, with Manusmriti serving as the definitive guide. It was an era of truth (Satya Yuga), where people would leave their country upon witnessing sinful deeds. Even conversing with a sinner was considered a transgression, and curses uttered by the profoundly virtuous would immediately take effect. Generosity reached such heights that donors personally sought out the needy to fulfil their desires.

Treta Yuga witnessed a slight decline in ethical standards, with knowledge (Jnana) taking precedence. The Gautama Dharma Sutras became the authoritative text, and people would abandon their villages if sinful acts were observed. Accidentally touching a sinner was deemed a sin, and curses would manifest within ten days. Donors, though still generous, would call or invite the needy before offering gifts.

Dwapara Yuga saw a further decline in dharma, with a fifty percent decrease. Vedic rituals (Yajna) became prevalent, guided by the Shankha-likhita-dharmasutras. Families would be abandoned if even one-member transgressed dharma, and accepting food from a sinner was considered sinful. Curses took a month to take effect, and gifts were given after the person begged for them.

Kaliyuga (the current age), considered the worst, witnessed a significant reduction in dharma, leaving only a quarter behind. Giving gifts (Dana) became the primary righteous act, guided by the Parasara Smriti. If a person committed a sin, only he had to be abandoned. Those engaging in sinful deeds were seen as depraved, and curses took a year to manifest. Gifts were given only after extracting service.

In Kaliyuga, dharma and truth (satya) succumbed to adharma and untruth (anrta). Demons ruled over good kings, women used lust over power men, and there was a decline in religious rites like Agnihotra. Respect for elders disappeared, and young girls gave birth to babies, marking an all-encompassing decline in values."

More about Kaliyuga [the present Yuga]:

## Exploring Kaliyuga in Indian Mythology: Unveiling the Meaning and Significance - By Nitten Nair

Indian mythology is a treasure trove of ancient wisdom, offering insights into various aspects of life, spirituality, and the cycles of time. One prominent concept within Indian mythology is "Kaliyuga," a term that holds deep meaning and significance. In this blog, we will delve into the meaning of Kaliyuga, its characteristics, and its role in the cosmic timeline.

## Understanding Kaliyuga

Kaliyuga, often referred to as the "Age of Kali," is one of the four Yugas or cosmic ages in Hindu cosmology. These Yugas are cyclic periods that depict the rise and fall of human virtues, morality, and spirituality, as well as the varying levels of righteousness in society. Kaliyuga is considered the last and darkest of the four Yugas, symbolizing a period of moral decline, discord, and spiritual degradation.

The Length of Kaliyuga

Each Yuga has a specific duration, which collectively makes up a Mahayuga or Great Age. According to Hindu cosmology, a Mahayuga consists of four Yugas: Satyuga, Tretayuga, Dvaparayuga, and Kaliyuga. The duration of Kaliyuga is believed to be 432,000 years. This age is marked by a gradual decrease in the virtuous qualities of humanity, leading to an era characterized by greed, deceit, and moral decay.

Characteristics of Kaliyuga

Kaliyuga is described in various Hindu scriptures, such as the Puranas and the Mahabharata, as an age of spiritual darkness and moral degradation. Some of the prominent characteristics of Kaliyuga include:

1. Decline in Dharma: Dharma, the righteous path, is believed to be weakened during Kaliyuga. People become more self-centered and less inclined to follow moral principles and ethical values.

2. Lack of Spiritual Practices: The practice of meditation, self-discipline, and devotion to the divine becomes rare in Kaliyuga. Material pursuits take precedence over spiritual pursuits.

3. Shortened Lifespan and Weaker Health: As Kaliyuga progresses, human lifespan and overall health are believed to decline. This deterioration is seen as a reflection of the decreasing spiritual and moral vitality of the age.

4. Increase in Conflicts and Wars: The scriptures depict Kaliyuga as a time of heightened conflicts, wars, and societal unrest. Discord and aggression become more prevalent.

5. Deception and Dishonesty: The prevalence of deceit, hypocrisy, and dishonesty is believed to increase during Kaliyuga. People become more prone to lying and manipulation.

6. Diminished Wisdom: Intellectual capacities decline, leading to a lack of discernment and understanding of spiritual truths.

7. Loss of Virtue: Virtues such as compassion, truthfulness, and kindness become rare, as selfishness and ego take center stage.

Significance of Kaliyuga

While Kaliyuga is often portrayed as an age of darkness, its significance extends beyond the surface understanding. From a spiritual perspective, Kaliyuga is considered an opportunity for individuals to cultivate inner strength, resilience, and self-awareness amidst the challenges and distractions of the age. <u>It is believed that even a small effort toward spiritual growth during Kaliyuga can yield significant results due to the heightened difficulties faced</u>. [Emphasis added by the author]

Furthermore, Kaliyuga also signifies the cyclical nature of time and the cosmic order. Just as day turns into night and then back into day, the Yugas follow a similar pattern. After the culmination of Kaliyuga, the cycle begins anew with Satyuga, an age of heightened righteousness and spiritual purity.

Kaliyuga, the final and darkest age in Hindu cosmology, holds profound meaning and significance within the tapestry of Indian mythology. It serves as a reminder of the cyclical nature of time and the challenges humanity faces in maintaining spiritual and moral integrity. While Kaliyuga is marked by moral decline, deceit, and spiritual degradation, it also provides individuals with an opportunity to shine amidst adversity and cultivate their inner strength.

As we navigate the complexities of our lives, understanding the concept of Kaliyuga offers a broader perspective on the ebb and flow of human virtues and challenges. It encourages us to reflect on our actions, make conscious choices, and strive for personal growth and spiritual upliftment, even in the face of adversity. <u>Ultimately, Kaliyuga invites us to seek the light within ourselves, fostering a deeper connection with our spiritual essence and the cosmic rhythms that shape our existence.</u>" [Emphasis added by the author].

## KALI YUGA [WIKIPEDIA]

"Kali Yuga, in Hinduism, is the fourth, shortest, and worst of the four yugas (world ages) in a Yuga Cycle, preceded by Dvapara Yuga and followed by the next cycle's Krita (Satya) Yuga. It is believed to be the present age, which is full of conflict and sin.[1][2][3]

According to Puranic sources,[a] Krishna's death marked the end of Dvapara Yuga and the start of Kali Yuga, which is dated to 17/18 February 3102 BCE.[9][10] Lasting for 432,000 years (1,200 divine years), Kali Yuga began 5,125 years ago and has 426,875 years left as of 2024 CE.[11][12][13] Kali Yuga will end in the year 428,899 CE.[14][b]

Near the end of Kali Yuga, when virtues are at their worst, a cataclysm and a re-establishment of dharma occur to usher in the next cycle's Krita (Satya) Yuga, prophesied to occur by Kalki.[15]

Etymology

[edit]

Yuga (Sanskrit: युग), in this context, means "an age of the world", where its archaic spelling is yug, with other forms of yugam, yugānāṃ, and yuge, derived from yuj (Sanskrit: युज्, lit. 'to join or yoke'), believed derived from *yeug- (Proto-Indo-European: lit. 'to join or unite').[16]

Kali Yuga (Sanskrit: कलियुग, romanized: kaliyuga or kali-yuga) means "the age of Kali", "the age of darkness", "the age of vice and misery", or "the age of quarrel and hypocrisy".[17]

A complete description of Kali Yuga is found in the Mahabharata, Manusmriti, Vishnu Smriti, and various Puranas.[18]

Epigraphy

[edit]

According to P. V. Kane, one of the earliest inscriptions with one of the four yugas named is the Pikira grant of Pallava Simhavarman (mid-5th century CE):[19][20]

Who was ever ready to extricate dharma that had become sunk owing to the evil effects of Kaliyuga.

—*Pikira grant of Pallava Simhavarman, line 10 (3rd plate, front)*

Other epigraphs exist with named yugas in the Old Mysore region of India, published in Epigraphia Carnatica.[21]

Start date

[edit]

Information kiosk at tiBhalka, the place from where Krishna left for His realm in 3102 BC.

The start date and time of Kali Yuga was at midnight (00:00) on 17/18 February 3102 BCE.[9][22][14][23][10]

Astronomer and mathematician Aryabhata, who was born in 476 CE, finished his book Aryabhatiya in 499 CE, in which he wrote "When the three yugas (satyug, tretayug and dwaparyug) have elapsed and 60 x 60 (3,600) years of kaliyug have already passed, I am now 23 years old." Based on this information, Kali Yuga began in 3102 BCE, which is calculated from 3600 - (476 + 23) + 1 (no year zero from 1 BCE to 1 CE).[24]

According to K. D. Abhyankar, the starting point of Kali Yuga is an extremely rare planetary alignment, which is depicted in the Mohenjo-daro seals.[25]

## Duration and structure

[edit]

See also: Yuga Cycle, Hindu units of time, and List of numbers in Hindu scriptures

Hindu texts describe four yugas (world ages) in a Yuga Cycle, where, starting in order from the first age of Krita (Satya) Yuga, each yuga's length decreases by one-fourth (25%), giving proportions of 4:3:2:1. Each yuga is described as having a main period (a.k.a. yuga proper) preceded by its yuga-sandhyā (dawn) and followed by its yuga-sandhyāṃśa (dusk), where each twilight (dawn/dusk) lasts for one-tenth (10%) of its main period. Lengths are given in divine years (years of the gods), each lasting for 360 solar (human) years.[11][12][13]

Kali Yuga, the fourth age in a cycle, lasts for 432,000 years (1,200 divine years), where its main period lasts for 360,000 years (1,000 divine years) and its two twilights each last for 36,000 years (100 divine years). The current cycle's Kali Yuga, the present age, has the following dates based on it starting in 3102 BCE:[11][12][13]

Kali yuga

| Part | Start (– End) | Length |
|---|---|---|
| Kali-yuga-sandhya (dawn)* | 3102 BCE | 36,000 (100) |
| Kali-yuga (proper) | 32,899 CE | 360,000 (1,000) |

| Kali-yuga-sandhyamsa (dusk) | 392,899–428,899 CE | 36,000 (100) |

Years: 432,000 solar (1,200 divine)

(*) Current. [14]

Mahabharata, Book 12 (Shanti Parva), Ch. 231:[26][c]

(17) A year (of men) is equal to a day and night of the gods ... (19) I shall, in their order, tell you the number of years that are for different purposes calculated differently, in the Krita, the Treta, the Dwapara, and the Kali yugas. (20) Four thousand celestial years is the duration of the first or Krita age. The morning of that cycle consists of four hundred years and its evening is of four hundred years. (21) Regarding the other cycles, the duration of each gradually decreases by a quarter in respect of both the principal period with the minor portion and the conjoining portion itself.

Manusmriti, Ch. 1:[27]

(67) A year is a day and a night of the gods ... (68) But hear now the brief (description of) the duration of a night and a day of Brahman [(Brahma)] and of the several ages (of the world, yuga) according to their order. (69) They declare that the Krita age (consists of) four thousand years (of the gods); the twilight preceding it consists of as many hundreds, and the twilight following it of the same number. (70) In the other three ages with their twilights preceding and following, the thousands and hundreds are diminished by one (in each).

Surya Siddhanta, Ch. 1:[28]

(13) ... twelve months make a year. This is called a day of the gods. (14) ... Six times sixty [360] of them are a year of the gods ... (15) Twelve thousand of these divine years are denominated a Quadruple Age (caturyuga); of ten thousand times four hundred and thirty-two [4,320,000] solar years (16) is composed that Quadruple Age, with its dawn and twilight. The difference of the Golden and the other Ages, as measured by the difference in the number of the feet of Virtue in each, is as follows : (17) The tenth part of an Age, multiplied successively by four, three, two, and one, gives the length of the Golden and the other Ages, in order : the sixth part of each belongs to its dawn and twilight.

10,000-year sub-period

[edit]

A dialogue between Krishna and Ganga found in the Brahma Vaivarta Purana describes that for the first 10,000 years of Kali Yuga, the ill effects of Kali Yuga will be reduced due to the presence of bhakti yogis and the ability to nullify sinful reactions, after which Earth will be devoid of devout religious people and be shackled by Kali Yuga.[29][non-primary source needed] Gaudiya Vaishnavism believes this sub-period started later in Kali Yuga with the birth of Chaitanya Mahaprabhu (1486 CE).[30]

Characteristics

[edit]

Hinduism often symbolically represents morality (dharma) as an Indian bull. In the Satya Yuga, the first stage of development, the bull has four legs, which is reduced by one in each age that follows. The four legs of Dharma are Tapas lit. 'austerity', Śauca lit. 'cleanliness', Dayā lit. 'compassion' and Satya lit. 'truth'.[31] By the age of Kali, morality is reduced to only a quarter of that of the golden age, so that the bull of Dharma has only one leg, the one representing Satya.[32][33]

## References in the Mahabharata

[edit]

The Kurukshetra War and the decimation of Kauravas thus happened at the Yuga-Sandhi, the point of transition from one yuga to another.[34]

## Prophesied events

[edit]

A discourse by Markandeya in the Mahabharata identifies some of the attributes of people, animals, nature, and weather during the Kali Yuga.[35][36]

Other usage

[edit]

The Kali Yuga is an important concept in both Theosophy and Anthroposophy,[37][38] and in the writings of Helena Blavatsky, W.Q. Judge, Rudolf Steiner, Savitri Devi, and Traditionalist philosophers such as René Guénon and Julius Evola, among others. Rudolf Steiner believed that the Kali Yuga ended in 1900.[37]"

Let us also consider how the Universe works according to Islam, Christianity, Buddhism, Jainism and Sikhism. The versions of these Religions on the working of the

Universe are given below based on the Articles posted by the knowledgeable writers on the Google Website:

## Islam and the Nature of the Universe posted Online [https://islamonline.net/en/islam-and-the-nature-of-the-universe/] enlightens the humans as under:

"[It is God who raised the skies without support, as you can see, then assumed His throne, and enthralled the sun and the moon (so that) each runs to a predetermined course. He disposes all affairs, distinctly explaining every sign that you may be certain of the meeting with your Lord] (Ar-Ra`d 13:2)

The last of the Abrahamic religions, following Judaism and Christianity, Islam considers the creation of the universe as ultimate proof of the existence of one Creator who "is that dimension which makes other dimensions possible; He gives meaning and life to everything" (Rahman) According to the teachings of Islam, Allah (God) is the one and only god, the absolute Creator of the universe, its components and its laws. Allah is the beginning and the end of all things, and this is the foundation for Islam's teachings.

The Qur'an is the word of Allah as passed down to Muslims through the Prophet Muhammad (peace be upon him) and the existence of only one version of the Qur'an (there are no dissimilarities between any two copies) attests to the reverence in which Muslims hold it. For Muslims, the Qur'an, containing the word of Allah, provides irrefutable proof of His existence. Along with the Qur'an, nature provides another source for the proof of Allah's existence. This intimate relationship between the Qur'an and nature is shown in the phrase ayat, which refers to signs of Allah's existence in nature and also refers to the verses in the Qur'an.

The Creation

In Islam, the world as man knows it, begins and ends with Allah. Unlike Christianity and Judaism, the creation process is not described in detail, but referred to as a starting point for Allah's power. The creation story in Islam is described in the Qur'an as the creation of the universe by Allah's will with a single command: "Be!" Several verses in the Qur'an highlight Allah's power of creation: [Creator of the heavens and the earth from nothingness, He has only to say when He wills a thing: "Be," and it is] (Al-Baqarah 2:117) and, [That is how God creates what He wills, when He decrees a thing, He says "Be," and it is] (Aal `Imran 3:47).

In this manner, Allah created the heavens and the earth, the sun and the moon, and the rest of the universe. He created the plants and the animals, and placed them on Earth, and He decreed upon them the laws by which the natural order of all creation functions. The universe is an independent entity, it exists according to those laws and does not require (divine) intervention, yet it cannot "warrant for its own existence and it cannot explain itself" (Rahman). In Islam, this in itself is considered conclusive proof of Allah's existence. The laws placed by Allah take into account all natural phenomena and provide further proof for Allah's greatness, which the Qur'an describes in detail. [He ushers in the dawn, and made the night for rest, the sun and moon a computation. Such is the measure appointed by Him, the Omnipotent and All-Wise] (Al-An`am 6:96). Natural law, as decreed by Allah, "reflects and issues from the order that exists in the Divine Realm" (Nasr) where Allah exists.

Mankind & Nature

Man was created from clay, and is thus part of nature, not separate from it. This relationship with nature materialises in Islamic living in several ways, the most significant and obvious being death. Muslim burials require the corpse to be washed, have all items removed, and placed in the ground within three days—for an easier return to the earth whence it came.

Within Allah's universe, man was given a special place. In Islamic teachings, in contrast to those of Christianity, man was not made in God's image. Rather, Allah distinguished man from His other creations by breathing His own spirit into man. This preferential treatment of God's creation gave man two privileges not made available to the rest of creation: (1) freedom of choice and (2) specialised knowledge or "creative knowledge" (Rahman).

Freedom of choice allows man the ability to make the decision whether or not to worship Allah and follow His will. The universe, as described before, is governed by the laws decreed for it by Allah, and has, therefore, been in submission to Allah since its creation. Man, however, was given the ability to think, rationalize, and argue the presence of a creator, and then decide whether to submit to Him or not.

An Open Invitation to Knowledge and Learning

Creative knowledge was first displayed—according to the teachings of Islam—when, after the angels questioned Allah as to why he had created man in the form of Adam, Allah challenged the angels and Adam to name objects. The angels were unable to bestow names upon things, whereas Adam could, giving him superiority over those that he had named and demonstrating his Creator's power.

As part of man's privilege, Islam, through the Qur'an, invites man to discover the laws of nature and the ways in which the universe exists. There is no threat to Allah's supremacy in this way, because if Allah wills something to remain a mystery (such as Himself) then man has no possible way of discovering whatever Allah chooses to remain hidden. On the contrary, when man sees for himself the extent to which the universe has been meticulously planned and provided for, Allah's infinite wisdom becomes apparent. Man is invited to question, discover, explore, and manipulate the world around him and use it for his benefit.

There are three types of learning encouraged in Islam, all of which will (or should) inevitably lead to acknowledgement and recognition of Allah's power. These are: (1) the discovery of nature, its laws, and how it can be used for the benefit of mankind; (2) the exploration of the history and the geography of the physical world and its peoples; and (3) knowledge of oneself (Rahman).

This encouragement to learn and discover has led to a proliferation of Arab scholars in the fields of the natural sciences and mathematics. In Islamic philosophy, one must always seek knowledge, both within and without, as knowledge illuminates the path on which one must travel. Ignorance is an unfavourable state of being, as the process of acknowledging the existence and power of Allah is one of enlightenment through knowing.

"Nature exists for man to exploit for his own ends, while the end of man himself is nothing else but to serve God, to be grateful to him, and to worship him alone" (Rahman). Islam suggests that nature was created by Allah specifically for mankind's use and so must be recognised and respected as a gift for which man must be grateful. There are three reasons for creation: (1) "to serve as a collection of signs, or ayat, of the power and goodness of Allah"; (2) "to serve Allah and to be submissive to God's will"; and (3) "for the use of humans" (Timm).

Natural law in Islam is based on the laws Allah created for nature, which as mentioned earlier, reflected the laws of Allah's divine realm. Man is expected to discover Allah's will and to follow it, because "Islam suggests that discovering the truth, learning the truth, and believing in the truth are all possible" (Ezzati).

Allah created the universe, bestowed human beings with a privileged position within it, and left the world to function under the laws He had decreed for it. Allah observes how people treat the bounty He has given them, and the universe is allowed to exist, with little intervention, for a certain length of time. At the end of this time, following portents of the end of the world as we know it, mankind is brought in front of Allah for Judgment Day. Islam's eschatology places Allah's role as mankind's judge as the progression from His role as mankind's Creator, and man will be punished or rewarded for his deeds in Allah's universe.

Islam is a natural religion, in that its teachings advocate the utilisation of nature for man's benefit, along with the preservation of the universe that Allah has placed in mankind's safekeeping."

Human Nature and the Purpose of Existence [https://www.patheos.com/library/christianity/beliefs/human-nature-and-the-purpose-of-existence#:~:text=Christianity%20teaches%20that%20the%20universe%20was%20created%20through,universe%20is%20not%20morally%20neutral%2C%20but%20fundamentally%20good.]

Christianity teaches that the universe was created through love by an intelligent power, namely the God of the Bible. Creation was purposeful, not arbitrary, and therefore the universe is not morally neutral, but fundamentally good. In this purposeful creation, everything and everyone is intrinsically valuable. God's design or purpose for creation reflects God's intention that all creatures enjoy perfect love and justice. God works in human history to fulfil that purpose. God created human beings in the divine image, enabling humans to have some understanding of God and of God's vast and complex design. The purpose of life is to love and serve God in order to help bring about God's glorious plan for creation.

Reason is a unique gift bestowed by God on humans and enables them to reflect on their own nature and conscience, and from that derive knowledge of God's will for creation. But a complete understanding is beyond human reach. To fulfil the goal of wholeness in an existence perfected by both justice and love, something more is needed. Humans are not expected to accomplish the divine plan alone. The fulfillment of God's purpose depends on God's grace. For Christians, grace is God's freely-given favor and love.

Reason is a good gift, sometimes misused for selfish, wilful, or prideful purposes. The substitution of selfish ambition for God's will is a condition that Christians call sin, meaning separation or alienation from God.

The Christian concept of sin originates in the story of Adam and Eve found in chapters 2-3 of the Book of Genesis, a story that has central importance for Christians. The story relates the creation by God of the first humans, a man and woman. God placed them in a beautiful garden called Eden, which provided for all their physical needs, as well as companionship with each other and fellowship with God. For these first humans, God had but one rule. In the garden stood "the tree of the knowledge of good and evil," whose fruit Adam and Eve should not eat. When Adam and Eve later broke the rule and ate the fruit, God banished them from the garden, condemning them and their descendants to a life of hard work, pain, disease, and eventual death, and submitting the earth itself to "bondage." Christians call this humanity's "fall" from innocence.

Some Christians believe that these events actually took place, while others understand this story to be symbolic of the human condition. But all Christians tend to view the story as essentially meaningful for all of humanity–that God is in a personal relationship with humans who must decide how to respond to God. They can obey God's will, working together with God to take care of each other and creation, or they can follow their own desires, rebelling against God's will and design.

The story illustrates the Christian belief in the inevitability and universality of sin. Throughout their lives, people will pursue their personal interests instead of seeking to serve God and follow God's will. Some believe in the doctrine of original sin, following Augustine, Bishop of Hippo in North Africa, who theorized that the rebellion of the first human parents is physically passed on to all human beings from one generation to the next. Others believe that sin originates with **Satan**, who first tempted Eve and now preys on humankind, seeking souls to devour. Many contemporary Christians seek ways of understanding sin separately from the story of Adam and Eve, believing that we must take responsibility for our tendency to sin and the harm it does to our loving fellowship with both God and each other.

Christianity teaches that everyone is equally prone to sin and so it focuses not only on human behavior, but also on human nature. In his letter to the Romans, Paul wrote that "there is no difference, for all have sinned and come short of the glory of God" (Romans 3:22-23). Even though there can be a considerable scale of wrongdoing in sinful human activity, a person's sin does not make him or her less valued by God; everyone is equally a candidate for **redemption**.

The Buddhist universe - *Last updated 2009-11-23* - This article examines Buddhist concepts of the universe, life and reincarnation, suffering and human existence –

[https://www.bbc.co.uk/religion/religions/buddhism/beliefs/universe_1.shtml#:~:text=Buddhism%20has%20no%20creator%20god%20to%20explain%20the,events%20and%20become%20the%20cause%20of%20future%20events. ]

The Universe - Last updated 2009-09-10 - This article looks at Jain concepts of the universe, space and time. [https://www.bbc.co.uk/religion/religions/jainism/beliefs/universe_1.shtml#:~:text=Nothing%20in%20the%20universe%20is%20ever%20destroyed%20or,and%20kept%20going%20by%20its%20own%20energy%20processes. ]

The universe

**Jain beliefs about the universe**

Jains believe that the universe we perceive really exists and is not an illusion. It contains two classes of thing: jivas - living souls, and ajivas - non-living objects, which include everything else, including space.

Nothing in the universe is ever destroyed or created; they simply change from one form to another.

Jains believe that the universe has always existed and will always exist. It is regulated by cosmic laws and kept going by its own energy processes. This concept of the universe is compatible with modern scientific thinking.

Jains do not believe that the universe was created by any sort of god.

The Jain word that comes closest to the western idea of the universe is "loka".

The loka is the framework of the universe. It contains the world we experience at the moment, as well as the worlds of heaven and hell.

The loka exists in space. Space is infinite, the universe is not.

**The nature of the universe**

The Jain universe is in five parts:

- **The supreme abode:**
- The region where liberated beings live for ever.
- **The upper world:**
- the region where celestial beings live, but not for ever
- **The middle world:**
- the region where human beings live
- this is the only part of the universe from which a being can achieve enlightenment
- **The lower world:**
- this region consists of seven hells where beings are tormented by demons and by    each other
- their torment does not last for ever
- **The base**
- the region where the lowest forms of life live

## Time

Jains regard historical time as cyclical. The universe moves through lengthy eras of time which Jains usually describe as like the series of downward and upward movements of a point on the rim of a turning wheel.

The downward movement is called avarsarpini and the upward movement is called utsarpini. Each full turn of the wheel is called a kalpa.

Each cycle is divided into 6 ages, represented by spokes. The first three spokes of a downward cycle are a golden age after which conditions decline until Jainism dies out in the 6th spoke. This is reversed in the following upward cycle, and so on.

Each full turn of the wheel takes a very long time: effectively infinity - long enough for the lives of 24 tirthankaras.

Substances (Dravyas)

## Substances: astikaya

Jains believe that everything falls into one of five or six categories of substance that are called astikaya.

All forms of substance except space are confined within the loka (universe).

## GURU GRANTH SAHIB ON THE UNIVERSE - NAVIGATION JUMP

"There are planets, solar systems and galaxies. If one speaks of them, there is no limit and no end. "The top line is the original text in Gurmukhi recited by Guru Nanak in about 1499 found in the Sikh holy scripture called the Guru Granth Sahib(SGGS p8)

The Sikh scriptures have said great many things about the Universe. However, although Gurbani has been in existence since about 1499 and the Guru Granth Sahib has been the Guru of the Sikh since 1708, the world has not been listening. It is clear that there is very little that the world has learnt from the important points mentioned in the Sikh holy text regarding the cosmos.

Carl Sagan (1934 – 1996) was an American astronomer, astrochemist, author, and highly successful popularizer of astronomy, astrophysics and other natural sciences. He was the David Duncan Professor of Astronomy and Space Sciences and Director of the Laboratory for Planetary Studies at Cornell University. He was a consultant and adviser to NASA since the 1950's and briefed the Apollo astronauts before their flights to the Moon.

This is what Carl Sagan, wrote in his book the Pale Blue Dot:

"How is it that hardly any major religion has looked at science and concluded, 'This is better than we thought? The Universe is much bigger than our prophets said, grander, more subtle, more elegant'? Instead they say, 'No, no, no! My god is a little god, and I want him to stay that way.' A religion, old or new, that stressed the magnificence of the Universe as revealed by modern science might be able to draw forth reserves of reverence and awe hardly tapped by the conventional faiths."

Well! The holy Granth of the Sikhs has said all these amazing things about the cosmos but no one is listening! The purpose of this article is not to criticise Carl Sagan but to bring home the point that most people pay little interest in studying our religious text with any real seriousness and that the many fascinating ideas within our religious texts are unknown to most of the world. Despite the wonderful things mentioned in the holy Granth, we continue to remain deaf to these ideas and hence continue to deny our spirits the wisdom that is contained therein.

What Gurbani says

Guru Granth Sahib states that, "There are planets, solar systems and galaxies. If one speaks of them, there is no limit, no end. There are worlds upon worlds of His Creation. As He commands, so they exist. He watches over all, and contemplating the creation, He rejoices. Nanak says, to describe this is as hard as steel!" (SGGS p8).

Despite this fact being clearly stated in the Guru Granth Sahib some 500 years ago, most of humanity is not aware of these sayings. Guru Nanak was an exceptional visionary and was responsible for bring some amazing ideas to the world.

The scriptures say that the universe consists of many different bodies including planets, solar systems galaxies, stars, suns, skies, etc and that the scale and extent of these bodies is unknown and that there is no end to their number. It is clear from this that probable size of the universe is beyond an exact evaluation or calculation by the human mind.

The holy text continues to state: "The limits of the created universe cannot be perceived. Its limits here and beyond cannot be perceived. Many struggle to know His limits, but His limits cannot be found. No one can know these limits. The more you say about them, the more there still remains to be said." (SGGS p5).

So it appears that as we get a better estimate of the size of the universe, in other words, the more we find, then the realisation will dawn that there remain even more outside our knowledge. Gurbani tells us that this is how we will progress when we try and calculate the size of the Universe. On a spiritual angle, the Guru tells us that the Lord is in his creation and the Creation is in the Lord; "All are in the One, and the One is in all." (SGGS p907). So the Universe is a manifestation of the Lord; He is found within the Universe. So from this we can see the extent of God as portrait by Sikhism.

Furthermore, it is stated that God created the whole universe including the earth: "You Yourself created the earth, and the two lamps of the sun and the moon" (SGGS p83); "He creates planets, solar systems and galaxies;" (SGGS p1162). And, "Many millions are the moons, suns and stars" (SGGS p275).

How was the world created?

According to Sikhism, God existed all alone in His abstract form - Nirgun - before He created the Universe. This may be called the state of precreation. God was in the state of sunn samadhi or primal void = state of pre-creation, state of contemplation of the void.

According to Guru Nanak, there was darkness and chaos for millions of years. There was only God and nothing else - no mists, no clouds, no vapours, nothing. None existed except God. Guru Nanak says:

"There was darkness for countless years.

There was neither earth nor sky; there was only His Will.

There was neither day nor night, neither sun nor moon.

He (God) was in deep meditation.

There was nothing except Himself." (SGGS p1035)

Guru Amar Das, the third Nanak further clarifies and reinforces this concept in the following lines found in the Guru Granth Sahib:

He created Himself - at that time, there was no other.

He consulted Himself for advice, and what He did came to pass. At that time, there were no Akaashic Ethers, no nether regions, nor the three worlds. At that time, only the Formless Lord Himself existed - there was no creation. As it pleased Him, so did He act; without Him, there was no other. ||1||" (SGGS p509)

Then God willed the creation of the universe. He became manifest: Sargun. He diffused Himself in nature. Guru Nanak says:

"Thou created all Thy Universe to please Thyself, to enjoy the spectacle, the reality, which is the light of Thy own Reality-self."

When was the world created?

This is a mystery. Was this process of creation a sudden and impulsive one or was it one of evolution and slow growth? Only God who created it knows. Like a spider, God spun Himself into a web. A day will come when He will destroy that web once again to become His sole self again.

The holy Granth tells us clearly that the time of the creation of the Universe is beyond human knowledge and that this was not known to the scholars of the Vedas, nor the Qazi who have studied the Koran; in fact this moment cannot be known by mankind. Only the Lord Himself knows about this instant of creation.

"What was that time, and what was that moment? What was that day, and what was that date?

What was that season, and what was that month, when the Universe was created?

The Pandits, the religious scholars, cannot find that time, even if it is written in the Puraanas.

That time is not known to the Qazis, who study the Koran. The day and the date are not known to the Yogis, nor is the month or the season. The Creator who created this creation-only He Himself knows." (SGGS p4)

Attributes of His Creation

The Parkriti of three attributes (Rajas, Tamas, Sattva) was created by God. Maya, attachment and illusion are also His creation: Guru Gobind Singh, the tenth Sikh Master writes:

"He created the Shakti (power) of three Gunas (attributes) The great Maya (world illusion) is His shadow."

The Universe is not an illusion. It is reality, not final and permanent but a reality on account of the presence of God in it.

This world is the abode of the Almighty and yet He transcends it.

Key features

"You created the vast expanse of the Universe with One Word! Hundreds of thousands of rivers began to flow." (SGGS p3)

"The limits of the created universe cannot be perceived. Its limits here and beyond cannot be perceived. Many struggle to know His limits, but His limits cannot be found. No one can know these limits. The more you say about them, the more there still remains to be said." (SGGS p5)

"So many worlds beyond this world-so very many! What power holds them, and supports their weight?" (SGGS p3)

"All are in the One, and the One is in all. This is what the True Guru has shown me.(5). He who created the worlds, solar systems and galaxies - that God cannot be known.(6). From the lamp of God, the lamp within is lit; the Divine Light illuminates the three worlds.(7)." (SGGS p907)

Beginning of the Universe

"For thirty-six ages, He created the darkness, abiding in the void. There were no Vedas, Puraanas or Shaastras there; only the Lord Himself existed. He Himself sat in the absolute trance, withdrawn from everything. Only He Himself knows His state; He Himself is the unfathomable ocean.(18)" (SGGS p555)

"For so many ages, there was only pitch darkness; the Creator Lord was absorbed in the primal void." (SGGS p1023)

"For endless eons, there was only utter darkness. There was no earth or sky; there was only the infinite Command of His Hukam. There was no day or night, no moon or sun; God sat in primal, profound Samaadhi.(1) There were no sources of creation or powers of speech, no air or water. There was no creation or destruction, no coming or going. There were no continents, nether regions, seven seas, rivers or flowing water.(2)" (SGGS p1035)

"From this primal void, came the moon, the sun and the earth....From this primal void, the earth and the Akaashic Ethers were created....From this primal void, came the four sources of creation, and the power of speech....They were created from the void, and they will merge into the void....." (SGGS p1037)

"The Supreme Creator created the play of Nature; through the Word of His Shabad, He stages His Wondrous Show.(7)....From this primal void, He made both night and day;" (SGGS p1037)

"Creating the Universe, He made the expanse....The True Guru, the Primal Being, is sublime and detached...." (SGGS p1038)

The existing state

"Creating the sun and the moon, He infused His Light into them. He created the night and the day; Wondrous are His miraculous plays." (SGGS p1279)

"Beauty fades away, islands fade away, the sun, moon, stars and sky fade away. The earth, mountains, forests and lands fade away." (SGGS p1354)

"His Power supports the moon, the sun and the stars, and infuses light and breath into the body." (SGGS p1358)

"He established the earth, the sky and the air, the water of the oceans, fire and food. He created the moon, the stars and the sun, night and day and mountains; he blessed the trees with flowers and fruits." (SGGS p1399)

"The continents and the solar systems rest in the support of the One Lord. The Guru has removed the veil of illusion, and shown this to me." (SGGS p205)

"He is the Supreme Lord God, the Perfect Transcendent Lord; O my mind, hold tight to the Support of the One who established the solar systems and galaxies. Chant the Name of that Lord.(1)Pause." (SGGS p209)

"Many millions are the fields of creation and the galaxies. Many millions are the etheric skies and the solar systems....So many times, He has expanded His expansion....Many millions are created in various forms......His limits are not known to anyone." (SGGS p276)

And this is how it will end

"The earth, the Akaashic ethers of the sky, the nether regions of the underworld, the moon and the sun shall pass away." (SGGS p1100)

"Night and day, and the stars in the sky shall vanish. The sun and the moon shall vanish. The mountains, the earth, the water and the air shall pass away. Only the Word of the Holy Saint shall endure." (SGGS p1204)

Space Topics: Voyager

Can you find the pale blue dot? This is the planet earth!
*(Click on the image to enlarge)*

## An Excerpt from A Pale Blue Dot by Carl Sagan Co-founder of The Planetary Society 1994

The Pale Blue Dot of Earth - Detail Credit: NASA / JPL

This excerpt from A Pale Blue Dot was inspired by an image taken, at Sagan's suggestion, by Voyager 1 on February 14, 1990. As the spacecraft left our planetary neighbourhood for the fringes of the solar system, engineers turned it around for one last look at its home planet. Voyager 1 was about 6.4 billion kilometers (4 billion miles) away, and approximately 32 degrees above the ecliptic plane, when it captured this portrait of our world. Caught in the center of scattered light rays (a result of taking the picture so close to the Sun), Earth appears as a tiny point of light, a crescent only 0.12 pixel in size.

Look again at that dot. That's here. That's home. That's us. On it everyone you love, everyone you know, everyone you ever heard of, every human being who ever was, lived out their lives. The aggregate of our joy and suffering, thousands of confident religions, ideologies, and economic doctrines, every hunter and forager, every hero and coward, every creator and destroyer of civilization, every king and peasant, every young couple in love, every mother and father, hopeful child, inventor and explorer, every teacher of morals, every corrupt politician, every "superstar," every "supreme leader," every saint and sinner in the history of our species lived there--on a mote of dust suspended in a sunbeam.

The Earth is a very small stage in a vast cosmic arena. Think of the rivers of blood spilled by all those generals and emperors so that, in glory and triumph, they could become the momentary masters of a fraction of a dot. Think of the endless cruelties visited by the inhabitants of one corner of this pixel on the scarcely distinguishable inhabitants of some other corner, how frequent their misunderstandings, how eager they are to kill one another, how fervent their hatreds.

Our posturings, our imagined self-importance, the delusion that we have some privileged position in the Universe, are challenged by this point of pale light. Our planet is a lonely speck in the great enveloping cosmic dark. In our obscurity, in all this vastness, there is no hint that help will come from elsewhere to save us from ourselves.

The Earth is the only world known so far to harbor life. There is nowhere else, at least in the near future, to which our species could migrate. Visit, yes. Settle, not yet. Like it or not, for the moment the Earth is where we make our stand.

It has been said that astronomy is a humbling and character-building experience. There is perhaps no better demonstration of the folly of human conceits than this distant image of our tiny world. To me, it underscores our responsibility to deal more kindly with one another, and to preserve and cherish the pale blue dot, the only home we've ever known.

-- Carl Sagan, Pale Blue Dot, 1994"

**Understanding your Dharma**

There is a popular saying in Sanskrit, 'dharmo rakshita rakshatah,' which means if you protect your religion or dharma, your dharma will protect you. Now what do we mean by the word dharma?

Actually, there is no equivalent to the word dharma either in English or in any other language. In our tradition, the word has many meanings and many connotations. But at the most basic level, dharma means your natural activity or propensity.

For example, in case of an animal like the dog, its dharma, among other things, is to eat and procreate, to be friendly with human beings, and to bark and bite if it is subjected to intense fear or agitation.

The dharma of a snake is to crawl, live in dark places, to store poison in its teeth, and bite its prey or anyone who tries to harm it. As far as the animals are concerned, their dharma is to fulfil their respective roles in creation, living according to their natural instincts, serving as food to other animals and surviving against threats and harsh nature. Since they lack intelligence, their roles are performed mostly by Nature.

The dharma of gods or divinities is to help people and other living beings and assist God in enforcing His laws, protecting people from evil and maintaining righteousness in the world.

When it comes to human beings, we know that we are not mere animals, although some people prefer to live that way. We are rational beings who are endowed with reasoning power, which we call buddhi or discriminating intelligence.

We are also endowed with intelligent self-awareness and the ability to direct our will in whatever way we deem fit. So in case of human beings, dharma means to live according to their highest nature, controlling their lower nature, animal instincts, natural urges and baser desires.

**THE DUTY OF HUMAN BEINGS IS TO LIVE INTELLIGENTLY, HELP THE BEINGS OF LESSER INTELLIGENCE, AND NOURISH THOSE WHO DEPEND UPON THEM. THEY ARE**

**ALSO EXPECTED TO SERVE THE PURPOSE OF CREATION, DO THEIR PART IN MAINTAINING THE ORDER AND REGULARITY OF THE WORLD AND SOCIETY. A DEVOUT HINDU IS EXPECTED TO PERFORM FIVE OBLIGATORY DUTIES: NOURISHING GODS, NOURISHING ANCESTORS, NOURISHING NEEDY HUMAN BEINGS, NOURISHING OTHER LIVING BEINGS AND SERVING THE SEERS AND BRAHMANAS.**

These are called obligatory duties because their practice leads to harmony, peace, order and regularity. [Emphasis added by the author]

If you analyze carefully, you will realize that all religions aims to accomplish this only: enforce discipline among humans and make them to look to the heavens and God to manifest good in their lives. In their own ways, they teach that we should live with a certain sense of moral and spiritual responsibility, curbing our baser instincts and controlling our evil and immoral thoughts. The language and expression many be different but the essential philosophy is the same.

Hence in ancient India, spiritual teachings were equated with dharma. Following the same tradition, the Jains called their faith Jain Dharma and the Buddhists also called the teachings of the Buddha as Dharma or crudely, Dhamma.

All Dharma arise from God only. We do not have to argue which Dharma is the best. Every dharma has its own value, just as every duty. All duties flow from God and all dharmas also flow from Him only. Each caters to certain needs and fulfils certain aims. Every living being who lives upon earth is an embodiment of God's eternal duty.

Therefore, we have to be careful when we speak ill of others or degrade their faith. Agreed that not all duties are equal, but all duties are sacred since they flow from God.

However, if we perform actions selfishly for our own end, then we are not performing God's duties anymore and we become subject to their consequences (karma).

Since the actions of animals are guided mostly by Nature, they do not incur karma as much human beings who are intelligent and who can exercise their will for good or bad.

Now what is the higher nature or the true dharma of a human being? According to Hinduism, as a human being, you have a responsibility or a duty towards yourself, towards your family, towards your society, towards your ancestors, towards your divinities and towards all living beings in general. These duties are essentially meant to establish peace and stability within yourself, in others and in the world in general.

God is the upholder of dharma and the order of the universe. He makes sure that the fire burns, the wind blows and the water flows because these are their essential dharmas. In case of living beings, He enforces the law of karma and allows them to indulge in wilful actions out of their desires and natural instincts.

However, if the world becomes too chaotic or disturbingly disorderly, on account of their activities, He incarnates upon earth and sets things right.

Our dharma also depends upon our births, the circumstances in which we live and the profession we choose to follow.

It is better if you choose your profession according to your natural inclination, or what you love most.

But if you are unable to do that, whatever may be the profession you choose, you should do it with sincerity, discipline and dedication, as an offering to God, because although we may think ourselves to be independent individuals, we are part of the universe and our actions have a bearing upon others and the world in general.

Manifesting the Eternal Dharma in your life

Whatever may be the religion or the personal philosophy you follow, make sure that you contribute to peace and harmony and do not disturb yourself or others in harmful and evil ways. According to the Bhagavadgita, a true yogi does not disturb others nor is disturbed by them. He does not create any ripples in the lives of other people or beings. He lives peacefully, without imposing himself or trying to control others. He is at peace with everyone. That is the true purpose of yoga.

If you are for peace, harmony and order and if you strive to establish them and maintain them in your life and your environment, it is deemed that you are following your dharma and you are in tune with your spiritual nature. God and all the divinities whom we worship will be happy with you and respond to you promptly whenever you pray to them sincerely.

It is through your adherence to dharma that you become a true devotee of God and fulfill the central purpose of your life. Here are a few simple ways in which you can practice your essential dharma.

Curb your baser desires and your animal instincts. Refuse to be guided by your lower instincts.

Identify yourself with your inner self, knowing that you are neither your body nor your mind but the immortal self, who is caught in the whirlpool of life.

Offer whatever you have and whatever you do to God or the divinities whom you love most. Make your life and your activities an offering to God.

Practice detachment so that emotionally you will be more stable and peaceful.

Cultivate sattva or purity by practicing virtue and avoiding wrong doings so that you can experience affinity with your spiritual side.

Practice non-violence and compassion towards other living beings. It will set you apart from animals and provide you with an opportunity to practice universal friendliness (mitrata).

Avoid thinking and harbouring evil and immoral thoughts.

Practice yoga and meditation so that you can control the modifications of your mind and experience peace and harmony within yourself.

Worship your gods and divinities so that they will be active in your consciousness as well as in the cosmos and express themselves through you.

Do your duty, whatever it is, without expectation and with a sense of sacrifice.

Fill your mind with positive and spiritual thoughts.

Speak right words, think right thoughts and do right deeds.

It is the dharma of the animals to live for themselves as intended by Nature. It is the dharma of humans to live wisely and intelligently and work for their liberation as intended by the Creator. The dharma of gods is to exist for others and help them according to their merit. As far as we are concerned, we have a choice. We have the freedom to live like animals or live like gods and accept the consequences.

We have a choice to live in whatever way we want, provided we are willing to pay the price. We can live for ourselves, living selfishly, fulfilling our material desires, which is what most people do, or live for others, to the extent we can, living according to our spiritual aspirations and expressing the divinity that exists within each of us.

We can live as if this is the only life we have or live with the awareness that our current life is a preparation for the next life or afterlife.

We have the freedom to live the right way or the wrong way or move towards darkness or light. This is an unique opportunity given to human beings.

Hence it is said that even gods, if they want to progress to still higher planes, have to be born upon earth as human beings and practice dharma to qualify for their further advancement."

From Wikipedia, the free encyclopedia

*"Sanatan" and "Sanatana" redirect here. For Sanatana the rishi, see Four Kumaras.[Author's Note: Reproduced below]:*[Excerpts]

The **Kumaras** are four sages (*rishis*) from the Puranic texts of Hinduism who roam the universe as children,[1][2] generally named **Sanaka, Sanandana, Sanatana**, and **Sanatkumara**.[3] They are described as the first mind-born creations and sons of the creator-god Brahma. Born from Brahma's mind, the four Kumaras undertook lifelong vows of celibacy (brahmacharya) against the wishes of their father. They are said to wander throughout the materialistic and spiritualistic universe without any desire but with the purpose of teaching.[1] All four brothers studied Vedas from their childhood, and always travelled together.[4]

The *Bhagavata Purana* lists the Kumaras among the twelve *mahajanas* (great devotees or bhaktas)[5] who although being eternally liberated souls from birth, still became attracted to the devotional service of Vishnu from their already enlightened state.[6] They play a significant role in a number of Hindu spiritual traditions, especially those associated with the worship of Vishnu and his avatar Krishna, sometimes even in traditions related to Shiva.

Names

[edit]

The group is known by various names: "Kumaras" (the boys/male children/young boys), "Chatursana" or "Chatuh Sana" (the four with names starting with Sana) and "Sanakadi" (Sanaka and the others).[7] Individual names usually include Sanaka (ancient), Sanatana (eternal), Sanandana (ever-joyful) and Sanatkumara (ever-young).[1][2][8] Sometimes, Sanatana is replaced by Sanatsujata. A fifth Kumara named Ribhu is sometimes added. Sometimes, the Kumaras are enumerated as six with Sana and Ribhu or Sanatsujata added.[9]

Though in Mahabharata, a total of seven sons are mentioned, namely: 1) Aniruddha, 2) Sana, 3) Sanatsujata, 4) Sanaka, 5) Sanandana, 6) Sanatkumara and 7) Sanatana and further mentions that, "Knowledge comes to these seven rishis, of itself (without being dependent on study or exertion). These seven are wedded to the religion of *Nivritti* (inward contemplation).[10] ............"

SECTION 7

MORAL VALUES

1. Learning Outcomes [Omitted being not in conformity with the Title of the Section 'Moral Values' which is supposed to embrace every religion and not merely Hinduism]

2. **Introduction**

Human values can be described as science of morality. Morality is the choice of righteous or good intentions, decisions and actions over the wrong or bad actions. Human values are governed by a large number of factors-biological, genetically, social cultural, religious factors. In addition, human values are inculcated through practice. Values are also transferred through stories and illustrations. Inner consciousness of man also affects the morality and values. When ones heart is pure and free from greediness and lust, then any actions performed with self-control by the person will definitely include high human values. Five basic values- truth, love, peace, right action and non-violence will help one to attain high level of morality. This will help the society and enhance the welfare.

## 1. Hinduism

Hinduism is the world's most prominent and oldest religion. Some practitioners refer it as 'Sanatana Dharma'. Hinduism believes in attaining materialistic ambitions like wealth recognition, progeny etc. to attain the higher level of satisfaction in the objective world. But the actions to achieve these material things should be governed by self-consciousness. The self-consciousness gives origin to reality of ideas, mind and soul. Therefore, Hinduism believes in evolution of human soul and mind. There are basically two general ethical and moral principles in the world that are followed by every Hindu – Dharma & Karma.

## 2. Hindu Scriptures

There are numerous scriptures in Hinduism like Mahabharata, Ramayana, Vedas etc. The most important scripture in Hinduism is 'Hindu Vedas'. Ancient Hindu scriptures are in Sanskrit and are composed & transmitted verbally. Hindu Scriptures are classified into two categories- 'Shruti' and 'Smriti'. 'Shruti' primarily refers to Vedas. Hindu Vedas are subcategories into four Vedas – 'Rig Veda', 'Yajur Veda', 'Sama Veda' and 'Atharva Veda'. These four Vedas include details of 'Karma Kanda' and 'Janana Kanda'. 'Karma Kanda' includes rituals and prayers to be followed by Hindus. 'Jnana Kanda' includes ontological realities like self-consciousness, Brahman, God.

**Classification of Hindu Scriptures**

Each Veda is subcategorized into four texts – Samhita, Aranyakas, Brahmans, and Upnishads.

'Samhita' includes prayers (mantras) and benedictions. 'Aranyakas' include text on rituals and ceremonies. These two parts of Vedas are called as 'Karma Kanda'. 'Brahmanas' include commentaries on rituals and ceremonies. 'Upnishadas' includes text related to philosophy, meditation and spiritualisms. These two parts of Vedas form Jnana kanda.

'Smriti' includes Hindu epics – 'Mahabharata' and 'Ramayana' as well as Puranas. 'Bhagavata Gita' is also included as integral part of Mahabharata. 'Puranas' contain Hindu mythologies.

The set-of teachings included in Jnana Kanda is termed as Vedanta. However, Vedanta is not limited to one book as a source of Vedanta philosophy. The important constituents of Vedanta are Upnishads, Bhagwad Gita, Braham sutras.

'Upnishads' are foundation of Hindu Philosophical thoughts. These are philosophical in nature and core of Vedic wisdom. 'Braham sutras' logically explain the teachings of 'Upanishads'. These include systematic strands of 'Upanishads' and form the background of orthodox system of thoughts. 'Bhagwad Gita' includes the teachings of Lord Krishna. It is considered as essence of all Hindu scriptures. The details of battle between 'Pandavas' between 'Kauravas' i.e. between righteous and wrong are given in this scripture. Though, Lord Krishna was Arjura's charioteer in battlefield but actually was his spiritual guide. The teachings of 'Bhagwad Gita' help human to choose and perform action that are normal and righteous especially when one is in emotional dilemma.

Moreover, there are other scriptures for children like 'Panchtantras'. 'Panchtantaras' are very popular in India and includes wonderful ancient Indian social stories that teach the lessons of morality to children.

### 3. Hindu Beliefs

In Hinduism there is no static and single belief. It includes a variety of beliefs and practices. The code of ethics followed by Hinduš in one part of the world may completely differ from code of ethics followed in other part. Hindu scripture clearly discuss three items – concepts, values and practices. The teachings of Hinduism are based on general principles of dharma and karma as well as desire to discern truth from illusion i.e. to achieve 'Moksha'. Hinduism believes in ontological nature of existence and to attain that through 'Dharmas' and 'Karmas'. Hindu beliefs include 'Dharma', 'Karma', 'Moksha', 'Samsara' and various 'Yogas'. 'Samsara' is continuing cycle of birth, life death and rebirth. 'Yogas' are path and practices opted by Hindus The Various Hindu beliefs are:-

## 5.1 Purusharthas

These are objective of human life. Hinduism includes four types of 'Purusharthas'.

'Dharma' embraces righteous conduct, selfless action. It covers all the aspects of life – religious as well as secular. It lays stress on performing the duties appropriately and sincerely. Appropriateness is determined in context in which action is performed. Nature of 'Dharmas' differs according to gender, caste and age of person. For example, Child Dharma is to obey parents. Parents Dharma is to protect, feed, educate and shelter children.

'Artha' refers to pursuits of securities. 'Artha' includes all activities and resources which help one to achieve higher levels of wealth, career and financial security. It aims at allowing economic prosperity and material well being.

'Kama' refers to fulfillment of sensual pleasures. It includes pleasure of senses, aesthetic enjoyment of life, fulfillment of desires, longingness. Any action performed to achieve 'Artha' or ''Kama' should be associated with 'Dharma'. This will help the individuals to evolve as responsible human beings on one hand. On the other hand, it will benefit the society as a whole.

As per teaching of Hindu scriptures, ultimate human Endeavour is to attain 'Moksha'. Every 'Karma' should be put into action in such a way that one should not be attached to it one should have freedom from travails to achieve 'Moksha'. One should have real & righteous knowledge about nature of one's own consciousness. This will bring one towards God i.e. towards 'Moksha'. The knowledge of your own consciousness is the knowledge of God and is called as 'Moksha'. Therefore, one should pursue knowledge and evolve into superior personality constantly through righteous actions associated with moral and ethical values. This will help one to go beyond knowledge for self-realization and hence God realization.

5.2 Karma and Samsara

'Karmas' are actions performed by individuals. Hinduism believes in law of 'Karmas'. Every individual is responsible for his own actions. One has to reap what one's seed. One has to face the results of one's actions; not only for present actions but also for actions performed in past. Every good or bad action has consequences. According to 'Karma' theory, present situation of individual is result of his actions in the past. An individual remains in 'Samsara' i.e. continuous cycle of birth, life, death and rebirth due to 'Karmas'. Therefore, 'Karmas' are also the basis of reincarnation. He can liberate himself from 'Samsara' and reach the ultimate happiness and peace through self-realization and realization of one's eternal relationship with God.

5.3 Concept of God

According to Hinduism, God is not separate from the world and is within one and everything. Hindu believes that God is within everyone. Each living creature has soul. The soul is believed to be eternal and is indistinct from God. Therefore God is formless and one. This is the root of secularism of Hindu beliefs. In Hinduism, God is also worshipped in form of Hindu deities like 'Shiva', 'Brahma', 'Vishnu', 'Ganesha', Goddesses etc.

5.4 Hindu Practices

Hindus generally practice their religion through rituals and prayers. In general, all Hindus follow 'Yamas' and 'Niyamas'. 'Yamas' are moral values to be followed while performing any action. 'Niyamas' are the practices followed in daily routine. Hindu follow certain practices like chanting (Japa), Austerity (Tapas), Sacred vows (Vrata), Purity (Shaucha), Remorse (Hare), worshipping, donations, modesty etc. All these practices help them to be ease at moral values and evolve into better individuals.

## 6. Human Values in Hinduism

The religious life is considered as system of education. Likewise, Hinduism is based on inculcating and practicing certain basic human value which are termed as 'Yamas'. 'Yamas' refer to behavior of individuals in daily life. These are the essential morals which every Hindu must have. The basic human values in Hinduism are described as follows:

6.1 Truthfulness (Satyam)

In Hinduism everyone should speak the truth with kindness and compassion. Truth is always ultimate winner. It is possible that in short run untruth may appear to win but in long run truth will always win. But if truth causes harm, it is better to be silent rather than speaking it. Therefore, one should speak the pleasant truth.

'Satyam Brooyat, Priam Brooyat '

For example, if a person is ill and there is risk of his life then telling truth about illness and risk of life to patient may cause harm to patient. So, in that case it is better to be silent.

6.2 Non Voilence (Ahimsa)

Hinduism teaches us to follow the principle of non-violence. According To Hinduism 'Ahimsa Paramo Dharma '

Best Dharma is not to harm others one should not harm others for his personal benefits. In Hinduism, one should not opt for non-violence at least not beyond bare minimum without which one could not survive. It also means that one should prefer to be vegetarian and should refrain from overeating and consuming meat.

6.3 Non Stealing (Asteyam)

Hinduism teaches us not to steal or enter into debt. One should not be greedy and selfish. This may result in stealing & non-violence. The person should not take the things which do not belong to him. The individuals should use their hard earned assets and money. They should not take other's things through stealing or cheating them.

6.4 Honesty (Arjavam)

Hindus should follow the principle of honesty. One should be simple, straight forward, open as well as honest and should not follow hypocrisy. There should be integration between physical body, mind and soul.

'Kayena Manasa Vacha '

6.5 Compassion (Daya)

Every Hindu must have callous, compassionate and intensive feelings. He must have sympathy, kindness, love, mercy for all. One should do his deed selflessly and for the benefit of society. One should always be ready to provide services to needy ones; even at one's own sacrifice, if needed.

6.6 Forgiveness (Kshama)

Hinduism teaches us forgiveness one should restrain oneself from intolerance and ill will. The individuals can forgive only if they have combined characteristics of patience, tolerance and bear sufferings. Forgiveness will ultimately result in peacefulness. It creates the basis of non-violence.

6.7 Sweet speech (Madhuryam)

Hinduism teaches us sweetness of speech and personality. One should not be rude harsh & impolite. The individual should be pious and should always use sweet words. One must be firm but at the same time he must be pure, pleasant, delightful and kind hearted.

6.8 Tithing (Dana)

Hindus should be generous. It is believed in Hinduism that more you give more you get. One should give or donate to others without any intention of reward. Tithings helps in purity by teaching us the lessons of distributing and sharing others.

6.9 Free of Sin (Akalkata)

Hinduism teaches us not to perform any action that is sinful. According to law of Karmas, everyone is rewarded according to his karmas, sooner or later, in absolute and correct measure. Every karma is rewarded whether good or bad, positive or negative, virtuous or vicious, loftier or sinful. If one will do sin or bad deed then bad will come back to him. Therefore, one should always do good deed so that good wills come back to one. So, one should always try his level best to stay away from sinful.

## 6.10 Self-Control (Dama)

Hinduism teaches us control over passion and senses. Self-control will result in limited desires. Self-controlled person will led by wisdom and kindness rather than desires. Self-control not only encourages humility but elevates man to level of God. However lack of self-control may take an individual to wrong path. A self-controlled person has neither fear of criticism nor impression of praise. His each and every action is according to moral and ethical values. For example, one should observe celibacy when single and faithfulness in marriage.

## 6.11 Contentment (Santosha)

Contentment is state of complete satisfaction. It is basic nature of soul. Hinduism believes in liberation of soul which is possible only if a person is contented. When a person attains contentment, he will experience mental peace, ease in life and feel free from all worries and tensions. A contented person will experience introversion as well as steadiness and will attain the highest transcendental meditation.

## 6.12 Acceptance

Everyone should do selfless deeds according to 'Dharmas and without concern of outcome. Whatever the outcome of any action should be accepted as 'Prasada'- the gift of God. Whether the Result is desirable or undesirable, one should not get emotionally disturbed or stronger. One should accept the result without anxiety. One should concentrate only on actions not on result. It is very truly said in Hinduism through a Sanskrit Shalok

'Maa Karma Phala Heterbhuh'

One should act as a matter of duty without being attached to fruits of activities. Any action performed without desired result will evolve individuals into superior personalities.

6.13 Each and every one is one

In Hinduism, it is believed that everyone is alike. 'Atma'- Soul is a part of God and exists in every one.

'Sarvabhootastam Atmanam, Sarva Bhootari Cha Atmani.'

One should follow inner consciousness and see everyone else in oneself. One should listen to other's problems and try to solve it as these problems are his own. When a person will experience everyone alike then he will transcended into an elevated soul.

6.14 Listen to self-conscience

Whenever a person is in dilemma whether the carrying out action is right or wrong then he should listen to his self-conscience. At that time almighty will guide him the right path and that person will be released from all the sins for that action. As said in Bhagwad Gita,

'Sarva Dharmaan Parityajya Maam Ekam Sharnam Vraja
Aham Twa Sarva Paapebhya Mokshaishyaami'

In Mahabharata when Arjuna was in dilemma whether it is appropriate to kill his own cousins. Lord Krishna enlightens him to choose and perform the action that is moral and righteous. Therefore, Arjuna fought the battle of Mahabharta and kill his cousins for the winning of righteous over wrong.

6.15 Enlightenment

Hinduism believes that one can evolve himself through continuous upgradation of knowledge. Knowledge of an individual is limited to his capabilities, likes, dislikes, upbringing background, and environment. One should always try to upgrade knowledge and reach the levels beyond the human capabilities. Then he can realize his 'self' and be fully enlightened.

7. Summary

Thus, it can be summarized that each and every individual should act and choose the righteous task. Actions of a person determine his personality. One should always try to graduate out of deception of world and achieve the ultimate goal of liberating himself from all the happenings of oneself and become a superior personality. This can be achieved only through following all the moral and ethical ideals of Hindus. Moral and ethical actions performed to achieve common goal with a spirit of sharing will definitely lead to progress of mankind. [Source: https://ebooks.inflibnet.ac.in/hrmp01/chapter/253/ ]

**Islam**

*"Religion without morality is a superstition and a curse, and morality without religion is impossible."*
*(Hopkins)*

Have you ever asked yourself these questions; How can we differentiate what is right from what is wrong? What are the sound principles that we should follow in life? I am sure you did. The right answer to these questions can be summarized in just one term which is "the moral values". Moral values are the principles that guide our life in the righteous path, help us to handle any situation and do not allow us to do any harm to others.

In addition, these values help us to stand as unique creatures in this world. So, from where do we get these values that we learn since childhood? Every religion has its own basic values and in Islam, the Holy Qur'an and the traditions of the Prophet Muhammad (PBUH) serve as the primary source of these values. There are several morals values we should follow and in this essay we will concentrate on three of them which are Honesty, kindness and forgiveness.

**1/ Honesty**

Honesty implies the meaning of sincerity in everything man does. It is related to all aspects of his life such as his actions, transactions and other dealings in which one should be fair and avoid deception and falsehood.

In addition, Honesty serves as an umbrella term that has some basic components such as fulfilling commitments, telling truth, keeping the promise, doing one's work as sincerely as possible, carrying out the duties as fully and completely as possible whether the person is under supervision or not and giving everyone their full deserved rights without their asking for them.

The importance of honesty lies in the fact that it has a great place in the Holy Qur'an as it is the core of the message of Islam and the main characteristic of Muslims. It also has a great role in strengthening the relationship between individuals and society members. The Holy Qur'an and the teachings of Prophet Muhammad (PBUH) orders people to be honest in their dealings with each other and always tell the truth even if it is against their own will or benefit.

Thus, Honesty is one of the greatest traits one must have as Prophet Muhammad (PBUH) was known as "the trustworthy Muhammad" and Allah the Almighty said in the Holy Qur'an:

**"O you who believe! Fear God, and be with those who are true (in word and deeds)." (Quran 9:119)**

**2/kindness (Ihsan)**

Kindness is one of the greatest moral values that man should have. The term kindness, in Islam, implies the meaning of giving charity and when the word kindness is mentioned, the first thing that comes into mind is giving or helping those in need from the provisions and sustenance bestowed by Allah to the rich. Allah the Almighty encourages the believers to practice kindness by declaring competition with each other in performing good deeds. This means that we are responsible for the money that Allah the Almighty bestowed upon us and on the Day of Judgment, we will be asked about how we earned and spent it.

Furthermore, the importance of kindness lies in the fact that when we give charity, we are rewarded in return. The forms of this reward are that charity atones for our sins, increases our good deeds, purifies our hearts from greed, increases our sensation of the poor, and protects us from Hell and the Angels pray on behalf of us when we give charity.

In Islam, The greatest character who gave charity is our prophet Muhammad (PBUH). Some features of kindness in the Prophet's life are that He fed the poor, gave water to the needy, took care of the widows, helped the orphans and said: "None of you have faith until you love for your neighbor what you love for yourself." (Muslim)

Prophet Muhammad (peace and blessings be upon him) said, "Every act of kindness is a Sadaqa (charity)" (Bukhari, Muslim). This text from the tradition of the Prophet (PBUH) shows the importance of kindness in Muslims' life.

### 3/Forgiveness (Afw)

We live in a world in which there are people with whom we have to interact. As a result of this interaction, there will be some fights or abuses due to any reason that will cause anger and violence. There may be some injuries or others harms and it will be difficult to forgive the offenders; However, Allah the Almighty orders us to forgive those who abused us and He will bless us with a lot of mercy after forgiving them due to complying with Allah's command.

Forgiveness in Islam can be taken into two forms; Allah's forgiveness of our sins and people's forgiveness of those who harm them and the earlier can be a result of the latter. Allah the Almighty said in the Holy Qur'an "whoever pardons [his foe] and makes peace, his reward rests with God – for, verily, He does not love evildoers" (Qur'an 42:40)

The importance of forgiveness is that it is a form of high morals that the human soul needs to get rid of all impurities and grudges that may be attached to the heart from the impact of harm. It is also a way to enjoy goodness and love between people. There is no doubt that preferring forgiveness and tolerance to punishment will prevent the individuals from the acute conflicts that may arise among them. Furthermore, forgiveness has a great effect in man's life as it helps to strengthen the social ties that are weakened and broken by abusing one another and it is reason for obtaining the pardon of Allah, his forgiveness and consent.

This shows us that forgiveness helps us to deserve Allah's mercy upon us as Prophet Muhammad PBUH said:

"Have mercy on those on the earth, and the One in heaven will have mercy on you" [Tirmidhi]

The role model of forgiveness in Islam is our Prophet Muhammad (PBUH) who was always forgiving those who wronged him and meets wrong with good deeds even the disbelievers. Prophet Muhammad was described as a "Mercy for all the Worlds". His mercy wasn't limited to his Muslim nation, but was extended to the non-Muslim nation. Aisha (may Allah be pleased with her) said that the Prophet never took revenge on his own behalf on anyone.

In the earlier portion of his mission, the Prophet traveled to the city of Taif, a city located in the mountains nearby to Mecca, in order to invite them to accept Islam. The leaders of Taif were tough and mistreated the Prophet Muhammad PBUH and the children followed him, threw stones and hurt him. The prophet endured all these injuries and more obstacles than he had to endure in Mecca. Out of his great tolerance and mercy, prophet Muhammad refused to punish them as one day, they may be guided to the right path. This shows us the importance of forgiveness in the earthy life and the hereafter.

In short, the importance of the three above-mentioned moral values, the sayings of the Prophet, the Qur'anic verses and the reward of these values urge all people to follow them." [Source: https://alquranworld.com/the-moral-values-in-islam/ ]

**Buddhism**

"1 .Learning outcomes-

1.1 To acquire the in depth knowledge of Buddha Religion.

1.2 To understand basic human values and teachings of Buddha

1.3 To acquire wisdom and knowledge like Buddhists.

2. **Introduction**

Buddhism is a worldwide religion. Its origin was by Siddhartha Gautama known as "Buddha". 'Buddha' means 'awakened one'. This religion was extinct in India due to Islam in 12th century. In the present time period, it remains a major religion only in Himalayan areas like

Sikkim, Arunachal Pradesh, Ladakh, Darjeeling hills in west Bengal, Lahaul and Spiti areas. But it has been gaining importance again by many Indians. There is a great contribution of Lord Buddha in inculcating good human values. He took birth in Lumbini in Nepal. He attained enlightenment sitting under a pipal tree, therefore, is also known as "The perfectly self-awakened one". He spread this religion in the whole world by forming the company of Buddhist monks. His first formation was Triple Gem i.e. Buddha, Dharma and Sangha with his fire companions. Now, there are many Buddhist councils in India. Dalai Lama presently is the 14th Buddhist leader of this religion. There is a big temple of Buddhist in Dharamsala or McLeod Ganj. It is one of the big centers of Buddhism in India. The religion has spread basic human values by providing awakening to mankind.

## 3. Basic teachings of Buddhism have been explained as under:-

**3.1 Believe in 'Karma'-** Human beings must believe in 'Karma' theory whatever actions we do, it has an effect on the next. There is a cause and effect relationship. One person is responsible for every wrong action committed by him. Everything exists in the world only with a change. We must believe in doing good change. Buddha remained in the heart of every person due to his true feelings. He taught them to differentiate between right and wrong and then only decide.

**3.2 Serve the Sicks-** Buddha and his discipline Ananda, one day visited a monastery. A monk was suffering from a chronic disease there. The Buddha himself took a good care of sick monk and also guided the other monks to look after each other. He said that serving the sick means serving the God.

**3.3 Morality-** One of the teachings of Buddha consists of 'Sila' which means Morality, good conduct and virtue. He believed in two golden rules of Christianity i.e. principle of equality and the principle of reciprocity. It means we must behave or act in the way, we expect from others. As per Buddha all human beings are equal and we must follow moral and ethical values being good human beings.

**3.4 Mental Development-** This is the only path which can strengthen and control our mind. Development of mind means wisdom, personal freedom and liberty. Mental Development is possible by concentration and meditation. This will help in maintaining good mental health and conduct. Buddha believed in 'Prajna' means wisdom and enlightenment. This can be gained with a pure and calm mind.

**3.5 Belief in Sufferings-** Sufferings is the truth of lie which means 'Dukkha' causing due to sickness, pain and failures. Suffering is only due to attachment, desires, fear, anger and jealousy. End of the sufferings is possible through...'Nirvana', in which mind is completely free and liberal with non-attachment. One has to leave all desires and a quest for fame. We must not harm anybody. We must avoid frauds and economic exploitations. One should always follow the path of truthfulness. One must not commit any sexual harassment. We should not consume alcohol or any other such drug or intoxicants. All these things spoil our mind and are the basic cause of human sufferings.

**3.6 Buddha's Eightfold Path-** the Buddha's eightfold path consists basically Panna: wisdom, sila: morality and Samadhi: meditation. He stressed upon right understanding of the noble truths and right thinking to follow right path in life. He also focused on right speech and to abstain from lying, criticism, gossip, harsh language etc. He also guided to follow right actions to away from killing and stealing. One should also avoid dishonesty and hurting others. We must put right efforts to conquer bad qualities. We must have awareness of our body, mind and emotions to overcome hatred and ignorance. Right concentration can be obtained through continuous meditation.

**3.7 Virtues for layman's happiness-** Once a man visited the Buddha to ask him some doctrines for happy life in the world. Buddha told him to follow four virtues in life. First, he should be quite skilled, efficient, energetic and earnest in his profession. Secondly, he should take care of his hard earned money from the stealers. He should have faithful, knowledgeable, liberal, intelligent and moral friendship to always show right path. He should avoid extravagance and try to live within his means. All these four virtues can make a person very happy and successful in his life.

**3.8 Love and Affection-** As per Buddha the end of hatred is to do love and compassion. We can conquer anger by love and affection to others. He asked the common man to think good, do good and pray good for the welfare of mankind. He said that Nirvana is the supreme bliss of the whole world so may God bless happiness to all human beings. Happiness for others may cause happiness to us and thus, the whole world will be happy.

**3.9 Individual Transformation-** Shakyamunl Buddha travelled throughout Indian and discovered that fundamental reason of suffering of human beings is not the external environment rather it is within the human heart. He tried to reform the hearts and minds of the individuals in the society. He was a moral leader and teacher. As per Buddha world peace can be attained through inner transformation in the life of each individual. He stressed on social reforms and morality as well.

**3.10 Harmony-** He strived to maintain a balance and harmony between all living and non-living things in the universe. It is a law of nature. Shakyamunl's enlightenment is the fusion of individual's own inner power and external power acts to bring out the individuals' own power completely for the restoration and rejuvenation of the humanity.

**3.11 Sila, Samadhi and Panna–** Buddhism is based on Sila, Samadhi and Panna which means precepts, meditation and wisdom respectively. These three trees are the way to salvation from all sufferings of this world. Combination of these three can make a perfect human being. Sila is concerned with rules, regulations, principles and discipline, which are helpful for building good character and nature. Mind can be kept very cool, pure and peaceful by practicing Sila. Moreover, one can abstain from all unlawful deeds. Samadhi means to control our mind for right action and welfare with concentration. Samadhi means meditation, yoga, bhavana and contemplation. With more efforts and strong determination, one can achieve right wisdom or Panna. Among the three wisdom is at the highest position, wisdom is most required in our daily life for the attainment of our goals and destination. It is not essential only to achieve salvation.

**3.12 National Integrity and humanity-** Buddhism is the religion in which more importance is given to humanity. Lord Buddha worked for the good of mankind. Buddha's preaching was not for a particular nation or community or group. Buddhism has no national boundary. The Buddha travelled from one place to another in his whole life by not giving any importance to their political ideology, constitution or administration. Both the greedy and rude emperors who were trying to conquer other's land, they all respected Buddha equally. The Buddha laid emphasis on ten duties of the kings. The ten rajadhamma, ten kingly attributes and seven unconquerable principles called the sapta aparihaniyo dhamma. This preaching of the Buddha was for the kings to protect their national integrity. There is inverse relationship between human beings and the society. Without society, there cannot be any human. Religious norms are no doubt essential, but to lead a social life, human beings have also to follow social norms. Humanity is the core of any society.

**3.13 Spread of Peace-** This was Buddha's main message, Buddha's aim towards all living beings was to spread peace,. Human society can be peaceful by accepting this very aim of Buddha. Peace can be attained through the practice of non-violence, equally brotherhood and friendship. This message of Buddha was not only for the Buddhists but for all human beings irrespective of any caste, creed and religion.

**3.14 Self- Reliance–** Human society and nation can be developed by self-power, unity and self- reliance. Unity got and grown by the strength of weapons is not last longing. True unity lies with courtesy and self-sacrifice. To develop morality, self-reliance and duty consciousness is must to proceed towards the attainment of our goals.

**3.15 Brahma Vihara-** Buddha advocated four kinds of right thinking called Brahma Vihara in Buddhist tradition. Aim was to control our unlimited human wants and aspirations, moreover to be free from greed in this world. It is the combination of four concepts-

I. Maîtree (friendship)- This means to have a desire for the happiness and welfare for all the living creatures in this world.

II. Karuna (compassion)- It means to have sympathy with all mankind and trying to reduce the pains and sorrow of others.

III. Mudita (sympathy or pity without any jealousy)- One should be happy for other's wealth and prosperity rather to feel any kind of jealousy.

IV. Upekkha (indifference)- We should try to apart from all kinds of jealousy, anger, ignorance, practicality and prejudice.

**3.16 Patience and Calmness–** One must have the ability to be calm and clear while facing various obstacles like delays, frustrations etc. Human beings should have ability to remain peaceful and abstain from anger during the time when other people try to harm them. With due patience, It is easy to control all unpleasant situations.

**3.17 Perseverance-** Human beings can achieve this perfection. It is the capability to utilize all of our energy into productive and constructive purpose which may benefit to all mankind. So, one should never indulge in wrong and useless activities. We should properly channelize our efforts.

**3.18 Clarity of objectives in life–** Maha-Mangala sutta in Buddhism says that a mind should be properly directed and guided. One should know his position and the place in the world. He must have clear vision and mission. He must acquaint with the way to achieve these goals. One must have a simple philosophy of his life, useful aims of life and clear plan of actions to follow. This is done only by a balanced person. Aims should be practical and feasible, only then we may be successful in life.

**3.19 Self- Analysis-** Self-analysis and self-observation is required for self-improvement. We should measure the degrees of our traits like kindness, honesty, truth, patience, tolerance, tactfulness etc. These are the qualities of a well-adjusted Buddhist. A little practice to improve ourselves is needed in every day of our life. Right practice will become our habit which ultimately becomes the part of our character. Meditative practices are independent of material things. A strengthen person is self-reliant and with self-sufficient mind. Material things become his servants and not his master. He lives his life with simplicity. He possesses a cool, calm, contended and controlled mind. As per Buddha, contentment is the greatest wealth. One can easily adjust himself to new environment.

**4. Schools of Buddhism–** There are various schools of Buddhism

4.1 Theravada

4.2 Mahayana

4.3 Tibetan

4.4 Zen

**4.1 Theravada–** This is the oldest school of Buddhism. It is found in southern Asia (Sri Lanka, Burma, and Thailand etc.) As per their thoughts Monasticism is the way to obtain Nirvana. Enlightenment is possible through our own efforts. So, one should focus on increasing wisdom and doing meditation. Their ultimate goal is to become a Buddha. The followers of this school are fairly unified in these believes and practices but there are some cultural differences.

**4.2 School of Mahayana-** Mahayana means the 'Great Vehicle'. This was developed in first century and found in Northern Asian (China, Japan etc.) They seek guidance from wise people called Bodhi Sattvas and heavenly Buddha, Their main focus was on compassion. Their basic aim is to become a Bodhi Sattva and help the people to get enlightenment.

**4.3 School of Tibetan-** It was development in 7th century. It is a combination of Theravada and Mahayana. They also focus on Meditation, monasticism, wisdom and compassion. Their Bodhisattvas include living Lamas (Dalai Lama)

**4.4 School of Zen-** It is the 'Meditation' school. They also focus on monasticism. They seek sudden enlightenment through meditation (satori), obtaining emptiness (sunyata) and the Buddha Nature. They stressed on beauty, arts and aesthetics in our life.

**5. Buddhism in the West-** Many people migrated from Asia to the west. But western Buddhists are stick to their own faith, believes and traditions. They find Buddhism a complement instead of conflict with other religions. The two groups Asian and Western remain independent of one another.

**6. Buddhist Culture–** A person is successful only when he has progressed in ethical discipline and mental culture. One should be self-less without any lust and greed. We must develop positive attributes in our life i.e. kindness, compassion, honest and truthfulness etc. Only then we can became cultured Buddhists. A person with such qualities is well trained in body, speech and mind. He will be able to live with calmness and harmony with himself and others. This is called in real sense 'Dhamma'. One should be super active and energetic rather than being lazy and lethargic. We may become cultured and civilized people of our society. We may become aware of our rights and duties. Social development is possible through transformation of each individual personally. Buddhism focuses on Art, which is a medium of human communication. Art is helpful in the education of feelings and it is the most civilized agency of humankind. The work of all artists highlights fresh insights, whether artist is a painter, writer or dramatist. They express the worldly objects in a different perspective and emotions creating new values e.g. when we observe the Samadhi statue of Buddha, it catches our mind, increases our confidence and our desire for the Dhamma. All the Buddhist paintings, sculptures and art work are the typical form of artistic expression. Buddhist culture is never obsolete. There is no moral blindness.

**7. Buddhism Today in India**: Buddhism has come back to India in the 20th century due to the prevalence of caste system. Top power of the society possessed economic and political powers and bottom i.e. Dalits were called untouchables. They had limited facilities for education, health, employment etc. There was oppression all over India. Dr Bhimrao Ambedkar, a dalit leader had done tremendous work to eradicate the caste system in India. Millions of people accepted the appeal of Dr. Ambedkar to adopt Buddhism to escape from the caste system. He was a man who is revered as a bodhisattva. Many Dalits from various villages and towns have shrines with pictures of the Buddha every year in October. Over a million dalit Buddhists go to Nagpur for rally at the place of the original conversion. Even though, many of them belong to a very low economic condition, they try to establish a Buddhist society to develop their understanding of the Dharma. These are many temples and places for meditation. Many social projects have been carried out by the younger generations to realize. Dr Ambedkar's vision of social justice and Indian growth based on the preaching of Buddha. There are various approaches and schools working in the different areas. Some of them are committed to Dharma and others are engaged in social welfare. Near Nagpur Nagaloka is a training center for Buddhist activities. This is a center for providing Buddhists knowledge by teachers like Dalai Lama and Thich Nhat Hahn. Thousands of pilgrims visit this place to see Buddha statute at the campus. Other centers are Triratha Bauddha mahasangha, National Network of Buddhist society and Manuski Institute. Important Buddhists temples are Bodhgaya, Sarnath (Varanasi) Shravasti, Kusinasa, Nalanda and Rajgir. Many of the dalit people have joined this religion to get self-respect and dignity. Most important movements in the world is the Buddhist revival in India. The focus of all the Buddhist centers is to spread the teachings of Buddha in the whole nation.

**Summary:-**

There are "Three Jewells" of Buddhism, Buddha the teacher, Dharma the teachings and Sangha the community. Buddha as a teacher through his teachings served the society a lot. His four noble truths consider sufferings in life of every human being, which are due to our desires and attachments. The solution is to attain Nirvana (extinction) by leaving our desires and belongingness. Nirvana can be attained by the "eight-fold path" given by the Buddha. Which are:-

- Right understanding
- Right motivation
- Right Speech

- Right Action
- Right livelihood
- Right efforts
- Right mindfulness
- Right mediation

To sum up Nirvana is the ultimate solution of all human problems which can be attained by wisdom, moral and mental discipline Buddhism totally rejects the philosophy of Hinduism, ancient Vedic texts, the Vedic caste system, Hindu deities, rituals and the concept of Brahman. They also differ from Jainism. They reject the concept of Atman (soul).

Buddhists believe in Rebirth (reincarnation) which is only the results of attachments (karma). They said that Nirvana is a peaceful and detached state of mind and it is also a way to escape from the cycle of rebirth. Buddha is not regarded as God but just a revered teacher. Everything in this world is im-permanent as per Buddhist philosophy. Buddhism shows a rational, practical and balanced way of overcoming all our pains and sufferings. Life is most important than any other thing."

[Source: https://ebooks.inflibnet.ac.in/hrmp01/chapter/264/]

### Jainism

1 .Learning outcomes-

1.1 To know about the religion of Jainism..

1.2 To understand basic human values and teachings of Jainism.

1.3 To inculcate basic values of Jainism in our youth.

## 2. Introduction

Jain Dharma is an old Indian religion. The basic idea of Jainism is non-violence and respect for all the living beings. 'Jain' word has been emerged from Sanskrit word 'Jina' which means conqueror. A 'Jina' as per Sanskrit language is a person who is away from all inner passions like wants, desires, attachment, greed, anger, pride etc. The followers of the path of 'Jina' are known as Jains. The revivers of the Jain path are known as Tirthankaras. History of the Jain teachers is concluded with Mahavira consisting of twenty-four teachers. The basic prayer of Jains is 'Namokar Mantra' which means we should always help each other. The main two sub traditions of this religion are –Digambaras and Svetambaras. These both traditions have different practices. Maximum Jains reside in India. Some of the big Jain communities are present in other countries like Canada, Europe, Kenya and The United States. Main festivals of the Jains are Paryushana, Daslakshana, Mahavir Jayanti and Diwali

3. Principles and practices of Jainism- Jainism is a source of core human values which have been explained as under:-

3.1 'Ahimsa' (Non-violence) as the main Dharma – The fundamental values of this religion constitute 'Ahimsa' which means non-injury or non-violence. This is a basic commitment of every Jain. Killing or harming any one physically or by the words of mouth, both are strictly abandoned by Jains. All the living organisms must help each other. The cause of violence is anger and hate. Violence destroys our soul and mind. This conduct of non-violence helps in spiritual development. Which also affects one's salvation and release from rebirth? Ahimsa may cause bad 'Karma' consequently future sufferings.

3.2 Anekantavada (Many-sided Reality) – The truth and reality can be experienced but with language or speech, we are not able to express or communicate them completely. Only through good actions and deeds, these can be experienced. The Jains religion teaches us to accept all the positive and negative facts of life. There is no God or creator but only one thing is permanent that is 'Jiva' or soul. From ancient times it goes parallel with other religion. i.e. Buddhism and Hinduism. But, sometimes it is very critical for the knowledge system and ideologies of other religions.

3.3 Aparigraha (Non-Attachment) - It concentrates on non-possession from worldly things or property. Followers of the religion must be satisfied with only hard earned limited money. Moreover, they must donate any surplus money. Non- Attachment may be of two types- Material and Psychic. Material possessions are relating to property and wealth. Psychic relates to emotions and feeling. Attachments may result in the direct harm to individual personality. Jain monk or nun is supposed to be homeless and family-less away from any belongingness. As per them, internal attachments are anger, ego, greed and deceitfulness. They also suggest that we can overcome anger by forgiveness and pride by humility. Deceitfulness may be conquered by straight forwardness and greed by contentment or satisfaction. Other internal passions are like, dislike, fear, sorrow, laughter etc.

3.4 Asceticism- Jainism follows strongest asceticism. Such life means nakedness or non-possession of even clothes, keeping fasts, body mortification etc. to be free from old Karma and a restraint on new Karma. This is most required for getting siddha and moksha(Salvation or liberalization form rebirth). Ascetic austerities constitute six outer and six inner practices. Commonly outer austerities include complete fasting, limited eating, only to eat few items, avoid tasty food, and avoid flesh. It means to avoid temptation of everything. Inner austerities include confession, respecting and assisting mendicants, study meditation and detachment from any wants. Ultimate aim is to purify our soul. Mahavira (Vardhamana) has set an example of a good ascetic life by adopting severe austerities for twelve years.

3.5 Asteya(Not stealing) – A Jain mendicant should always take necessary permissions to get anything from others. They should accept only those things which are given to them voluntarily by others. They are strictly opposed to theft and stealing.

3.6 Brahmacharya – It means "celibacy' or away from sex and sensual pleasures for Jain monks and nuns. But for laypersons or followers Brahmacharya means complete faith with our life partner.

3.7 Food and Fasting – Most of the Jain follow lacto vegetarianism. It means they don't take even eggs. Root vegetables like potatoes, garlic, onions are not eaten by monks and nuns. The plants are also considered as living things. They believe that when plants are pulled, they are injured. During festivals Jains fast, which is called Upavasa or Tapasya? Jain layperson eats only twice a day, drinks boiled water or sometimes complete fasting during festivals. Fasting practice is done to improve their Karmas or actions. Fasting is very common in Jain women. They observe fasts for religious purity, family goodwill and future wellbeing of her family.

3.8 Dhyana (Meditation) – It is a most essential practice in this religion. As per different views, Meditation is a form of austerity and ascetic practice. It means one has to be pure. One must leave selfless, rather to concentrate on enhancing knowledge. Jains believe that they must be on the right road to meditate on the soul, the pure self. They also focus on the periods or timings for meditation. Some of the Jains believe to meditate thrice in a day, especially mendicants. Some laypersons practice rituals as Puja in a Jain temple and charity work.

3.9 Rituals and Worship – Jains have faith in 'darsana' or watching of deva including Padmavati, Ambika and Brahmadeva. Digambaras have a sub-tradition called Terapanthi. They do not worship many of the deities. 'Devapuja' ritual is very common in all Jain sub traditions. This is practicised by Jain doing 'namsakara' to God in the temples. One of their practice include abhisheka i.e. ceremonial bath. These rituals are matched with the Hindu rituals. They also recite mantras. Most famous eternal mantra of Jainism is ''five homage (Panca Namaskara).

3.10 Monasticism- Jainism has further Digambara monks and Svetambara monks. Digambara monks and nuns carry with them the feathers of peacock and always sweep while sitting or walking in order to avoid small insects being crushed. Svetambara monks also follow the same type of practice. Four fold order of Jainism consists of muni (male ascetics), aryika (female ascetics), sravaka (laymen) and sravika (laywoman)..

3.11 Jiva (soul) - As per Jain philosophy body means matter and soul is consciousness. Soul (jiva) is different from other substances i.e. Matter, Time, Space, Dharma and Adharma. Other substances are called Ajiva. As per their ideology, all living beings are soul, immortal and perfect. Soul is embodied in our body just like in a prison.

3.12 Tattva (reality) – Tatvas are the ways to obtain moksha or salvation. This is the ultimate solution for attainment of the goal of liberalization. There are seven Tatvas:-

Jiva (the soul)

Ajiva (non-living things like matter, time, space etc.) Asrava (influx) – entry of evil matters in the soul

Bondha (bondage)

Samvara (stoppage) i.e. to stop the evil matters in the soul Nirjara (gradual dissociation)

Moksha (liberation)

3.13 Soul and Karma – Natural soul is a mixture of impurities like natural Gold. Soul is closely associated with Karma. For the refinement of soul, The Jain Karmic theory is important to explain pains, sufferings and inequalities. Realization of this reality is the supreme destination of Jainism.

3.14 Samsara (cycle of rebirths) – Jainism strongly believe in Samsara. As per their thoughts, soul passes through 8,400,000 birth situations. They believe that soul passes through five types of bodies i.e. earth bodies, water bodies, fire bodies, air bodies and vegetable lives. Soul changes the bodies again and again. Therefore, we should concentrate on Karmas.

3.15 Tirthankaras (God) – As per Jainism there is no existence of God. As per external universe Jain cosmology, the whole cycle of the world has been divided into two parts i.e. avasarpini and utsarpini. As per their thoughts twenty four Tirthankaras are present to bless the whole universe in every half cycle of time. 'Mahavira' Jain is regarded as the last Tirthankara of avasarpmi.Tirthankaras are the role models for Jains to show the path of liberation.

3.16 Salvation (liberation)- As per Jainism ideology three Jewels can show is the way to salvation. They are right view, right knowledge and right conduct. There is one more jewel which is also considered by them very significant that is right asceticism. Only following all these four practices "Moksha can be obtained. These four jewels practice under this religion is called 'Moksha Marg.' Morality and virtues- Jainism related to the interconnection between religion and morality. One must live a good life as well go higher to divine perfection. There are different ethical standards and values for laymen and monks. To avoid pain and loss in living beings practice of Dharma is most essential. Ten virtues of Jainism are humility, purity, non-attachment, self-restraint, super forbearance, straight forwardness, truthfulness and complete renunciation. Thoughts, actions and speech are governed by these virtues. Dharma (religion) and morality are related to each other.

3.17 Morality and virtues- Jainism related to the interconnection between religion and morality. One must live a good life as well go higher to divine perfection. There are different ethical standards and values for laymen and monks. To avoid pain and loss in living beings, practice of Dharma is most essential. Ten virtues of Jainism are humility, purity, non-attachment, self-restraint, super forbearance, straight forwardness, truthfulness and complete renunciation. Thoughts, actions and speech are governed by these virtues. Dharma (religion) and morality are related to each other.

3.18 Equality in men and women- A book on 'Jain system of education' clearly states that Jains laid stress on educating all the individuals, kings, princes, princesses and even laymen. Their main aim was to provide knowledge and wisdom to all men and women to build their character by practicing some discipline in their student life. Then, they could become good human beings and will facilitate nation building. As per their philosophy women should obtain respect and honour from their fathers, brothers, husbands and even brother-in-law. Women respect means pleasing God.

3.19 Education in Jainism- They consider education as very integral and intrinsic in their life. Knowledge acquisition is not education. Education means knowledge, vision and building a good sound character.

Education is a way to achieve the major aims of our life i.e. liberation. Jainism way of life is to educate on our own to get quality soul which will lead us to perfection and liberation from all worldly sorrows

4. Jain Schools – Two major sub-groups of this community are Digambara and Svetambara. Both have different dress codes. Their individual thoughts are also vary from each other. Monks of the Digambara sub-community never wear clothes, but female monastic of this tradition wrap white saree which is unstitched and plain. These are called as Aryikas. Svetambara monastic usually wear white seamless clothes. Digambara and Svetambara are further divided into sub groups with their own believe. AS per Jainism liberation can be achieved by males mostly. Women can get salvation only by improving their Karmic merit to take birth as men.

5. Jain Symbols – The main Jain symbols are as follows:-

5.1. Swastika – It is an important Jain symbol. It constitutes four states of existence.

– Devas (heavenly being)

– Human Being

– Hellish being

– Triyancha (subhumans like flora or fauna)

These symbolize the existence of beings in different states.

5.2. Symbol of Ahimsa – In this symbol there is a wheel inside it, there is a hand. In the middle, Ahimsa word is written. Wheel signifies Dharma chakra. It means non-violence is the ultimate religion of Jains.

5.3. Jain Emblem- Jain emblem represents heaven, hell and material world i.e. three Loks Beyond these three realms on the upper side, a part signifies Siddhashila, a zone beyond the three zones. On the emblem three dots symbolizes ratnatraya-right thinking, right knowledge and right conduct. Symbol of 'Ahimsa' is present on lower porton and 'swastika' is shown on top area. At the bottom, their main mantra is given, which means "All life is bound together by mutual support and interdependence."

5.4. Jain Flag – Jain flag contains five colours i.e. white, red, yellow, green and black. White colour shows that souls who are free from anger, attachments and all passions. Souls who have obtained self-realization. It also denotes peace and non-violence. Red depicts Siddha as the souls with truth and liberation. Yellow signifies the acharya, the masters of adepts and achaurva (non-stealing). Green colour shows Brahmacharya and Upadhyaya (who teach scriptures to monks). Black symbolizes Jain ascetics which mean non-possession.

5.5. Om- It represents Namokar Mantra. It is a short form of five parameshthis i.e. Arihant, Ashiri, Acharya, Upajjhaya and Muni. These are the Jain Gurus teaching Jains. These are the souls who are free from all passions.

6 .Mahavira and his teachings – One of the oldest religions called Jainism was established by Mahavira (Vardhamana). He presented the philosophy of Jainism

in different way. But he was not actually the founder of this religion. He was born in 599 BC. He belongs to a very wealthy family. But he spent his life with great hardships, doing meditation and fasting. He was related to 23rd Tirthankara of this religion. He showed the way to live happy and peaceful life. Right knowledge, Right faith and Right conduct are the ways to shape the life of an individual as per Mahavira. All the living beings i.e. human beings, animals and plants have pure souls full of knowledge. He strongly believed in Karma and also guided us to free from the miseries of karma to acquire Moksha or Nirvana. He had no faith on God. But, he had a faith in the powers of all the souls. Mahavira stressed upon five principals which are-

– Ahimsa (non-violence)

– Satya (truth)

– Asteya (no stealing)

– Tyag (no property)

– Brahmacharia (virtuous life)

As per Mahavira Moksha can be obtained by Karma theory. His teaching has a good impact on all the Indians, religions, culture and languages. It has also worldwide impact on countries like U.S.A., U.K. Canada and Eat Africa. He did not believe in castes, creed, rich and poor moreover any gender discrimination. He suggested us to be truthful and honest. He said that in every living being there is a spirit so he laid stress on vegetarianism and to avoid injury to animals. His ideology was equality, self control, spiritual liberation and non-violence. His life had a great impact on community. He advocated about universal brotherhood of man and human rights. He visualized of a democratic society. He stressed on the egalitarian society on the basis of non-violence to obtain a state of equilibrium, social peace and excellence. Jainism had unqualified faith in human rights.

Summary

As per Jain philosophy, violence is a sin which is against the dignity of human being. Human dignity means human rights. We must have 'maitri' or friendship with every living being. We should respect for mankind and all other living beings. We should do charity for needy people, which are called Karuna. Highest wisdom is to do generous service to mankind i.e. madhyasthya. Guiding force of non-violence is compassion (daya), which is the basis of religion. Jainism believes in rational consciousness (samyaktva). In our old Vedic values, compassion is a must. Such type of atmosphere will basically promote and protect the rights of men. Non-violence is means as well as end towards creation of a society. Mahatma Gandhi, a great political leader was also following the path of non-violence in the struggle for independence of India from the British rules. Gandhiji also had a good impact of Mahavira's teachings. The Jains also claim that compassion for all living beings is possible after self-realization and spiritual wisdom. An important maxim of Jains is-"First knowledge then compassion". The theory of their religion also depicts to live and let live. In today's era, when world is going very fast, the basic ethical and moral values have been deteriorated. It is essential for the educational institutes to provide guidance and training to the future of India i.e. our young students. Some of the part of religious teaching must be imparted to the students to follow the preaching of our old religions. This is most essential to produce good human beings. This is also a way to stop violence which has become a prominent feature today. The world peace and harmony can be obtained only by inculcating moral and ethical values in present and upcoming generations. The cause of the destruction of our society is that we have forgotten the basic rules, principles and values system of our old epics and religions. There is a great contribution of Jain religion to our society. But the present western culture has provided us a life full of comforts and luxuries. Such life is an obstacle in front of humanity. Indian a country of Vedas, Upnishdas, Vedic culture and religions is today facing a very chronic phase. Modernization and Westernization is trying to dominate our community. The ultimate solution is to practice our old religious values and customs.[Source: https://ebooks.inflibnet.ac.in/hrmp01/chapter/271/ ]

## Sikhism

Sikhs believe that the world is real. What and how individuals perform here in life has real consequences. One need not escape the world through asceticism or austerity. In fact, pursuing ethical conduct in line with the Guru's teachings bestows gifts that even ascetics cannot reach. Guru Nanak (1469-1539) writes:

*Contemplating the word brings a benevolent attitude Destroying self-pride brings austerity's fruits The one who has heard the word is liberated-in-life Right conduct brings true peace.* **(GG 1343)**

That is, the opportunity for spiritual cultivation exists in social life, and does not require austerity or renunciation of social ties. As a believer in the universal accessibility of the spiritual path, Guru Nanak was vehemently opposed to those who retreated from the world to seek their spiritual cultivation.

Guru Nanak's sense of moral responsibility required fair interaction between people under the watchful sight of a just God. Guru Nanak spoke out against lying lawgivers (GG 662) and officials who accepted bribes (GG 951). Taking more than one's fair share is expressed as a social taboo for Sikhs, comparable to eating beef for Hindus and pork for Muslims (GG 141). On the flip side, charity is key to the good life. Guru Nanak teaches that the person who gives from his or her rightful earning is surely on the path to liberation.

These kinds of ethical injunctions are echoed in the writings of the later Gurus, and especially in the writings of the Sikh savant Bhai Gurdas. He made the first attempt to systematize Sikh ethics in organizing codes of conduct in consecutive, coherent stanzas of poetry. For example:

*Waking at the ambrosial hour, the Guru's Sikh bathes at the tank Repeating the Guru's words, he arrives at the place of worship. Arriving at the holy congregation, he listens lovingly to the holy word Dispelling doubts from his heart, he serves the Guru's Sikhs Earning from his hard work, he takes sacrament and distributes it Serving the Guru's Sikhs, he eats from what's left Lighting the way in this Dark Age, the Guru is the disciple, and the disciple meets the Guru* Gurmukhs *travel the straight path.* (Var 40, Stanza 11)

Another way Gurdas proliferated Sikh morals was to expound upon words and phrases containing pithy kernels of Sikh teachings that the common person could remember and enact. *Gurmat* ("Guru's advice") is the word for the Sikh teachings and the Sikh way of life in accordance with scripture. *Parupkari* ("benevolence") is the highest aim in this way of life. Ethics, and enacting the right things in life, take precedence over all else, and Guru Nanak proclaims that rightful living (*sach achar*) is far higher than proclamations of truth. Knowledge, and reflection on that knowledge, allow for right actions, which culminate in benevolence. We ought to seek virtue by aligning our mind, words, and actions (*man bach karam*) with Sikh teachings.

Along the way, remembrance of the Lord's name, charity, and spiritual ablution (*nam dan isnan*) guide our actions. Bhai Gurdas reflects on the Sikh Path:

***Waking at night's end, hold steadfast to* nam dan isnan *Speak sweetly, tread softly, give from your hands, give thanks Sleep little, eat little, speak little, and receive the Guru's teachings Eat of your labor, perform good deeds, be great but remain unnamed Day and night, congregate with the holy, sing Acquaint yourself with the sound of the word, thus know the true Guru and satisfy your heart***

***Amidst temptation, remain untempted.* (Var 28, Stanza 15)**

Elsewhere, Gurdas expresses the Golden Rule in his own unique way: everyone loves their son, trade, and religion like you love yours.

Some aspects of Sikh morality have been misunderstood by Western scholars, particularly the issue of Sikh justifications for violence. A typical, but incorrect, understanding of Guru Nanak's message is that it is pacifistic, and that later tradition contradicted this in its militarization. It is more accurate to see that Guru Nanak was a politically engaged religious teacher, and even activist. His poetry expresses concern for the weak and the meek. He even writes that violence between equals is acceptable, and military targeting of civilians is absolutely and deeply unjust.

Most Sikhs believe that the increased politicization of the community from its inception into the 18th century was not a qualitative shift. That is to say, violence may be justified as a final means for political engagement. As an act of last resort, the use of violence must be tempered by moral deliberation. Sikh morality abhors violence of aggression, the killing of innocents and non-combatants, and policies of environmental destruction like "scorched-earth."

Overall, specific questions of ethics, sexuality, and abortion are left to individuals, congregations, and families to decide. The Sikh conduct code is clear, however, that no gender-based feticide is allowed and that women must be treated with proper respect. This code of conduct, called the Sikh Rahit Maryada, is a mid-20th-century product that has its roots in the Guru's teachings, the works of Bhai Gurdas, and 18th-century

Rahit literature." [Source: https://www.patheos.com/library/sikhism/ethics-morality-community/principles-of-moral-thought-and-action ]

# SECTION [18]
# HUMAN & HUMANITY

"What's the Difference?

Human refers to an individual belonging to the species Homo sapiens, while humanity refers to the collective qualities and characteristics that define human beings as a whole. While human describes the physical and biological aspects of an individual, humanity encompasses the emotional, social, and moral aspects that make us unique as a species. In essence, human is the individual, while humanity is the essence of what it means to be human.

Further Detail

| Attribute | Human | Humanity |
|---|---|---|
| Definition | A member of the Homo sapiens species | The quality or state of being human |
| Physical Characteristics | Biological features such as height, weight, skin color | N/A |
| Emotions | Feelings such as happiness, sadness, anger | Compassion, empathy, love |
| Intelligence | Cognitive abilities such as reasoning, problem-solving | Collective knowledge and wisdom |
| Behavior | Actions and reactions of an individual | Actions and values of the human race as a whole |
| Definition | A member of the Homo sapiens species | The quality or state of being human |
| Physical Characteristics | Biological features such as height, weight, skin color | N/A |
| Emotions | Feelings such as happiness, sadness, anger | Compassion, empathy, love |
| Intelligence | Cognitive abilities such as reasoning, problem-solving | Collective knowledge and wisdom |
| Behavior | Actions and | Actions and |

| | reactions of an individual | values of the human race as a whole |
|---|---|---|

Definition

Human and humanity are two terms that are often used interchangeably, but they have distinct meanings. The term "human" refers to an individual member of the species Homo sapiens, characterized by their physical and mental attributes. On the other hand, "humanity" refers to the collective qualities, characteristics, and behaviors that define human beings as a whole.

Attributes of Human

Humans possess a wide range of attributes that set them apart from other species. These include their ability to think critically, communicate effectively, and experience a wide range of emotions. Humans are also known for their capacity for creativity, innovation, and problem-solving. Additionally, humans have a unique sense of self-awareness and consciousness that allows them to reflect on their own existence and purpose.

Attributes of Humanity

Humanity, on the other hand, encompasses the collective qualities and behaviors that define human beings as a species. These include compassion, empathy, kindness, and a sense of morality. Humanity is also characterized by a sense of community, cooperation, and the ability to work together towards common goals. Additionally, humanity encompasses the values and beliefs that guide human behavior, such as justice, equality, and respect for others.

Relationship between Human and Humanity

While human and humanity are distinct concepts, they are closely interconnected. The attributes of individual humans contribute to the overall quality of humanity as a whole. For example, acts of kindness, compassion, and empathy by individual humans can have a ripple effect on society, leading to a more compassionate and caring humanity. Similarly, negative behaviors and actions by individual humans can have a detrimental impact on humanity as a whole.

Impact on Society

The attributes of human and humanity have a significant impact on society as a whole. A society that values the attributes of humanity, such as compassion, empathy, and cooperation, is likely to be more harmonious and peaceful. On the other hand, a society that lacks these qualities may be characterized by conflict, inequality, and injustice. Therefore, it is essential for individuals to cultivate the attributes of humanity in order to create a more compassionate and caring society.

Conclusion

In conclusion, human and humanity are two closely related concepts that play a crucial role in shaping the world we live in. While human beings possess unique attributes that set them apart from other species, it is the collective qualities and behaviors of humanity that define us as a species. By cultivating the attributes of humanity, such as compassion, empathy, and cooperation, we can create a more harmonious and peaceful society for all individuals to thrive in." [Source: https://thisvsthat.io/human-vs-humanity

## What Are The Human Traits? | Essential – Characteristics - Diet & Glucose / By Mo [Source: https://wellwisp.com/what-are-the-human-traits/ ]

"Understanding Human Traits

Human traits are the characteristics that define us as individuals and collectively as a species. They range from physical attributes to emotional responses and intellectual capabilities. These traits can be innate or developed over time through experiences, culture, and social interactions. Understanding these traits is crucial for comprehending human behavior, relationships, and societal structures.

Physical traits are the most visible aspects of humanity. They include features such as height, skin color, hair type, and eye color. These traits are largely determined by genetics but can also be influenced by environmental factors. For instance, exposure to sunlight can affect skin pigmentation, while diet can influence overall health and physical appearance.

Emotional traits refer to the ways in which individuals respond to experiences and stimuli. These include temperamental qualities like optimism, resilience, empathy, and anxiety. Emotional intelligence plays a significant role in how we interact with others and manage our own emotions. It's fascinating to observe how these emotional traits can vary significantly from one person to another.

Intellectual traits encompass cognitive abilities such as problem-solving skills, creativity, analytical thinking, and memory. These traits often determine how effectively a person can navigate challenges in life or contribute to society. Education and life experiences shape these intellectual capacities over time.

The Role of Genetics in Human Traits

Genetics plays a foundational role in determining many human traits. Every individual inherits a unique combination of genes from their parents that influences their physical appearance and predisposition to certain behaviors or conditions. For example, some people may inherit genes that make them more prone to anxiety or depression due to family histories of mental health issues.

Moreover, research into the human genome has revealed specific genes associated with various traits. The study of genetics has expanded our understanding of hereditary conditions and has paved the way for advancements in medicine and psychology. However, it's essential to recognize that genetics is just one piece of the puzzle; environmental factors also significantly impact how these traits manifest.

**Nature vs. Nurture**

The debate surrounding nature versus nurture has been a longstanding discussion in psychology and sociology. Nature refers to genetic inheritance while nurture encompasses all environmental influences after conception. This dichotomy raises questions about how much of who we are is predetermined by our DNA versus shaped by our experiences.

For instance, two siblings may share similar genetic backgrounds but lead very different lives based on their upbringing, peer influences, education opportunities, and personal choices. This variability illustrates that while genetics provide a blueprint for potential traits and behaviors, life experiences play an equally crucial role in shaping an individual's personality.

**Cultural Influences on Human Traits**

Culture significantly impacts human traits by shaping beliefs, values, customs, and social norms that guide behavior within communities. Different cultures promote various attributes as desirable or undesirable; for example, some cultures value collectivism over individualism while others emphasize independence.

Cultural practices can also influence emotional responses; in some societies, expressing emotions openly is encouraged while others may view it as a sign of weakness. This cultural lens affects interpersonal relationships among individuals from different backgrounds.

Furthermore, cultural narratives often dictate what it means to be successful or fulfilled in life—shaping aspirations accordingly. Understanding these cultural influences allows for greater empathy towards diverse perspectives on human experience.

## Socialization's Impact on Human Traits

Socialization is the process through which individuals learn behaviors appropriate for their society—this begins at infancy through family interactions before expanding into schools and communities later on. Through socialization processes such as imitation or reinforcement learning (where behaviors are encouraged based on positive outcomes), individuals develop various human traits over time.

For instance, children raised in nurturing environments tend to develop higher emotional intelligence than those exposed only to neglect or abuse—demonstrating how critical early experiences are in shaping character development throughout life stages.

Socialization also includes exposure to societal expectations regarding gender roles which contributes further complexity into understanding what constitutes typical masculine or feminine behavior within differing contexts across cultures globally.

Common Human Traits Across Cultures

| Trait | Description | Examples Across Cultures |
|---|---|---|
| Empathy | The ability to understand | Caring for elderly |

| | | |
|---|---|---|
| | others' feelings. | relatives; charitable acts. |
| Curiosity | A desire for knowledge or exploration. | Children asking questions; adults traveling. |
| Resilience | The capacity to recover from difficulties. | Overcoming poverty; adapting post-disaster. |
| Creativity | The use of imagination or original ideas. | Artistic expression; innovative solutions. |
| Cooperation | The ability to work together towards common goals. | Community projects; team sports. |

Despite variations across cultures regarding specific values or norms surrounding behavior—certain universal human traits emerge consistently around the globe:

These universal characteristics illustrate fundamental aspects of humanity that transcend cultural boundaries—highlighting shared values within diverse societies worldwide.

The Evolutionary Perspective on Human Traits

From an evolutionary standpoint—human traits have developed over millennia shaped by survival needs within varying environments. Natural selection favored certain characteristics that enhanced survival chances leading toward adaptation over generations.

For example—traits associated with cooperation likely evolved because they provided advantages when hunting or gathering food within groups rather than acting alone—a strategy yielding higher success rates overall!

Similarly—emotional expressions serve vital functions facilitating communication among individuals fostering social bonds crucial for group cohesion necessary during challenging times throughout history!

Understanding this evolutionary perspective offers insight into why certain human behaviors persist today despite technological advancements altering lifestyles dramatically compared with those faced by earlier generations!

The Impact of Technology on Human Traits

In recent decades—the rapid advancement of technology has introduced new dynamics influencing human behavior patterns! Social media platforms allow individuals across vast distances instant connectivity reshaping communication styles impacting emotional expressions too!

While technology enables convenience—it also poses challenges like diminished face-to-face interactions leading potential erosion empathy levels among users accustomed solely virtual engagement! Balancing online presence alongside authentic interpersonal relationships remains essential navigating modern complexities surrounding evolving definitions belonging community!

Despite these changes—the core essence humanity persists reflecting timeless qualities resilience compassion curiosity creativity vital navigating ever-changing landscapes life presents us daily!

The Significance of Emotional Intelligence Among Humans

Emotional intelligence (EI) refers ability recognize manage one's emotions while understanding those experienced others—a critical component successful interpersonal relationships! High levels EI correlate positively outcomes personal professional realms alike fostering collaboration trust among peers enhancing productivity overall workplace environments!

The Future of Human Traits: Adaptation and Change

As society continues evolve rapidly—the landscape surrounding human traits will undoubtedly shift reflecting changing values technological advancements societal norms! Increasing globalization fosters cross-cultural exchanges encouraging blending diverse perspectives enriching collective understanding shared humanity!

Individuals possessing strong EI display heightened self-awareness enabling them navigate challenging situations effectively maintaining composure under pressure! This trait proves invaluable during conflicts negotiations where empathy understanding play pivotal roles achieving resolutions acceptable parties involved!

Moreover—individuals with developed EI exhibit greater adaptability facing change demonstrating openness learning new perspectives enriching personal growth journeys throughout lives!

Recognizing importance cultivating emotional intelligence empowers individuals strengthen connections enhance quality relationships ultimately contributing healthier happier societies collectively thriving together!

Future generations may prioritize different attributes emphasizing sustainability inclusivity innovation responding pressing global challenges facing us today climate change inequality etc.! Embracing adaptability becomes paramount ensuring resilience amidst uncertainties navigating complexities ahead collectively striving create better world future generations inherit legacy built compassion cooperation creativity resilience! In conclusion—it's evident exploring myriad facets defining what it means be human reveals intricate tapestry woven through shared experiences challenges triumphs defining essence existence itself! Key Takeaways: Human Traits

➤ **Human traits** include physical, emotional, and intellectual characteristics.

➤ **Genetics plays a role** in shaping traits but is influenced by environment.

➤ **Cultural influences** shape our behaviors, values, and emotional expressions.

➤ **Emotional intelligence** is crucial for successful relationships and adaptability.

> ► **Adaptation is key** as societal values and technology continue to evolve.
>
> .

Conclusion – What Are The Human Traits?

What Are The Human Traits? They encompass our physical attributes alongside emotional responses intellectual capabilities shaped both genetically environmentally over time! Recognizing diversity inherent within humanity enriches understanding fosters appreciation unique journeys each individual undertakes navigating intricate tapestry life presents daily!

# SECTION [19]
# HUMANS TREATMENT OF OTHER LIVING BEINGS

### DIFFERENT RELIGIONS, DIFFERENT ANIMAL ETHICS? LOUIS CARUANA SJ 1,

> [Source: Anim Front - . 2020 Jan 10; 10(1):8–14. doi: 10.1093/af/vfz047 - Different religions, different animal ethics? Louis Caruana SJ 1, ✉ - https://pmc.ncbi.nlm.nih.gov/articles/PMC6952866/
> Implications.
> 
> - Religions, in spite of their differences, converge on some fundamental points, and some of these points concern our responsibility toward animals.
> 
> - Human superiority over all other creatures is to be understood in terms of caring for creation.
> 
> - Moral questions concerning our treatment of fellow humans are linked to those concerning our treatment of animals. Animal care is an obligation, both moral and religious.

"Introduction

Interest in animal ethics has recently increased considerably. This is due to various factors like technological progress, the sharp rise in human population, and the consequent pressure on global ecology. In this area, do traditional religions have anything to offer? It is obvious that religion still plays an important role in many areas of individual and communal life, for better or for worse. As regards animals, religious traditions affect the subliminal conscience and moral dispositions of billions of people. This paper explores this effect in three sections. The first section will be about religion, the second about conceptual clarification, and the third will be about morality.

At the very start however, an important general point needs to be highlighted. The paper's title may give the impression that the overall argument will defend some form of relativism. The final result, however, will pull in the opposite direction. Accepting a plurality of perspectives is not the same thing as embracing relativism. The method adopted in this research acknowledges that, within the global, complex cultural landscape, each individual sees things from his or her own specific location. It acknowledges also however that being situated does not necessarily block the researcher from objective truth. Those who accept the relevance and importance of different cultural perspectives can still arrive at objective truths, just as observers can arrive at some truths about the room they are sitting in even though they are seated at different places.

Religions and Animals

Starting with the most ancient traditions and proceeding chronologically, the following selective overview will first consider the main religions that emerged from India before spreading across East Asia: Hinduism, Buddhism, and Jainism; it will then deal with the Abrahamic religions, those that consider Abraham as their founder. In most religious traditions, animals play a symbolic role, but such symbolism will not be the focus of this paper. It will concentrate rather on moral issues, not limiting the discussion to animal-friendly teachings but mentioning also some problematic or negative aspects.

In Hinduism, the majority view as regards animals highlights two basic ideas: the idea of a hierarchy of living things with humans enjoying the highest status and the idea of reincarnation (Krishna, 2010; Kemmerer, 2012). The position of each animal within the hierarchy of life is not random, but determined by the fixed law of *karma*. Good deeds contribute to the believer's promotion within the hierarchy, bad ones to a demotion. The idea of a hierarchy determines a kind of sacred inequality differentiating all biological species, differentiating even the various ethnic groups within humanity. This idea functions well within Hinduism for promoting good behavior, but it assumes that animals are situated at a significantly inferior level when compared with the lowest caste of humans. This devaluation of animals is counterbalanced by the many sacred texts, for instance in the Rig Veda and the Atharva Veda, where we find praise toward anyone who shows sensitivity toward animals. It is counterbalanced also by the belief that Hindu deities reincarnate as animals, especially as monkeys and cows, for instance Rama and Krishna. In fact, detailed studies indicate that the respect Indian religions show toward animals is supported by the strong symbolic link eventually established between the various animal species and the various divinities (Krishna, 2010). According to Nanditha Krishna, the cow veneration arose during the Vedic era. As is well-known, the cow occupies a special place in Hinduism, even today. In giving us milk, it represents our source: our mother or mother Earth. A relatively recent text, the Chandogya Upanishad, which appeared about 800 BC, confirms that nonviolence, or *ahimsa*, should be observed not only toward humans but also toward all beings (Figure 1).[Author: Not reproduced in this book]

As regards Buddhist traditions, one can start by highlighting a very general point. According to most interpretations, the goal of Buddhism is to overcome suffering and free oneself from the cycle of death and rebirth. One notices therefore that Buddhism retains from Hinduism the hierarchical view of beings and also the idea of reincarnation. It adds however the idea of personal liberation through enlightenment. The main goal for humanity is to find the right spiritual practice to end the suffering that results from rebirth. Later Buddhist interpretations hold that the painful cycle of rebirth occurs in six realms of existence: the heavenly, the demi-god, the human, the animal, the hungry ghost, and the hellish realm. The last three of these realms are evil, the animal realm included. Does Buddhism admit of a creator? This is a disputed question even today. One school holds that all phenomena originate from other phenomena and that the cycle of originating dependence is closed within itself. The universe therefore does not need a first cause. Other forms of Buddhism however admit the ultimate reality as the source of all things. For instance, Mahayana Buddhism describes the ultimate reality as the Womb of all Buddhas or as the Primordial Buddha. Regarding the status of animals, Buddhism shows trends that apparently pull in different directions. On the one hand, one maxim of the Noble Eightfold Path is that all Buddhists should refrain from killing. On a broad interpretation, this maxim includes all sentient life (Kemmerer, 2012). Consequently, vegetarianism is a highly respected ideal. On the other hand, Buddhism retains not only the hierarchy of life but also the idea that the animal realm is evil, in the sense that it is a realm that humans should avoid by living virtuous lives.

Jainism is another ancient Indian religion. It is founded on the four main ideas of nonviolence, many-sidedness, nonattachment, and asceticism. Jain lifestyle is marked by vegetarianism and the avoidance of all harm to humans and animals. It is the strictest religion as regards avoiding harm to animals. All living things are meant to help one another. Killing is not allowed, even in self-defense. Going further than Hinduism and Buddhism, Jainism considers nonviolence the highest moral duty. The background cosmology is similar to what we saw in Hinduism and Buddhism, namely a hierarchy of living things and the cycle of rebirth, from which humans need to be liberated. According to some Jain traditions, killing is to be avoided not because of the inherent value of living things but to keep one's soul pure, ensuring thus a better rebirth. One important prayer includes a plea for forgiveness from all living beings. The idea of *Jiva* corresponds somewhat to what Western thinkers call consciousness or soul but Jainism sees *Jiva* as present everywhere, in gods, humans, animals, plants, hell beings, and even in inert matter (Figure 2) [Author: Not reproduced in this book]. There is, therefore, an emphasis on a common hidden vital principle that joins all things into a kind of brotherhood. The universe in all its realms is eternal and self-sufficient. There is no creator God who rewards and punishes. Instead, there is the law of *karma*. This plays the role of delivering reward and punishment and it does it through necessity.

We move on now to the Abrahamic religions, starting with Jewish traditions. In the Jewish Bible, one finds that God created all things and that all creatures are good in themselves. There are also some specific moral obligations toward animals, for instance the injunction not to muzzle an ox while it is working (Deuteronomy 25:4), and to help a fallen overloaded donkey, even if it belongs to your enemy (Deuteronomy 22:4). The prophet Qohelet, speaking about the prospects after death, holds that "man has no superiority over beast" (Ecclesiastes 3:19 NRSV). More noteworthy still, one finds passages where the author describes animals as part of the human community. God commissions Noah to save not only his family but all creatures in view of a new world order (Figure 3) [Author: Not reproduced in this book]. Moreover, after the flood, God establishes the new covenant with all creatures: "I am establishing my covenant with you [Noah] and your descendants after you, and with every living creature that is with you, the birds, the domestic animals, and every animal of the earth with you, as many as came out of the ark" (Genesis 9:9 NRSV). In the book of Jonah, the King's call to fast, repent and return to living well, in line with God's will, includes domestic animals (Jonah 3:7–9 NRSV). One could mention also human fellowship with animals as regards rest and as regards praise: "that your ox and your donkey may have rest" (Exodus 23:12 NRSV); "Let everything that breathes praise the Lord!" (Psalm 150 NRSV). The kosher slaughter of animals is allowed but it involves minimizing pain and draining away the blood to show respect toward the animal's soul (Leviticus 17:10–13). Although a discussion on the related issue of animal sacrifice lies beyond the scope of this paper, one needs to mention at least one other somewhat disputed point. In the book of Genesis, there is an explicit reference to human authority and supremacy. "Then God said, 'Let them [humans] have dominion over the fish of the sea, and over the birds of the air, and over the cattle, and over all the wild animals of the earth, and over every creeping thing that creeps upon the earth'" (Genesis 1:26 NRSV). According to many Jewish commentators, the idea here is that, since God is merciful toward all creation, humans should do likewise. They should imitate God by extending His mercy toward all creatures (Seidenberg, 2008; Kemmerer, 2012).

Christianity retained nearly all the religiosity of Judaism, articulated it to some extent in terms of Greek philosophy, and added its own original elements. As regards animals, the New Testament makes few direct references. Jesus did say of the birds that "not one of them is forgotten before God" (Luke 12:6 NRSV) but the main thrust of his message concerned humans. According to the Christian doctrine of the Incarnation, Jesus is both divine and human, and he invites humans to follow him and to become children of God. This idea entails a strong form of anthropocentrism. Nevertheless, it includes also a cosmological aspect. As explained by St. Paul, Christ's salvific act embraces not just humans but all creation, including animals. Paul writes, "the creation itself will be set free from its bondage to decay and will obtain the freedom of the glory of the children of God. We know that the whole creation has been groaning in labor pains until now; and not only the creation, but we ourselves, who have the first fruits of the Spirit" (Romans 8:21–24 NRSV). Humans are definitely more important than animals. Nevertheless, many prominent Christian figures in history, like Francis of Assisi, became famous for their inclusion of animals as close friends, deserving love and mercy. For Catholics, official doctrinal statements focus not so much on whether animals have rights per se but on the moral constraints that apply to humans in their treatment of animals. The current position defends not only the unquestionable dignity of the human person but also the reality of moral obligations toward animals. On the one hand, the Second Vatican Council documents affirm that the human person is "the only creature on earth that God has willed for its own sake" (Paul VI, 1965, paragraph 24) and the Catechism of the Catholic Church (1994) adds that animals are "by nature destined for the common good of past, present, and future humanity" (Catechism, 1994, 2415). On the other hand, the same Catechism affirms that humans are obliged to "respect the particular goodness of every creature" (Catechism, 1994, 339). The recent encyclical *Laudato Sì* is more explicit. Pope Francis writes, "The ultimate purpose of other creatures is not to be found in us. Rather, all creatures are moving forward with us and through us towards a common point of arrival, which is God" (Francis, 2015, Section 83). Moreover, "our insistence that each human being is an image of God should not make us overlook the fact that each creature has its own purpose. None is superfluous" (Francis, 2015, Section 84). The overall current position emphasizes the urgent need for reconciliation with all creatures. Christianity is not a vegetarian religion. Nevertheless, it has always highlighted the importance of abstaining from the eating of flesh as a way to help realize the purity of life before the Fall, and thus prepare for the full realization of the new creation (Berkman, 2004).

The final point in this quick overview of major religions deals with Islamic traditions. Just like Judaism and Christianity, Islam recognizes God as Creator of a hierarchy of beings with humans on top. Humans enjoy a special status because they have a far higher dignity than animals. For Muslims, God created animals for the use of humans. For instance in The Qur'an (2004) Surah 16:5, there is the claim that "And livestock – He created them too. You derive warmth and other benefits from them: you get food from them." Surah 40:79 says, "It is God who provides livestock for you, some for riding and some for your food." Humans however are God's vice-regents on Earth and are obliged to make decisions for the benefit of creation as a whole. Within Islam therefore, there is the same kind of anthropocentrism as in the other Abrahamic religions. Nevertheless, Muslims see animals as creatures that enjoy their own communities. Animals praise God in their own way, which we do not understand. For instance, the Qur'an (2004) Surah 6:38 explains that "all the creatures that crawl on the earth and those that fly with their wings are communities like yourselves." Later holy writings support these foundational ideas in The Qur'an (2004).

Most significantly, the important Islamic collection, the Hadith, often describe the Prophet Muhammad's special concern for animals. The central Islamic message of love, compassion, humility, submission, and almsgiving (*zakat*) is applicable not only for humans but also in the broader context of human-animal relations. The overall picture therefore has two sides. On the one hand, since humans are the centerpiece of creation, the killing of animals is permissible. On the other hand, maltreatment of animals is recognized as wrong. Killing for food therefore needs to be minimal and regulated carefully to minimize the painfulness of the procedure. The Qur'an (2004) in fact allows the eating of certain animals only, and only when slaughtered in a specified way.

Conceptual Clarification

Each religion responds to the restlessness of the human heart by offering a particular viewpoint. Because of the various ramifications of religious traditions in the course of history, the overall stand as regards animals is not always clear. Nevertheless, we can still identify at least two areas of global convergence, one dealing with the interdependence between all living things and the other with the significance of the triad animality–humanity–divinity.

First then: the interdependence of all creatures, material and spiritual. The very use of the word "creatures" reflects a common kinship. The universe, charged with its own dynamism, shows how most creatures flourish by using other creatures. Religions see therefore the entire biosphere as a unified, dynamic whole. This universal creaturely kinship is not a flat or chaotic landscape. It is a hierarchy. All living things occupy a specific position within this hierarchy. Humans may be the highest within the material realm but they are certainly not the highest overall. Our position bestows on us not only power and authority but also special responsibilities. The major religions accept that a lack of human respect toward animals often generates a corresponding lack of human respect toward other humans, especially the poor, the underprivileged, the physically or mentally challenged, the sick, and the old (Figure 4).[Author: Not reproduced in this book]

The second area of convergence involves the relation between the concepts of animality, humanity, and divinity. Religions go beyond the direct interest of animal ethicists, who normally focus on the animality–humanity relation. Religions add another dimension.

Many philosophers of ancient times, most notably Aristotle, had correctly recognized that humans are indeed animals, animals of a special kind. Nevertheless, our use of the term "animality" as distinct from "humanity" remains useful. Such use highlights the gap between us and other animals. "Animality" is sometimes used to refer to the bodily instincts of humans as distinct from human intellectual or spiritual nature. In what follows however, the focus will be mainly on animality as a generic characteristic of nonhuman animals. As regards animality in this sense, one notices first that it is not a human construct. Animality is a given. Although we can care for animals, manage them, dominate them, and eat them, we cannot construct them ourselves. Sometimes the expression "animal production" is indeed used, but this use is misleading. What we produce are things like tables and chairs. They are artifacts. Had humans never existed, the world would be bereft of tables and chairs. Not so as regards animals. They constitute part of the fundamental givenness of the world. Moreover, animality comes across to us as a realm of innocence. It is a morality-free zone. Sometimes, we might feel nostalgic about this zone. We might yearn for this state of life. We do share in animality but we are burdened, one might say, by another realm, the realm of thought and morality.

Animality acts like a mirror that reveals something of our own nature to us. The gap is highly instructive (e.g., Derrida, 2002). It is certainly different from the gap between machinery and humanity. When we insert animals within complex input–output structures, designed for our benefit, we overlook the specific integrity that each animal represents. Factory farming degrades animality by confining it within the rigidity of machinery, within the restrictions of artificiality. In fact, in plain pragmatic and utilitarian terms, factory farming is nothing but the project "to raise as many animals as possible in the smallest possible space in order to maximize profits" (Degrazia, 1998, p. 281). The integrity of the individual animal does not count in any way. The problem here does not concern the factory only. It concerns the factory and all its links to society at large. The machine in this case includes its human administrators, its animal constituents and also the human consumers. The fact that consumers are far away, are ignorant of the conditions involved, or are unwilling to find out, does not detached them completely from the problem. By buying its products, consumers are in fact collaborating with the malpractice. The "social distance" between the perpetrator and the supporter of the system is never enough to render the supporter totally innocent. Some researchers therefore rightly support the demand for transparency and for boycotting. Current empirical studies have confirmed that many animals have rudimentary forms of beliefs, desires, and self-awareness (Degrazia, 1998; Lurz, 2009). Nevertheless, current levels of cruelty to animals are unacceptably high. For some people, awareness of this is like a personal wound, a wound that cannot heal. They carry it with them, hidden in their hearts, wherever they go, like a kind of original sin (e.g., Agamben, 2004; Cavell, 2009, p. 128–130)

Cruelty is pleasure in inflicting suffering or inaction towards another's suffering when a clear remedy is readily available. Sadism can also be related to this form of action or concept. Cruel ways of inflicting suffering may involve violence, but affirmative violence is not necessary for an act to be cruel. For example, if a person is drowning and begging for help and another person is able to help with no cost or risk, but is merely watching with disinterest or perhaps mischievous amusement, that person is being cruel—rather than violent. George Eliot stated that "cruelty, like every other vice, requires no motive outside itself; it only requires opportunity." Bertrand Russell stated that "the infliction of cruelty with a good conscience is a delight to moralists. That is why they invented Hell." Gilbert K. Chesterton stated that "cruelty is, perhaps, the worst kind of sin. Intellectual cruelty is certainly the worst kind of cruelty."{Source: Wikipedia Free Encyclopaedia

As regards divinity, one needs to acknowledge that some religions, for instance Buddhism, apparently do not refer to God at all. Nevertheless, one can take divinity in a broad sense as a common element for all religions. Divinity in a broad sense refers to a transcendent order to which people aspire. The transcendent order is the ultimate goal and the source of moral insight. Religions talk about divinity in this sense in various ways, for instance in terms of union with a loving God or in terms of the dissolution of the self as a result of liberation from the cycle of rebirth. Whether Buddhism is fundamentally atheistic is a debated question and there is apparently no clear agreement between the various traditions. For instance, on the one hand, some argue that Buddhism is ultimately atheistic because of its deep conviction that the sense of unity between different aspects or experiences, as in our own subjective experiences, is an illusion. Therefore, things, although many, are not bound together by any kind of real unity (Hayes, 1988). On the other hand, in the Buddhist scriptures known as the Nibbana Sutta of the Udana Nikaya (the Pali Canon), one finds the Buddha himself teaching as follows: "there is, monks, an unborn-unbecome-unmade-unfabricated. If there were not that unborn-unbecome-unmade-unfabricated, there would not be the case that escape from the born-become-made-fabricated would be discerned. But precisely because there is an unborn-unbecome-unmade-unfabricated, escape from the born-become-made-fabricated is discerned" (Udana Nikaya, 2012). Such a statement indicates an ultimate One analogous to what the Abrahamic religions and various philosophies refer to. How does divinity, understood in this way, affect the animality–humanity conceptual relation? The divinity dimension opens up the horizon of religious believers to ideas about a common source and a common goal to all life. This horizon introduces a common ultimate relation of order and interdependence. Religious people feel obliged to care for animals, remaining nevertheless fully aware of their own human specificity of superior intellect and power. Are we ashamed of being so different from animals, so superior to them? The givenness of all life-forms includes the givenness of our own specificity. It includes our responsibility and the alarming ecological imperative that we are discovering nowadays, namely to care not just for ourselves but for all living things. This is a divine imperative, a commandment.

**Moral Implications**

How does religion affect the foundational source of people's action? Of course, actions speak louder than words. Religious doctrine therefore remains ineffective until it takes up concrete form in deliberation and action. Some personal traits or habits, attributes of the person as a whole, are crucial for that person's morally good life. These traits are called virtues. Most religions and philosophical traditions agree that the basic virtues are not culturally dependent. They are the same for all people, whatever their culture or religion. Virtues like prudence, temperance, justice, and fortitude are universally indispensable for genuine human flourishing. How are these virtues applicable as regards animals? Let us consider them briefly one by one (Schaefer, 2008). In general, prudence makes one identify real needs and judge well as regards the best means to adopt. It ensures that one makes judgments in the light of all the available data. As regards animal welfare, this means that religious believers are motivated to collect all available data, including embarrassing data like appalling farming conditions and cruel slaughtering methods. Temperance, as sustained by religious discipline, helps believers avoid inordinate and immoderate desires, for instance excessive meat-consumption. Justice motivates religious believers to give to each his or her due, and to extend this imperative to all creatures. And finally fortitude: sustained by religion, this virtue makes believers act fearlessly even when opposed. With fortitude, they respond effectively to ecological concerns and are ready to revise well-entrenched practices. They are ready to engage in self-corrective procedures, even as regards their own belief systems, and to learn from past mistakes.

## Conclusion

This paper's title was in the form of a question: "Different religions, different animal ethics?" Although most of the arguments presented deserve further exploration and analysis, the overall result is clear enough. There is considerable support for the claim that religions, in spite of their differences, do converge on some fundamental points; and some of these points regard animals. The conclusion can be formulated in two points. Firstly, a point about human superiority. The major religions indicate that it is indeed possible to affirm two apparently opposing claims: the claim that humans have a higher dignity than that of all other creatures and the apparently opposing claim that humans should not cause suffering to creatures. The way to hold these two affirmations together is to see human superiority in terms of caring for creation. Even though humans count more than animals, animals count as well. Indeed, they should count much more than what we have been assuming for centuries. Secondly, a point about urgency. One way of reacting to cruelty is to say that animals must wait. First, we need to learn how to eradicate cruelty to humans and then, once this is accomplished, we will sort out our relations with animals. This kind of response however is deceptive. We need to address all moral fronts together, in the right way. Practices like factory farming, irresponsible genetic manipulation, excessive meat-consumption, the use of animals for experiments, cosmetics or entertainment should all be thoroughly revised accordingly. Animal care is an obligation—both moral and religious."

The above Article though appears to be realistic assessment of the subject matter, the crucial aspect of the matter is that the human treatment of other living beings on Mother Earth the way it is now prevalent in the world is not comparable, the reason being that in the case of human beings, the cruelty and killing is considered to be crimes under the laws of the land. The other living beings also have the same Spirit as the humans have and, therefore they also need to be treated the way the humans want to be treated rather relaxations accorded to the humans under the governing laws of the land on cruelty and killings and denying the same under those laws of the land cannot be considered less than inhumanistic having accepted the fact that all the other living beings are alive there being Spirit in them. The Spirit cannot be differentiated between the humans and other living beings. The pain and the state of shock the other living beings undergo when those are subjected to cruelty and killings is not different from the ones the human beings undergo. The Article referred to above though gives reasoning on this differential treatment based solely on the religious biases that include mainly the permissibility of cruelty and killings in some religions and prohibition of the same in some other religions. The religions are born based on the creation and evolution by the Great Saints and Sages who were also had the same Spirit as we and other living beings are having. Author finds himself in great perplexity to understand the reasoning that the cruelty and killings in the case of other living beings is based on the Faith to which one belongs. That raises a question WHETHER FAITH IS SUPERIOR THAN SPIRIT [GOD]? God created the Faith through respectful Saints and Sages and the Faith cannot question the Godly Qualities. Let us read the following Article to enlighten ourselves:

**"ANIMAL SUFFERING AND THE GOD QUESTION" - DR. MICHAEL W. FOX -** https://drfoxonehealth.com/post/animal-suffering-and-the-god-question/

In these difficult times many people are becoming increasingly affected by global problems of cruelty and suffering of humans and non-humans throughout the world. Animals have enough to cope with in the wild in extremes of weather and often starving, afflicted by injuries and disease as do many domestic animals left to fend for themselves; not to forget the whales, tigers, elephants and other endangered species likely to become extinct in the near future. So caring people ask what kind of God could create a world of so much suffering and killing. A God who stands for all that is good? Or did God create the natural world for our own exclusive use no matter the cost to other inferior beings.

As a child I witnessed creatures killing and consuming each other in the ponds and meadows I explored and what I saw I felt was part of Nature's laws and order and all was created by God. There was neither right nor wrong in that sentient realm that filled my spirit with awe and wonder—the stepping stones of reverence for all life.

Many animal species must kill or parasitize others to survive and continue their species. (Few enslave). If there were no predators would vegan gazelles and deer be swift of foot and sharp of horn, embodying speed and grace and even magnificence to us? Robinson Jeffers, in his poem The Bloody Sire writes: "What but the wolf's tooth whittled so fine/The fleet limbs of the antelope?") Would they not suffer more from devastating cycles of overpopulation and habitat destruction without becoming the food of carnivores? Predation is not the same as humans killing each other even in the name of God but warfare may be our biological response to overpopulation and dwindling natural resources.

More people are protesting and lament our specie's violent propensity and cry for the billions of creatures, from fish to fowl and pig to kid and lamb captured and slaughtered daily around the world for human consumption and at ever increasing environmental cost. Over one hundred and fifteen million animals are experimented on world-wide each year to find cures for essentially anthropogenic diseases, cancer in particular.

We dissected frogs in high school biology class: Frogs like those from my childhood's ponds whom I observed for hours and once when I was nine years old found several along the bank blown to pieces with straws impaling them. The cause of the killing was evidenced by the small boot -prints around the bloodied remains—a gang of my peers.

The normalization of cruelty by common practice becoming acceptance means the end of empathy with erosion of moral sensibility and ethical responsibility in civil, secular and religious communities. Yet still, some religious leaders assert that animals were created for man's use and that animal experimentation is justified it for human benefit.

If there was not sentience there would not be consciousness to experience physical pain and emotional suffering and associated mechanisms to avoid pain, injury, infection and motivation to protect others. But the suffering of other animals on the scale that we humans impose is unnatural, a biological aberration and, according to many sacred scriptures, sinful and forbidden along with slavery. Few are those who see trees and wolves as sacred but many who dedicate their lives to rescue and protect enjoy a life worth living for others through the power and grace of love.

Those who believe there is a God must help bring good into the world if we equate divinity with goodness in God's name, for God's sake. Atheists and agnostics can accept this ethic of the common good which includes the good of the forests, oceans and all of Nature: Earth's life community that sustains us all.

Surely if God is love then we should treat His/Her creations as we would have Him/Her treat us. We do have a choice, which some say is God-given, to harm or not to harm; to eat animals or change our diets. The problem is in our psychobiology as the most carnivorous of the apes, a super-predator, occasionally cannibalistic and known for pushing other species and entire plant, animal and human communities into extinction. So people ask what kind of God could make a species like us and a world like this where there is predation and so much strife and suffering. Others say if wolves and cougars can slaughter other animals for food then why can't we? And eliminate them as competitors especially when they kill "our livestock." These carnivores have no choice. But we do.

The anthropomorphization of God, (making God in our own image and believing only we are made in God's image) is compounded by the ultimate hubris of fabricating a supreme andromorphized (masculine) God. This has given divine authority to the world's three monotheistic religions, (still at war with each other) to sanction male dominion, chauvinism, cults of self-worship and now the global tyranny of what Pope Francis calls "unbridled anthropocentrism" which is harming all of "God's creation" on Earth. Ultimately only that which we hold sacred is secure.

Around the advent of the industrial revolution biological scientists and others had the arrogance to proclaim Homo sapiens as the scientific name for our species: Man the wise. In setting ourselves apart as superior, perhaps to make us feel more comfortable, even good about killing others for whatever reason—for food, sport or revenge, we widen the divide between self and other. We objectify and set in motion the process of disconnecting of what philosopher Martin Buber called the I-Thou relationship, that sense of spiritual communion with another, through what psychiatrist Prof. Robert Jay Lifton described after interviewing Nazi concentration camp doctors as splitting and doubling. Such disconnectedness is at the root of our inhumanity and of racism, sexism and speciesism; genocide and ecocide. In contrast the love that sustains us through hardship and loss, injustice and inhumanity is that illimitable love that some call God; the universal and universalizing affinities—our sacred connections—that make us whole and one and which many peoples celebrate in music, prayer, ritual and dance.

Self-realization and God-realization are claimed by some in incremental steps of personal development and collective cultural evolution. The more conscious and empathetic humans become, the more aware they are of the nature of divinity and the divinity of nature, the two being as inseparable as self-awareness and God-awareness and self-realization and God-realization. German theologian Meister Eckhart asserted "Every creature is a word of God and is a book about God." St. Francis of Assisi preached that it was through animals and nature that one can have communion with the divine. An indirect affirmation of the benefit of extending the Golden Rule to include other sentient beings is captured in the Qur'anic statement "Whoever is kind to the creatures of God is kind to himself." The Holy Prophet Mohammed also said "A good deed done to a beast is as good as doing good to a human being; while an act of cruelty to a beast is as bad as an act of cruelty to a human being." Echoing the Hippocratic Oath to first do no harm, the principle of ahimsa is the central ethic of Jainism and Hinduism. Buddhism, along with all major religions, advocates the Golden Rule of treating others as we would have them treat us, Buddhism, arguably, having suffered less from anthropocentric restrictions through extending the Rule to embrace all sentient beings.

The notion of a Heaven is different for different religions and was often used as political tool to make people conform to certain values and beliefs otherwise they would go to Hell. The German philosopher Goethe contended that "the mind is its own place and in itself can make a heaven of hell a hell of heaven." Accepting that there are different physical and mental states of being then Goethe is surely right: Heaven is in the embrace of all we love and suffer for. Ignorance, indifference, fear and hatred of each other and other animals, along with outright cruelty, turn Heaven into Hell. We are living spirits experiencing life in human form whose lives are enriched and even healed by other spirits in dog, cat and other sentient forms. As the

Australian aborigines say, "Dingo (feral dog) make us human". Indeed, other animals can awaken our humanity and touch our spirits and we must protect them from those who are not yet so touched, help them connect—and not treat other beings as objects and have neither compassion nor empathy for their Earthly relations nor respect for their ancestors.

The Christian Church Blessing of the Animals on the Feat Day of St. Francis is a hallowing affirmation of those many people with animals in their lives whom they regard as blessings. The Hindu sacred festival of Divali, celebrates the lights of life which includes decorating their animals, especially milk cows and working bullocks in gratitude. The Tihar festival is the Nepali equivalent of Diwali with one major difference, the Nepalis dedicating the second day to the worship of dogs. As man's best friend, the dogs are paid respect with garlands and a lot of food. In many countries religious and community leaders have traditional ceremonies blessing natural springs, ancient trees, groves, lakes and other subjects of natural creation that draw and sustain the human spirit. These "pagan" sentiments and praxis are shared by millions of different faith traditions, many ancient indeed and grounded in the primal religious rituals and spirituality of animism (see Leslie E. Sponsel's Spiritual Ecology, Prager, 2012) such as those of Native American Indians, Australian aborigines and other near-extinct indigenous peoples.

Incorporating such views under the banner of Creation Spirituality, Dominican priest Fr. Matthew Fox, author of several books including Original Blessing was silenced by Cardinal Ratzinger in 1988 for promoting pagan heresies and was excommunicated in 1993 when Ratzinger assumed the papacy as Pope Benedict XV1. Clearly, we are a chimeric species which, through reason, arrogance, belief and ignorance, or openness, humility and compassion can chose to harm or avoid harming others. Our biological past and genetically wired mental capacity to become a territorial predator enabling us to objectify, separate from and kill another, must be recognized and tempered for the common good including that of other animal species as well as of our own kind. This atavistic propensity for killing may lead to the depravities of subjugation, oppression, sadism and torture when there is power and control over others, be they prisoners of war, weaker minorities or captured elephants being broken for a life enslaved: and ultimately to genocide and ecocide.

The degree of self-awareness in the sacred union of the universal in the particular and of the particular in the universal brings humility and compassion since no one is God because all is in God and God is in all. This conceptualization of divinity, termed panentheism, resonates with pan-empathy (feeling and caring for all sentient life) and with the process theology of an emergent universe where human consciousness and conscience, emotional and scientific intelligence and purposive, mindful action are developed and refined as we strive to avoid causing harm and establish mutually enhancing relationships.

Yet some religious traditions perpetuate and condone animal cruelty, as with ritual Islamic and Judaic slaughter practices; animal sacrifices in Hindu temples. Many Hindus and Jains oppose euthanizing terminally ill and suffering animals because killing makes one spiritually impure by violating the principles of ahimsa and of non-interference with another's karma. They have also imposed their religious vegetarian dictate on captive, obligate carnivores such as hawk eagles and lions resulting in chronic malnutrition, deficiency diseases and death.

Atheists and agnostics can accept the bioethical principle of treating others as we would have them treat us (the Golden Rule) as the path of empathy, loving kindness and altruism's enlightened self-interest. Similarly, atheists, theists and agnostics alike must sense the joy of animals at play and tending and defending their young and wonder at the numinous quality of Nature's beauty and diversity. All of this which touches the rational soul and renews the spirit with or without belief in God, impels us to respect life and strive to live in accord the Golden Rule as we step out from egocentrism and techno-centrism to a more encompassing, body, mind and soul-sustaining and affirming eco-centrism.

If we agree with avowed atheist the late theoretical physicist Stephen Hawking, who uses the word God figuratively, on why the universe exists that "If we find the answer to that, it would be the ultimate triumph of human reason—for then we would know the mind of God" then similarly biology reveals the living expression of divinity and DNA the words.

May we all find the way of peaceful co-existence with better, less harmful ways to control pests, parasites and diseases increasingly of our own making as well as our own proliferating numbers and celebrate and protect the life and beauty on planet Earth. Surely it is our duty to take action against inhumanity; seek justice in the name of loving concern and give equal consideration to all beings, especially those whom we may fear or have no feeling for.

Postscript

The fifth Pillar Edict of early Buddhist King Ashoka of India ( 304-BC-232 BC) proclaimed:

Beloved-of-the-Gods, King Piyadasi, speaks thus: Twenty-six years after my coronation various animals were declared to be protected – parrots, mainas, //aruna//, ruddy geese, wild ducks, //nandimukhas, gelatas//, bats, queen ants, terrapins, boneless fish, //vedareyaka//, //gangapuputaka//, //sankiya// fish, tortoises, porcupines, squirrels, deer, bulls, //okapinda//, wild asses, wild pigeons, domestic pigeons and all four-footed creatures that are neither useful nor edible.[42] Those nanny goats, ewes and sows which are with young or giving milk to their young are protected, and so are young ones less than six months old. Cocks are not to be caponized, husks hiding living beings are not to be burnt and forests are not to be burnt either without reason or to kill creatures. One animal is not to be fed to another. On the three Caturmasis, the three days of Tisa and during the fourteenth and fifteenth of the Uposatha, fish are protected and not to be sold. During these days animals are not to be killed in the elephant reserves or the fish reserves either. On the eighth of every fortnight, on the fourteenth and fifteenth, on Tisa, Punarvasu, the three

Caturmasis and other auspicious days, bulls are not to be castrated, billy goats, rams, boars and other animals that are usually castrated are not to be. On Tisa, Punarvasu, Caturmasis and the fortnight of Caturmasis, horses and bullocks are not be branded. (From https://www.cs.colostate.edu/~malaiya/ashoka.html).

As various sacred scriptures intimate, we are living spirits consciously experiencing life, transiently if not gratefully, in human form. When we have close, respectful and caring engagements with other animals and their environments we ennoble ourselves. The less we engage the more we dispirit ourselves and the living world in our ignorance, limiting the possibilities of personal "growth" and our specie's evolution. The Kurumba tribal elders of the Nilgiris recall a time when they had no word for "weed" and could walk among the wild elephants without fear, intimating that colonialism created weeds, killer elephants and their mutual suffering and near-extinction.

The adversarial state of mind of the human primate species forever at war with itself and against other species and their communities from wolves and lions consuming invasive livestock to crop consuming insects and birds is the way to mutual extinction. Globally, humanity is moving inexorably and quickly toward the horizon of nihilism without better controls on population and consumption growth rates. The "anthro-apologists" (Mother Frackers) cannot continue to justify the mining, sucking and burning of ever more fossil fuels that turn into toxic waste and contribute to climate change. Ever increasing production and consumption is the goal of extractive, non-sustainable and ultimately pathogenic economies and government-industrial-military complexes. The more affluent now demand more meat and wine, increasingly at the expense of biodiversity and planetary health.

A less destructive and harmful state of mind and civilization, more befitting of Homo sapiens, cries for the life and beauty of the Earth's creation and all who dwell therein, seeing how different animal, plant and microscopic species help maintain the health and integrity of the natural world/environment. It is ours only to share "in sacred trust" according to the teachings of many indigenous people' spiritual and once highly sustainable socio-economic traditions like the practices and teachings of the Toda mamas of Colombia, Hopis of North America, Kurumbas of the Nilgiris and the Gaguji Australian aboriginals. We must care and share with all life and have the wisdom to respect the bacteria in the soil and in our guts and break our anti-bios habits, from antibiotics to pesticides as well as from narrow science-based "solutions" such as genetically modified insect resistant crops and vaccines that are pathogenic responses to pathological conditions. Only with a clearer perspective (and conscience) devoid of self-interest and irrational fears and ultimately enlightened, will we know when we must strike back and kill or contain with humility and loving kindness and cope with remorse and regret assuaged by the knowledge of serving the common good.

For more discussion and documentation visit www.drfoxvet.net and the author's book *The Boundless Circle: Caring for Creatures and Creation.*"

The foregoing Article categorically and convincingly states what should be the relationship between the humans and the other living beings. It is heartening to note the grounds that emphasize the humanistic approach to the cruelty and killing of other living beings and calls upon the humans for greater sense of love and affection towards the other living beings as well as the need for reversing our present thinking and practice for the common good between the humans and the other living beings. Author appreciates the Articles as of high thinking and endorses the views put forth in the Article in support of the other living beings that could be possible if the humans realize that they should not be so keen to fulfil their desires using the other living beings as part of their regular food. It may be more sumptuous for humans failing to understand that such act amounts to seeking for the sacrifice by the other living beings. Though the humans rely upon in such cases that the Holy Saints of their Faith have considered it permissible, author begs to differ here for the reason that the same Holy Saints have impressed upon the humans that they should treat the other living beings in the same manner as the humans expect them to treat. Author is not a highly learned man as to assert what the Holy Saints stated to have said and, with full respects to them, wishes to submit that one Life should not snatch away the life of the other living beings which don't enjoy any protection of law as enjoyed by the humans.

There appears to be mistaken notion on the part of the humans and, as a matter of fulfillment of the desires, has become a normal practice or habit. Author is also a being on Mother Earth and by virtue of ancestral culture is a purely vegetarian and believes in protecting the other living beings to the best of his ability. This should not be misconstrued that the author is criticizing or against non-vegetarians and that he is not in agreement with them. He is and will continue to be there as long as he is destined to live his life on Mother Earth. Every human being on Mother Earth is at full liberty to consider and decide his or her own course of life as long as his or her Atman [Soul, Conscience and Faith satisfies him or her]. This is a subjective and not objective choice on the part of the humans to be guided by their own Faith.

## Aristotle's Concept of Eudemonia: The Quest for Human Flourishing - September 30, 2023 [Source: https://philosophy.institute/ethics/aristotles-eudaimonia-human-flourishing/ ]

"Aristotle's vision of the good life

Aristotle saw life as a quest for something greater than mere survival or fleeting pleasures. He proposed that the ultimate goal of human existence was *Eudaimonia*, often translated as 'happiness' or 'flourishing'. But this wasn't happiness in the sense of how we often think of it today; it was deeper, encompassing a life lived in accordance with virtue and reason. Aristotle believed that achieving Eudaimonia was akin to fulfilling our potential as human beings, but how do we go about this?

Intellectual virtues: The role of reason

For Aristotle, rationality was what set humans apart from other animals. He categorized virtues into two types: intellectual and moral. Intellectual virtues are those related to the mind and our ability to reason. They are acquired through teaching and include:

- **Knowledge:** Understanding of the world around us.
- **Wisdom:** The ability to discern the true nature of things.
- **Insight:** The application of knowledge and wisdom to real-life situations.

These virtues enable us to make wise choices and lead a life that aligns with our inherent purpose.

Moral virtues: The significance of character

While intellectual virtues deal with the realm of thought, moral virtues are all about action. They arise from habit and shape our character, influencing how we interact with the world and those around us. Moral virtues are the golden mean between two extremes – excess and deficiency. Some key moral virtues include:

- **Courage:** Bravery in the face of fear, avoiding both recklessness and cowardice.
- **Temperance:** Moderation in pleasurable activities, steering clear of overindulgence and insensitivity.
- **Generosity:** The giving of resources or time, balancing miserliness and wasteful extravagance.

Moral virtues are developed through practice and repetition, much like a skill. By habitually acting in virtuous ways, we craft a moral character that leads to Eudaimonia.

The Doctrine of the Mean: Finding balance

Aristotle's *Doctrine of the Mean* advises us to navigate the path between excess and deficiency. But this isn't a call to mediocrity; rather, it's about finding the right amount of virtue that is appropriate for each situation. For instance, the mean of courage lies between the extremes of recklessness and cowardice. It's about context and understanding that different situations call for different measures of virtue.

Living the Eudaimonic life in the modern world

It's all well and good to discuss ancient philosophy, but how can we apply Aristotle's concept of Eudaimonia to our lives today? It's about striving for personal excellence, making choices that foster growth, and engaging with our community in meaningful ways. Here are some practical steps to living the Eudaimonic life:

- **Self-reflection:** Regularly take stock of your actions and decisions, aiming to align them with virtuous principles.
- **Continuous learning:** Commit to lifelong education and the development of intellectual virtues.
- **Community involvement:** Participate in civic activities and contribute to the betterment of society.

- **Mindful practice:** Cultivate moral virtues through conscious habit formation and ethical decision-making.

By integrating these practices into our daily lives, we can move closer to the ideal of Eudaimonia, creating a life of purpose and fulfillment.

Conclusion

In our pursuit of happiness, Aristotle's concept of Eudaimonia offers a timeless guide. It's not about chasing fleeting pleasures or material success, but about developing a balanced character grounded in virtue and reason. By embracing both intellectual and moral virtues, we can navigate life's challenges with wisdom and grace, and ultimately, experience the profound satisfaction of flourishing as human beings."

Author now deals about the Nature and its relationship to humans. Nature has dominant influence over the human beings. The God on Earth is also manifested in the nature. Planet Earth is home to trillions of organisms (living things), including animals and plants. They are found on land, in lakes, rivers, and oceans, as well as in the air. Scientists use Classification to show how different species, or types, of organisms are related. If an individual feels connected to nature (possibly by spending time in it), they may be more inclined to care about nature, and protect the environment. Recent research has found that nature exposure (and feeling connected to nature at a trait level) provides many benefits to humans such as well-being. The God on Earth being manifested both in Humans and the Nature, the identity being the same, how both the Beings live together or co-exist and the extent to which conflict, if any, exists between them. The impact of nature of human behavioural pattern is also immense. Nature brings to humans joyous times and moments as well as sorrows. It is not known yet the causes of the sorrows the nature forces upon humans. Some say it is because of humans' way of treatment of nature, at times cruel, some others say it is because of the wrath of the nature arising from the kinds of the injuries humans inflict on the nature, especially from unfriendly environment point of view. These factors contribute to some or other extent to the tragedies contributing to negativity and depression among the humans. There seems to be a kind of struggle between the humans and the other beings (Nature), each possessed with one's own right and might that each claim over the other, the difference being, the humans have higher consciousness factor whereas it doesn't exist in other beings.

According to Wikipedia, "Animal consciousness, or animal awareness, is the quality or state of self-awareness within an animal, or of being aware of an external object or something within itself. In humans, consciousness has-been defined as: sentience, awareness, subjectivity, as: sentience, awareness, subjectivity, qualia (a quality or property as perceived or experienced by a person)., the ability to experience or to feel, wakefulness, having a sense of self, and the executive control system of the mind. Despite the difficulty in definition, many philosophers believe there is a broadly shared underlying intuition about what consciousness is. The topic of animal consciousness is beset with a number of difficulties. It poses the problem of other minds in an especially severe form because animals, lacking the ability to use human language, cannot tell us about their experiences. Also, it is difficult to reason objectively about the question, because a denial that an animal is conscious is often taken to imply that it does not feel, its life has no value, and that harming it is not morally wrong. The 17th-century French philosopher René Descartes, for example, has sometimes been blamed for mistreatment of animals because he argued that only humans are conscious..........................................................."

Also, according to Wikipedia, "Humans – who enslave, castrate, experiment on, and fillet other animals – have had an understandable penchant for pretending animals do not feel pain. A sharp distinction between humans and 'animals' is essential if we are to bend them to our will, make them work for us, wear them, eat them – without any disquieting tinges of guilt or regret. It is unseemly of us, who often behave so unfeelingly toward other animals, to contend that only humans can suffer. The behaviour of other animals renders such pretensions specious. They are just too much like us. (Carl Sagan, the American cosmologist, points to reasons why humans have had a tendency to deny animals can suffer)";

"Be in communion with nature, not verbally caught in the description of it, but be a part of it, be aware, feel that you belong to all that, be able to have love for all that, to admire a deer, the lizard on the wall, that broken branch lying on the ground. Look at the evening star or the new moon without the word, without merely saying how beautiful it is and turning your back on it, attracted by something else, but watch that single star and new delicate moon as though for the first time. If there is such communion between you and nature, you can commune with man, with the boy sitting next to you, with your educator or with your parents. We have lost all sense of relationship in which there is not only a verbal statement of affection and concern but also this sense of communion, which is not verbal. It is a sense that we are all together, that we are all human beings, not divided, not broken up, not belonging to any group or race or some idealistic concepts, but that we are all human beings, living on this extraordinary, beautiful earth. To live in harmony with nature brings about a different world. If you lose relationship with nature, you lose relationship with humanity. (Krishnamurti in Ojai 1983, Talk 1- Posted on the Website of Krishnamurti Foundation Trust)."

So much is the relationship between the humans and the nature. The nature has a higher level of relationship with human rather human with the nature. Nature doesn't express but only gives human so much that human goes back to nature asking more and more. Nature does not refuse because its very essence is to remain in relationship with human. Human knows how to benefit from the nature's generosity but does not think to protect the nature with the same spirit and generosity. This is so because the human lives more under the influence of consciousness and not conscience while the nature has no such consciousness. Human also does not understand that all that he has to survive is gifted by the nature and without that he succumbs. A look at the inside and outside of the home brings more clarity of relationship because what one sees within or outside one's home is the existence and presence of nature in one form or the other. Inside home we find so much of what nature has gifted to human, all of which is the product or the by-product of the nature.

Humans feel proud of possessing them and exhibiting them. Outside home, the phenomena of nature are indescribable and beyond the human concept, howsoever, the human may be learned and knowledgeable. That is the secret of nature known only to the Creator and that Creator is manifest in the nature and human as well. Yet, there is delinking between the two. The nature does not understand the human psychology while human, through years of research and experiments, has been and continuing to try the psychological aspects of every being in the nature. This includes both positive and negative considerations in the human mind of which the nature and living beings in the nature cannot comprehend and ready to give up to humans either voluntarily or by force the human uses thinking much superior to others. This is where the delink between the two is visible. The Creator in them being one and same, the living beings in nature believe human is good and generous, placing the onus on humans. When human thinks of living beings in nature, his immediate inclination is how to use them for his satisfaction without linking mind to the Creator in him that has conscience for consultation.

To the extent the nature considers affordable meets the human wants that should be accepted with gratitude to the nature and its living beings. The nature does it as part of its natural duty to help humans to survive and live happily. Such attitude is absent in human who feels insatiable with whatever nature is endowed with and given to human. A sense of concern and respect for the nature seems to have been now growing among the humans. It is a good sign and should be taken upwards and upheld for the goodness of the nature and human. There is also increasing flow of thoughts between the nature and human with the humans undertaking tours and visits to various places lying in the nature's lap including famous zoos preserved by the government with least hurting and realizing great pleasure and praise of what the nature is bestowed with for the benefit of humans. This way, connectivity between the nature and humans is being re-established, the essence of co-existence. In a way, the nature is born as benefactor of humans.

Some people assert that using the animals and birds flesh as part of food is necessary firstly, it also being part of food lawfully permitted and secondly, this process reduces uncontrolled and increasing populace of the animals and birds considered harmful to the world as a whole. Fact, however, remains, it amounts to blindest torture when one looks that populace as having born to live and enjoy with the nature so long the Spirit residing in them as manifestation of sustenance permits them to live. This is cyclic. Same is also human life and survival on earth. Law does not permit torture and injury to humans, the greatest protection human enjoys on earth. It may be right for the humans couched in fundamental rights or otherwise enforced in the world. Carol Kaesuk Yoon notes- '………Why would we expect any organism to lie down and die for our dinner? Organisms have evolved to do everything in their power to avoid being extinguished. How long would any lineage be likely to last if its members effectively didn't care if you killed them? Question, therefore, is whether awareness (consciousness) which is wholly present in the human in such cases, should it not be subjected to test through the application of conscience also existing in the human body?' Think it over. Nature also demands, according to author, equal rights. This is only a pleading and not a complaint or contest against anyone including the Faiths to which the humans belong.

Our present understanding of the word 'civilized' lacks 'humane and reasonable that are integral part of the word civilized even though it satisfies its other meaning 'intellectual' [Meaning of 'civilized' has been derived from Online Free Dictionary]. In the foregoing context, the word civilized becomes irrelevant for want of humane and reasonable. The kinds of act the humans are committing against the other living beings on Mother Earth who are the cohabitants of human or for that matter, the race of hatredness, inimical terms and threats of arms conflicts also deficient of the word 'civilized' that is crossing the Divine Border with consequences unpredictable. Do we deserve to be called civilized? The greatest thing that God has given to the humans and the other living beings is Life which is none other than God in the form of Spirit. Knowing this, we are unable to appreciate the difference in the meaning of 'cruelty' and 'compassion', the absence of which makes the human as inhuman. Author is aware that such statement by him is in the nature of pinching the humans but he is helpless himself because of our big claim that we are civilized. This is in lighter sense and has to be taken by the humans as such. Author is compelled to provoke this aspect because we are doing what is contrary to our claim that we are civilized. That means, we are aware of we being civilized but unaware of, for one or other self-reasoning that such act on our part is permitted. The greatest virtue of humans being the humane, we, as humans, cannot disown that the humane is not integral part of the humans. The sense of humane and humanness is bestowed by God only to the humans in order that the humans treat other living beings as they want to be treated. This is the missing link in between the humans and other living beings.

Some section of the humans state if we cannot act do so, then the growth of the other living beings will outgrow the humans at some time or the other when the humans may find it difficult to survive on Mother Earth. This is self-misleading assumption intended for the fulfillment of the humans' excessive desires multiplying every day. In thinking so, we forget the fact that the presence of the Spirit within us and other living beings is for a limited period as ordained by God but other living beings don't know nor can these living beings ask the same question the humans are asking the humans will outgrow them. Mother Earth knows the art of balancing both of the humans and other living beings, She being the God herself. The process of life whether of the humans or of the other living beings. The governing system is itself confused when at one time it introduces family planning for the people to plan for the size of the family providing the various kinds of incentives in the form of kinds or monetary benefit [as especially happened during the period of Emergency 1975-77] and as of now, the governing system tells the people to increase the population. There is no such system in the case of other living beings on Mother Earth.

It is also pertinent to touch a bit more about the population growth whether of humans or other living beings in the nature. The population growth is natural and has close relationship with nature. For the past about fifty years, there had been constant talk about the population control (humans). Basic necessities in both the cases, that is, human population and of the other living beings are the same. Human interpretation to this is that the uncontrolled growth of human population upsets socio-economic balancing factors difficult to manage due to constraint of financial and material resources. The population is not to be treated as a swinging ball. The entire economic and social development is planned duly taking into the projected growth of the population. Blaming the population growth is seeking self-excuse for not implementing the plans as projected or targeted. This is governance failure not attributable to the population. When there is an imbalance between them, the blame game starts in political governing system. Greatness lies in self-admission of the failure and not attributing it to the others such as growing population. How family planning affected the growth of the population in various countries where aging of the people was advancing should be an example for us. Other countries then started adopting the children from the populated countries. Let not the population measurement become a political tool. Let the government do its duty of managing economic growth based on the Census System and ensure that the implementation method is stronger than the targeting method for the economic development and welfare of the people. This is within the capacity of the governing system but on account of more mismanagement, leakage and corruption, the achievements go haywire compared to the targets thereby increasing the gap between the planning process and the population growth.

**"ONE OF THE MOST TRAGIC THINGS I KNOW ABOUT HUMAN NATURE IS THAT ALL OF US TEND TO PUT OFF LIVING. WE ARE ALL DREAMING OF SOME MAGICAL ROSE GARDEN OVER THE HORIZON INSTEAD OF ENJOYING THE ROSES THAT ARE BLOOMING OUTSIDE OUR WINDOWS TODAY." - DALE CARNEGIE**

One may think what relationship the growth of the population, the nature and economic development has to do with this book. Both are equal partners on Mother Earth. Artificial or human interventions in the natural growth whether of humans or of the nature have their own impacts. Both these were there from time immemorial. There are no revelations either in the ancient scripts or in the recent past historical events that suggested that the rulers and the people of those days were in any way concerned or conscious of the growth either of population or of the nature. They lived as natural and the economic constraints were also present in those days. They never believed that the population growth affected the economic growth. That was the concern of the kings and rulers how best they could maintain the economic growth to adjust with the population growth. This was because of the fact they were sincere, honest and devoted in what they did to the people with severest consequences for misuse of the resources intended for the welfare of the people and the nature. This is the missing link between the olden and present days. Few years that followed the independence testify this fact because those who spearheaded economic growth of the country were those who sacrificed their self-interest for the sake of attaining freedom and were fully conscious of values of the human life as well as of the nature. They tried to maintain a harmonious balance towards human development, economic development and nature development.

This book is dealing with "God on Earth". In the kind of situation stated before, how could one emulate and adore the Godly Qualities – Love, Kindness, Compassion, Forgiveness and Trust, without which the life becomes a barren? Tensions and turmoil in the society and social living are the cause of this barrenness. Outcome is presenting a precarious picture to the people, increasing poverty, multiplicity of crimes, insecurity, psychological and physical impacts, desperation, and frustration inviting suicides as an inevitable end. This is all because HUMANNESS AND HUMANITY which seem to have no consideration whatsoever with the Humans and the Nature. Let the nature and the population grow and let us be honest to ourselves how best we can serve both. Young generation is conscious and aware of how to plan their life and future whether in metros, urban or rural by now and leave the choice to them about the population growth. **Let us not invite a time when we would be needed to go to populated countries for adoption of the children.**

What Mark Twain thought about 'The real reason why you were born': "There are two great days in a person's life - the day we are born and the day we discover why." Have you ever wondered if there is a concealed, mystifying and gigantic reason for which god decided to send you on earth? God created each of us for a reason - and I think we can be the happiest when we are living in harmony with the purpose he has given us. But we need to know what it is…". What Maya Angelou said "One isn't necessarily born with courage, but one is born with potential? Without courage, we cannot practice any other virtue with consistency. We can't be kind, true, merciful, generous, or honest." What Virgin Group says: Togetherness is a hugely important aspect of life. It unites us, gives us security, much-needed support and a sense of belonging, and encourages us to love one another. What Henry Ford said: "Coming Together Is A Beginning; Keeping Together Is Progress; Working Together Is Success. What John Lennon/Yoko Ono said: "A Dream You Dream Alone Is Only A Dream. A Dream You Dream Together Is Reality." What Mother Teresa said "I Can Do Things You Cannot, You Can Do Things I Cannot; Together We Can Do Great Things."

All the Holy Scripts ingrained a sole message – kindness, affection, love, compassion and forgiveness, all of which together assume the underlying essence – Harmony both with humans and the nature. Marcus Aurelius, emperor of Rome and the author of the philosophical work Meditations said "He who lives with harmony with himself live with harmony with the universe." Understanding of this message sprinkles harmony in every individual; each individual together forms a group and each group form into a culture and religion. It is not that harmony is to be taught. A taught harmony does not last long. One who learns through self-learning while experiencing the life, of whatever nature, pastes that permanently in him or her. Harmony is one of them. It is the experience that teaches best in life. Those ideals of life learnt through life do not erase. They are based on incidents that happened in life. That is to say, whatever we learn through teachings in Life Experience, the highest learning School, as Swami Vivekananda has said which form into solidity in mind facilitating humans to practice them in real life.

Why the author has brought the topic of nature, having fairly dealt earlier? That is the temptation of the nature the author is caught in. Author is also a human being and has learnt the interaction process with the nature in life, having been born in a tiny village. Villages are the distinct class that live in and represent the true followers of the nature. Living with nature is Life and living apart from it, makes Life not to know what the nature is in its true sense. The ways of living are different in villages and cities.

The life in cities does not cherish the true happiness that one derives living with nature. It is not that those living in cities cannot experience the nature. They do. Human efforts continued since long have learnt to naturalize the cities bringing to the cities a character of nature. This is commendable because it acquaints those living in cities devoid of nature, what the nature means and how to live life together with the nature. This is receiving highest urgency and consideration among the authorities as well as the people with the authorities creating a natural environment adopting various features of the nature and the people started loving it. Most of the big and small cities are changing their landscapes in their outlook that is further changing the living style of the people. Eating habits also are showing signs of shifting towards natural products and produces beneficial for healthy living, especially for the newly born and growing children. There is also a keen competition between the natural and manmade products and produces and, to propagate the latter, the advertising agencies together with print and electronic media are making their best efforts to impress upon the manmade products and produces. Author's personal view is that it is for the people to ascertain and choose the one that is most beneficial. Author only wants to remind the readers that the Nature itself is 'The God on Earth' showering umpteen varieties of nature made products and produces for betterment and welfare of humans and every other living being on earth.

It is the mindset to think we are superior to the other living beings. This places added obligation on our part to care more for the other living beings. These are also born on Mother Earth and have to live as ordained by the God. This condition is equally applicable to both. How then, we consider ourselves superior to the other living beings. Our superiority can be our knowledge about the behavioural pattern of the other living beings. That knowledge is more for our selfishness than doing betterment for them. These are innocent and don't get provoked unless the humans try to harm them. Humans have learnt various methods how to use the other living beings even through following cruel methods. This doesn't touch our heart because we become impersonal in their treatment. Many of us made them as pets at home establishing thus our proximity to them where by these also respond to that and act like a family member. The dog pets even act as security guards for the owner's home. There are many instances where the pet dogs learnt to alert and wake up the owners while thieves attempting entry into home. These shower lot of love and affection to the owner that makes both of them as good friends. This shows the human compassion towards the other living beings brought up as pets. The love affection gets into so deep that we feel afraid of losing the pet and constantly remain in touch with it. This can also be practised by the human with other living beings not being pets at home. The god has given to humans sufficient capacity to understand them in the same manner we want others to understand us. The understanding grows only through kindness, compassion and love whether among the humans or with the other living beings. These qualities are those gifted by god to both but we feel indifferent with them compared to our following them among ourselves. Where the compassion, kindness and love exist, that brings the other living beings nearer to humans and evokes sympathy while the same humans think of cruelty towards them for fulfilling the selfish desires.

# SECTION [20]
# GODLY QUALITIES

**LIVING THE FIVE HUMAN VALUES FOR MOTHER EARTH Based on the universal teachings of Sri Sathya Sai Baba Truth v Right Action v Peace v Love v Nonviolence**

[Source: https://www.sathyasai.org/sites/default/files/pages/goggreen/HV%20for%20Mother%20Earth.pdf]

"The five universal human values of Truth, Right Action, Peace, Love and Nonviolence are found in all major religions, faiths and spiritual philosophies of the world, including indigenous cultures and traditions, and in all secular societies. They represent the highest ideals of humanity. Truth, right action, peace, love and nonviolence are the innate qualities of a human being. To lose awareness of these five values is to lose our humanity. The five universal human values are within us. They reside in the seat of our soul in our heart. The highest aim of education and our human experience is to elicit these values from within and to manifest them in all our interactions and experiences with other people and our environment, or Nature and Mother Earth. In this way, we begin to experience the Truth that we are in reality spiritual beings having a human experience. When we live our life in tune with the universal human values, Mother Earth is sustained and protected. Therefore, to protect Mother Earth we must first understand these values and then learn how to practise them in all that we think and do.

Truth is very much within each of us. The value of Truth is based on the omnipresence of God in the entire Universe as well as within ourselves. The qualities of living in Truth include faith, honesty, discrimination, goodness, respect, humility and integrity. Truth is eternal. The value of Truth is unchanging throughout time, even when we do not recognise or practice it. When we recognise Truth and align our lives with it, Mother Earth and indeed the Universe function in greater harmony. The opposite is also true. Understanding and practicing Truth helps us better care for each other and Mother Earth. When we live in Truth, we know that God exists as the unseen dynamic force or consciousness that sustains all of Nature and all beings. • We sense the presence of God in Nature. • We live our lives in such a way that we witness and experience the divine in all Creation, including within ourselves and all others as well as all matter. • Knowing the omnipresence of God, we cannot cause harm to the Earth and its beings, nor to the waters, atmosphere, or soil. • We spend time in Nature, not simply to enjoy the sights and sounds or to exercise, but as communion with its essence or Truth.

• We revere Mother Earth, pray to know Her better, and ask forgiveness for the harm we may have caused even unknowingly. This helps us realise the Truth of Nature that we are all one and there is only Oneness in God. • We bring our thoughts, words, and deeds into harmony. We walk our talk in an honest way. • We not only think and speak about the importance of protecting the planet;

we do so, even when others are not aware. • We understand that Truth tells us it is within our power to transform ourselves—to realise the spiritual beings that we truly are—such that we focus less on material goods and more on spiritual goodness. "First and foremost, establish Truth in your heart. Thereafter, the other four human values of Righteousness, Peace, Love and Nonviolence will reign in the world. Then, there will be no violence at all in the world and all human beings irrespective of religion and nationality will live in peace and harmony." (SSS Vol. 40:4, 2007)

When have you experienced the feeling of God in Nature?

## RIGHT ACTION

Right Action is following the moral path. It is characterised by holiness, good conduct, responsibility, virtue and fortitude. Its qualities include justice, sense control, sense of honour, moral behaviour, dignity, goodness, fairness, sympathy, simplicity and ethical living. Practicing Right Action leads us to universal love and unity, and to knowing ourselves as the divine beings that we are. Right Action is living in accord with our proper role as humans within the play of creation. All aspects of Nature have their own prescribed role, but human beings sometimes choose not to follow their prescribed duties. This is why Spiritual Teachers and Messengers of Truth are born—to remind us of our spiritual duty, including to Nature, and to show us how to live as moral beings. Like Truth, Right Action is unchanging and indestructible throughout time. What does it mean to follow the moral path of Right Action for Mother Earth?

- We acknowledge and serve God by lovingly and selflessly serving others and Nature.

- We seek to know Nature as a manifestation of the Will of God by spending quiet, meditative time in natural places.

- We know that anything we do for Mother Earth we are doing for God.

- We live with a sense of justice, knowing that all beings, including animals and plants and our future generations, depend on Nature. We become aware of our duty and responsibilities as custodians of the Earth's goodness.

- We are careful in our use of resources so that others have enough, and we support charities that provide for those less fortunate, including humans and all beings.

- We listen to the voice of God within our heart (our conscience) and act with love, reverence, gratitude, and the strength to do good always.

- We work at doing the right thing at the right time. Given the trauma we have inflicted on Mother Earth, there is no better time to act on Her behalf than now.

- We place a ceiling on our desires, such that we limit our use of natural resources, we don't waste food, and we use the money and time we saved to help others.

- We remain aware of the impact our actions may have far from our sight and avoid harming the Earth's atmosphere and climate by reducing energy use and our carbon footprint. When we follow Right Action, we experience the joy of knowing we are helping, not harming, Mother Earth. Our lives become more free and fruitful. Pathways to even more service open and we happily carry out our responsibilities. Walking with God in this way, our burdens become less heavy and our love glows more brightly. Eventually, we become one with the One behind Creation, which benefits Mother Earth and all beings even more.

**"Your duty is to yearn for the attainment of the consciousness of the One behind all this apparent multiplicity. Be centres of love, compassion, service, mutual tolerance, and be happy, very very happy." (SSS 11:28, 1971)**

**"What is the lesson to be learnt from the observance of Nature? It is…excellence in the performance of duty. It is because Nature ceaselessly performs its duty that the world is able to derive so many sacred benefits." (Summer Showers: 18, 1990)**

What are some other ways you can express your duty to protect Mother Earth?

### PEACE

Peace in the world is a sign that God's Creation is working in harmony. Peace within us is a sign that we are practicing Right Action that we are controlling our senses and mastering our mind. When we put Peace into action, we experience greater friendship, tranquility, harmony, equanimity and serenity. We keep greed, anger, and desire for possessions and material things in check and experience the peace and joy of pure consciousness. In such a state, we are in unity with Nature, the very embodiment of Peace. To cultivate the value of Peace in our interactions with Mother Earth,

- We foster peaceful qualities by spending time in Nature and learning the lessons of Peace that Nature teaches.

- We seek the peace and happiness that does not come from material wealth, comfort and excessive consumption.

- We serve as a model for living in Peace. In doing so, we help others to see the importance of seeking happiness within, rather than in worldly things. Such inner Peace helps us preserve Nature's bounty for essential needs.

- We recognise our unity with Nature and practice equanimity in the face of disturbances in the outside world.

- We show gratitude for all the gifts we receive from Nature. We demonstrate this through prayers that honour God and Nature as givers and we as grateful recipients.

- We cleanse the atmosphere with good thoughts, prayer, devotional singing, mantras and meditation, which also promotes our inner balance in tune with Nature.

- We place a ceiling on our desires such that we do not waste Nature's gifts in the form of food, time, money, or energy.

- We are true to our duty to promote peace within the community of humanity and thereby in harmonious relationship with Mother Earth and all beings… and better able to serve them.

- We endure triumphs and tragedies with equanimity. In so doing, we are better prepared to help others in distress—especially those harmed by disasters arising from human actions that disrupt Nature's balance.

Most of all, Peace teaches us to be happy with what we have and to calmly accept whatever difficulties come our way. It keeps us strong and able to stand up for Truth in the world. We do not fear what others think when we choose to tread lightly on the Earth. Instead, we develop our inner strength and step away from actions that may harm Mother Earth. We demonstrate a better way, a more peaceful way.

**"Peace does not exist in worldly things. Peace can only be found inside, within you. 'I want peace' consists of three words. 'I' is the ego, and 'want' is desire. If you remove these two, then you have Peace." (Sathya Sai Newsletter, 5 August 1988)**

How might you make time in your day to experience the peace of Nature? For example, walking to a destination through a park where possible and away from traffic and noise.

## LOVE

Love is the basis for all of Creation and is the very form of God. It springs forth as pure joy that flows naturally from the depths of our soul. The experience of Love fosters our understanding that all are One, meaning we are one with Nature, all beings, and Mother Earth. Love is selfless, universal, and unconditional. It seeks no rewards and knows no fear. It serves as the ever-pure spring of divine energy that motivates us to practice all the other human values. Love in action is experienced through unity, compassion, empathy, reverence and respect. When we act through Love for Mother Earth:

- We behave with full awareness of our oneness with all beings and Mother Earth.

- We reflect God's love in our life through our love for Nature.

- We spend time in Nature to reconnect and acknowledge the interdependence and interconnectedness of everything.

- We feel Nature's abundant beauty and bounty and show our greatest respect and reverence.

- We are prompted to serve selflessly, not looking for the fruits of our action. We give to Mother Earth in gratitude for all She provides, unceasingly. This may be through dedicated prayers, offerings, and heartfelt appreciation for Her material gifts that are filled with divinity.

- We practice selflessness as the full expression of the Love we feel, ever ready to help, not hurt, and willing to sacrifice as needed. This includes prayers for the wellbeing of all those we cannot directly serve.

- We demonstrate our compassion for the suffering of others and, thus, do our best to avoid polluting or wasting resources, while embracing opportunities to relieve suffering (like improving habitat, picking up trash, or helping to rebuild after disasters).

- We connect easily with other beings and Nature because divine sweetness, Love, and peace flows from us in a way that we feel one with them. We establish heart-to-heart relationships.

- We trust that our needs will be met and avoid striving for and using more resources than we need.

- We allow the wisdom that wells up from our heart to inform our actions, such that we are ready to do what is most needed at any moment.

**Love binds one person to another; Love attaches one thing to another. Without Love, the universe is naught… Life is Love; Love is Life. Without God, deprived of God, nothing and nobody can exist. We live on and on through Divine Will. It is His Will that operates as Love, in each of us. It is He that prompts the prayer, 'Let all the worlds be happy,' for He makes us aware that the God we adore, the God we love, the God we live by, is in every other being as Love. Thus Love expands and encompasses all Creation." (SSS 11:39, 1981)**

How do you express your love for Nature?

**NONVIOLENCE**

- Nonviolence is the natural expression of universal Love. It includes being nonaggressive, soothing, calming, gentle and serving as a peacemaker. The principle of "Help Ever, Hurt Never" best describes it. Nonviolence results from putting all four previous values into practice and is a natural outcome of developing unity and purity in thought, word, and deed. Practicing Nonviolence, we inflict the least harm possible at all times, in all ways, and in all circumstances, and are selflessly drawn to relieving the suffering of all beings. Nonviolence is an essential virtue for those wanting to live in harmony with Mother Earth. We express Nonviolence best when,

  - We live in awareness of our oneness and know that any harm we do to others is also harm to ourselves.

  - We are aware of the suffering we may cause by using too much energy or water, or by polluting the soil, water, and air. We try our best to avoid such harm.

  - We consume vegetarian foods that are grown organically.

  - We make sure any animal products we use are from animals treated humanely.

  - We live a simple, eco-friendly life as spiritual practice.

- We use household products that are produced from environmentally-friendly ingredients and are not polluting.

- We manage our landscape so that it provides opportunities for birds and other species to gain food, water, and shelter and avoids harming them.

- We demonstrate our inner strength by nonviolently opposing harm being done to others and supporting actions that help protect the environment.

- We listen for the call to relieve the suffering of any being and respond as best we can. This may take the form of direct help or it may be in the form of prayers such as "May all the beings in all the worlds be happy."

- We are ready and able to work cooperatively with others in selfless service to improve the environment. This may include litter pickups, planting trees, growing organic gardens, creating natural respite places in the midst of urban areas, writing and disseminating information about environmental protection, and helping to ensure waste is recycled to the fullest extent possible

**"We generally think that Nonviolence means not causing harm to some living being. Nonviolence is not just this. Even bad vision or bad hearing or bad talk is violence. Nonviolence really means that you should not cause harm to anyone through your vision, hearing, or talking. Buddha**

**also said, 'Nonviolence is the Supreme Right Action.' …We should interpret Nonviolence as not causing any harm to any individual by any means." (Summer Showers 1978)**

**Consider how practicing the other four values help us adopt nonviolent behavior. What are some other practical ways we can observe Nonviolence and help Mother Earth?**

**"Love as thought is Truth. Love as feeling is Peace. Love as understanding is Nonviolence." (SSS XII, ch. 15)**

The above Teachings of Shri Sathya Sai Baba are invaluable and everlasting. The human endurance must be to understand, realize and practice them in daily life in order to uphold not only the Balancing of the Mother Earth but also the Togetherness of humans and other beings, the greatest asset the God has bestowed upon the humans. The author considers himself a servant of the readers of this book and in that capacity has found the above teachings through Google Website to whom the author remains grateful for ever. The point here is not limited to author's learning of the Teachings. The author considers that his greatest ambition is that the humans [including the author] should respect those Teachings and mandate their practice in life for the wellbeing and goodness of the Nature as well as the humans and other living beings on Mother Earth. This is the craving of the author to the readers of this book. This is called for on the part of every one of us in order to humble and calm down the human disturbances among themselves and atrocities to other living beings as well as on Mother

Earth for the reasons the author has explained in the succeeding paragraphs.

The country is witnessing increasing negativity in socio-economic-politics over the last three and a half decades. Why it is so is difficult to explain. What is seen of what is going on since that period is much mud throwing against each other, whether it is the case of politics, religion, society, economics, media reporting, professional writings and sarcastic speeches of politicians and learned community rather than washing the face of those people whose faces are pasted with mud and are living in a state muddle. There are also people who have been enduring unpardonable crimes such as women, babies, children, parents, rage, atrocity, disregard to law and order, disorderly behaviour which are contrary to the apriorism and basis of human living and humanness.

These attitudes have outgrown their size and causing deep wounds in social ecology. The law enforcing authorities and the courts of law are assigned under the relevant laws to do justices in such cases. That is known and is very much in vogue. It is another matter this process is agonizing. How to cure them should receive greater attention than think of punitive measures. There is a cry and crisis of the victims of these crimes in every corner of the country and, most of them feel hapless and psychologically irretrievable. Those committing the crimes are humans and upon whom the crimes are inflicted are also human. The difference is former has the predominance of negativity driving recklessly towards the crimes. Those who are around, if there happens be one or more, are scared to intervene because instant threats of the criminals. Who is the God on Earth for the victims of such crimes? Could the Law enforcing force and the courts of law from lower court to highest court can be regarded so? Answer is No, the reason being they act within their own limitations of the law and it cannot be said that in all cases the criminals are punished. That is so because the punishment could happen if the legal and procedural compliances have been complied with and proved beyond reasonable doubt.

The proverb "Justice Delayed is Justice Denied' is based on two reasons. One, the apathy of the accused especially of innocents in criminal cases indirectly imposes upon the accused as a sense of mentally imprisoned due to prolongation of the trial, not in terms of days or months but in years that makes him or her livingly dead. Two, this drains out him or her physically and financially. Author is not dealing here presentation of any statistical account on the subject matter which is otherwise available through various information sources such as the Courts of Law and Google Website and is ascertainable by anyone. It is time it touches the heart of the judicial system for; there is also the human heart and the Spirit in the system which should awaken towards such accused on humanitarian consideration because the accused believes the Judicial System is God for timely relief as otherwise the accused continues to look at the God within him or her. This is also the case where, even after such inordinate process, the trial is yet to begin. Having spent such period, the accused will have to wait for the completion of the trial; the time it takes is unpredictable. Should we consider this as a curse of humans or the God?

The God on Earth is someone else who acts as the Spirit that has instinct to act and protect such victims without seeking any reward. The Spirit, Soul and Conscience are there in every human body. So also there are Conscious and the Mind in everybody. Then what is that difference someone else has? God, invisible yet everyone and everything on the earth is visible to Him. That is Divine Vision that has the eyes to embrace every aspect of the earth and the living beings on earth – good or bad or evil. The negativity does not pause over this and impulsively causes harm to self and to others. The positivity pauses over this and proceeds only towards goodness and understands the cries and crisis of the victims. Both these qualities nest in mind but their application in action rests upon humans who are controlled by Ego of the process followed. There also comes time when, by the time the trial is completed, the innocent accused would have dead. What the trial would do in such cases other than recording on the file as deceased. There ends the Justice to him or her.

Ego nested with negativity delinks with the Spirit where conscience resides while positivity is constantly linked to the Spirit. Who is then the God on Earth? The negativity and positivity are the products of the circumstances the human lives in. Both are interactive. If positivity overthrows the negativity, it creates a sense of eagerness and love to live on earth. If negativity overthrows the positivity, the events that follow in such a life are disastrous both for the self and other humans-unpredictable being impulsive and instantaneous. This is the birth place of self-inflictions and crimes against humans. The other living beings on Mother Earth are not within the reach of the Judicial System as there is no law of the land as such.

Cure lies within oneself, if not, within someone else who is capable to cure the negativity. That is awareness and awakening to be ignited in other humans having positivity that links automatically with the Spirit. That is, by another human or group of humans, the society or the entities and organizations created by humans. One can say it is easy to say but difficult to do. True. Yet, it has to be done for the sake of wellbeing of human and of other living beings on earth. Entities, organizations or group of humans should themselves first have the positivity with utmost desire to serve others. The religious bodies and organizations can be said to have this quality to a great extent as well as constant touch and interactions with the humans. This is one class created by God for carrying the message of goodness and wellbeing to other human beings and other living beings on earth. In author's view, the religious bodies and organizations by virtue of their holiness and sacrility are capable of bestowing upon the humans the real purposes and values of life.

**Article "Religion and Crime Studies: Assessing What Has Been Learned" by Melvina Sumter Wood, Ingrid and Dianne, Department of Sociology and Criminal Justice, Old Dominion University, Norfolk, VI 23529, USA published on MDPI Website - 18 June 2018. Only "Abstract" of the Article has been given below, being relevant in the context:**

**"Abstract**

This paper provides a review of the literature that assesses the relationship between religion and crime. Research on the relationship between religion and crime indicates that certain aspects of religion reduce participation in criminal activity. A review of the literature indicates religion reduces participation in criminal activity in two broad ways. First, religion seems to operate at a micro level. Studies have pointed to how religious beliefs are associated with self-control. Second, researches have examined the social control aspects of religion. In particular, how factors such as level of participation and social support from such participation reduces criminal activity. Likewise, findings suggest that although there has been a sizable number of studies and diverse interests of researchers examining the religion/crime nexus, the research has not identified which aspects of religion have the strongest influence on crime reduction. In addition, the specific ways in which these factors are associated with crime reduction have not been comprehensively identified. Similarly, more than 40 years of empirical scholarship suggests that religion suppresses criminal behaviour. Nevertheless, these findings remain controversial as the literature neither accentuates the mechanisms of religion responsible for suppressing criminal behaviour, nor does the literature reject the spuriousness of the religion-crime association relative to mediating effects of self-control and social control. Finally, our review suggests that methodological constraints infringe on the capacity for sociological and criminological to accurately ascertain the validity of the religion-crime nexus, often generating mixed or inconclusive findings on the religion-crime association. Our paper concludes with recommendations for future empirical scholarship that examines the religion-crime nexus."

**Excerpts from "WHAT RELIGIOUS COMMUNITIES CAN DO TO ELIMINATE VIOLENCE AGAINST CHILDREN** – Religions for Peace and UNICEF, with input from religious leaders and child protection specialists, have developed the guide as a tool to support religious communities' work to promote child rights and to prevent and respond to rights violations, in particular violence against children. UNICEF." (Website: www.religionsforpeace.org):

"We find strong consensus across our religious traditions about the inherent dignity of every person, including children. This requires that we reject all forms of violence against children and protect and promote the sanctity of life in every stage of a child's development. – Kyoto Declaration, Religions for Peace Eighth World Assembly, Kyoto, Japan 2006"

"This pain stays with you, you don't forget, doesn't matter if you forgive that person – it stays with you. – Teenage boy3"

"With these two hands my mother holds me, cares for me. This I love. But with these two hands my mother hits me. This I hate. – Young girl, East Asia3"

As seen from the available information on the website, there are no organizations sponsored by the religious bodies, government bodies, philanthropists, corporate for the prevention of crimes by and correctional measures for the people, more so, youths in the country who are committing crimes on woman, babies, children, elders and the ordinary people in cities, urban and rural areas, like the ones existing in other countries specially in western and European countries though there are a number of NGOs and organizations that provide various kinds of services for the inmates in prisons in all the States and UTs. There is no law that promotes and supports the private and non-government organizations on prevention of crimes through spiritual and religious practices considered to be effective and result oriented in prevention of the crimes. Lack of legal back up, moral obligation and incentives has to a great extent affected the establishment and growth such institutions in the country which is creating multiple criminal activities as one could observe from the media reports placing substantial stress on the law enforcing authorities.

The services provided by the NGOs and other organizations for the inmates in the prisons include moral, spiritual and psychological teaching; welfare services; spiritual awareness programs and meditation classes; programmes for upliftment of mental as well as physical health; medical health check-up camp; imparting motivational classes; imparting training on human spiritual development and meditation; provide spiritual awareness to create power to choose good and positive thoughts and thus to change the inmates in a very positive way; specialized Yoga & Meditation to inmates and staffs to build up good sound heath and mind for happy and peaceful life; Art of Living classes; recreational programmes, Music training;; regular arrangement of religious lectures for motivation;

Computer Training and Skill Development; moral lessons & cultural programmes; helping inmates for their rehabilitation once they are released from the prison; funding education of inmates as well as inmates children who are continuing their education; financial and moral support to the family members of (particularly convict prisoners) in the field of medical treatment and maintenance of livelihood rehabilitate and re-integrating the release convict in the main stream of the society; financial support to the children of prisoners in field of education and their rehabilitation and financial support to the needy probationer released under the Probationer offender Act (PO Act); conducting counseling and sports events; providing employment opportunities to the released prisoners; providing prisoner children's education and hostel accommodation to the children; conducting Small Industrial Training; conducting rehabilitation programmes like basic education and hand craft training to female prisoners for their welfare; developing agriculture in the prison campus and providing various seeds for plants to the prison garden; imparting Vocational Training like mat weaving for the livelihood of the prisoners and their families; etc. (Source: Compendium of Non-Government Organizations (NGOs) in India involved in Correctional Programmes 2017 - Bureau Of Police Research & Development Ministry of Home Affairs Government of India).

Though it is heartening to note the various kinds of services being provided to the inmates in the prisons by the NGOs and other organizations with or without government support, there are no signs of any initiatives so far from any side for motivational measures and spiritual promotion for prevention of the crimes; most wanted in the environment of criminality mindset among the youths and juveniles inflicting different kinds of crimes daily which include serious crimes. It is not known how this necessity rather a social obligation continued to be ignored by the society, religious bodies, government agencies and the corporate. The prevention of crimes being committed by the youths and juveniles by identifying high risk areas through passionate and positive treatment would contribute greatly in controlling the crimes, as the saying goes "to nip in the bud", should be the immediate concern and appropriate measures including a definite plan of action needs to be taken.

The central and state governments need to recognize the prevailing social tensions due to such crimes and enact suitable law with such incentives as considered appropriate that induces and prompts the religious bodies, private agencies, NGOs to actively participate in developing proper infrastructure and facilities that help motivate birth of new culture in the criminal and justice arena to reform at the root that is responsible for origination of crimes. Causes that drive the youths to commit crimes mainly could be said poverty ridden families, lack of employment opportunities according to their abilities and skills, want of humanness in the society, addictions which also happens either because of extreme poverty or excessive richness, ill treatment by the law enforcing authorities on one or the other excuse that hardens their sentiments and forces resorting to crimes, belittling their educational level and living standard in the schools, colleges, working places and the society. This entire negative process needs to be eliminated earliest the better through the dedicated organizations to reshape their orientation through spiritual, motivational means and methods including to build them to stand up of their own and act like the God on Earth for them. This is what the country demands from all those concerned who should passively participate to create a new life and hope in them for their happiness and for the happiness of the society in general.

Youths of the nature mentioned before are part of the humanity but looked upon differently in the society not for their fault but for the fault on account of the sociological compulsions which itself has evolved into an environment of hate and ill treatment. Beautiful structures have been built in ancient days as well as in the modern days and would continue to be built in generations to come just by chiseling and carving a stone which was believed to be hardest to break; so also let us chisel and carve the humans who stand with hardened habits and sentiments who feel as living in isolation like stone and make them worthy of humans that confers self-respect and appreciation as the structures built have the great appreciation of the people. One day, they will also become the God on Earth for a better human life and would do the services what others have done for them. LET THE HUMAN INSTINCT EXTEND A HELPING HAND FOR THE BETTERMENT AND WELFARE OF SUCH PEOPLE AND LET THAT HELPING HAND BE THE GOD ON EARTH FOR THEM.

Humanism is a philosophical and ethical stance that emphasizes the value and agency of human beings, individually and collectively, and generally prefers critical thinking and evidence (rationalism and empiricism) over acceptance of dogma or superstition. The meaning of the term humanism has fluctuated according to the successive intellectual movements which have identified with it. The term was coined by theologian Friedrich Niethammer at the beginning of the 19th century to refer to a system of education based on the study of classical literature ("classical humanism"). Generally, however, humanism refers to a perspective that affirms some notion of human freedom and progress. It views humans as solely responsible for the promotion and development of individuals and emphasizes a concern for man in relation to the world.[2] (Source: Wikipedia Free Encyclopaedia).

"Encyclopaedia Britannica defines and elaborates 'humanism' as:

".....................Humanitas, also known as humanism in some countries of Europe meant the development of human virtue, in all its forms, to its fullest extent. The term thus implied not only such qualities as are associated with the modern word humanity—understanding, benevolence, compassion, mercy—but also such more assertive characteristics as fortitude, judgment, prudence, eloquence, and even love of honour. Consequently, the possessor of humanitas could not be merely a sedentary and isolated philosopher or man of letters but was of necessity a participant in active life. Just as action without insight was held to be aimless and barbaric, insight without action was rejected as barren and imperfect. Humanitas called for a fine balance of action and contemplation, a balance born not of compromise but of complementarily.

The goal of such fulfilled and balanced virtue was political, in the broadest sense of the word. The purview of Renaissance humanism included not only the education of the young but also the guidance of adults (including rulers) via philosophical poetry and strategic rhetoric. It included not only realistic social criticism but also utopian hypotheses, not only painstaking reassessments of history but also bold reshaping of the future. In short, humanism called for the comprehensive reform of culture, the transfiguration of what humanists termed the passive and ignorant society of the "dark" ages into a new order that would reflect and encourage the grandest human potentialities. Humanism had an evangelical dimension: it sought to project humanitas from the individual into the state at large.................."

Time for the authorities, the judiciary and the human research organizations to think about the need for restructuring and reshaping the existing laws that could inculcate the sense of humanism in their spirit and substance which would enlarge the eyes of the society, the politicians, the police and judicial system would as "THE G|OD ON EARTH" for the persons who are termed as criminals mainly responsible due to their sociological condition, lack of opportunities to live with dignity of life and the hardening laws and rules they are subjected to. It is to be accepted that no person wants to become criminal rather the circumstances make him criminal and our whole object should be that once criminal should not again be criminal. This can be achieved through the process of humanism which strongly rests on the political will, generosity and divine approach. Otherwise, the courts of law will continue to be overburdened and opening up of more and more courts could be a political statement and not a solution to the problem.

The basic concept of "THE GOD ON EARTH" needs to be understood – UNLESS THERE IS A HELPING HAND IN ANY SPHERE OF HUMAN LIFE, THERE CANNOT BE CURE; THAT HELPING HAND IS GOD(THE SPIRIT) ACTING THROUGH HUMANS. IF WE WANT TO TURN THE CRIMINALS INTO HUMANS AND MAKE THEY LIVE WITH DIGNITY, MERE PUNITIVE LAWS WOULD NOT SERVE THE PURPOSE RATHER THEY FURTHER HARDEN THEM TO LEAD CRIMINAL LIFE. ALL THE PUNITIVE LAWS NEED TO BE HUMANIZED, THAT IS, SUCH LAWS ALSO SHOULD CLEARLY LAY DOWN HOW THEY SHOULD BE BROUGHT UP AFTER THEY ARE SENTENCED AND SENT TO JAIL. THE JAIL MANUAL BELONGS TO DIFFERENT CENTURY WHEN CRIME WAS TREATED AS ANIMALISTIC INSTICT. THERE IS IMMEDIATE NEED TO REFORM THE JAIL MANUAL, SO FAR IT IS CONCERNED WITH HUMAN UPBRINGING AND ITS INTEGRATION WITH THE CRIMINAL LAW. THE UPBRINGING NEEDS TO BE ACCORDING TO THE SKILLS OF THE PERSON SENTENCED. ALL THESE MEASURES WOULD ACT AS 'THE GOD ON EARTH' FOR THEM FOR, ONCE HE IS MADE KNOWN HOW TO SUSTAIN HIMSELF IN

SOCIETY, THE CRIMINALITY IN HIS MIND WOULD AUTOMATICALLY DISAPPEAR. THAT IS THE OBJECT FOR INJECTION OF HUMANISM IN CRIMINAL LAWS TO ELIMINATE THE CRIIMINALITY IN THE MIND.

FURTHER, THE EXISTING LAW ENFORCING SYSTEM BOTH IN THE SOCIETY AND IN THE JAILS ALSO BELONGS TO EARLIER CENTURY. BRUTALITY IS CONSIDERED THE BEST COURSE TO TREAT THE HUMANS. THIS HAS INCREASED THE CRIMES AND DISRESPECT TO RULE OF LAW MULTIFOLD. THIS SYSTEM ALSO NEEDS TO BE COMPLETELY HUMANIZED AND THE LAW BREAKERS SHOULD BE TREATED WITH HUMANISM.

BOTH THESE FACTORS OPEN UP A NEW HORIZEN IN THE CRIMINAL HISTORY AND THE ATTITUDANAL AND BEHAVIOURAL PATTERN OF THE CITIZENS AND THE SOCIETY WILL ALTOGETHER CHANGE AND WOULD EASE THE SOCIAL TENSIONS. THERE IS NO GREATER STRENGTH WHETHER IN LAW OR IN ENFORCING THE LAW THAN HUMANISM.

This is not to be misconstrued as author is supporting the criminals. Those persons who are leading good life having well educated; occupying higher position, the professionals, IT experts, belonging to rich community are yet committing crimes in the society including crimes against women and children, cheating and frauds both in the governmental and private spheres are to be dealt with severest punishments with no compassion or sympathy.

Because, this class of people are not committing crimes out of compulsive circumstances but are committing even having been well brought up and conscious of their action, the reasons for such acts could be extraordinarily selfish. Considering their status and standing, they should have rather been 'THE GOD ON EARTH' for the sake of others who would remain ever grateful to them. The very fact that they are attracted towards crimes shows their total delinks with the Spirit residing in them.

# SECTION [21]
# WHY HUMANS ARE INDIFFERENT WHEN THEY BELIEVE GOD IS ONE

There are many similarities between humans and other living beings in on the earth that one may have noticed. Humans as well as other livings eat, sleep, think, and communicate. We are also similar in a lot of ways our bodies work. But we also have a lot of differences. Are there any differences that set humans apart, uniquely, from all other beings? Some people think that the main differences between humans other species is our ability of complex reasoning, our use of complex language, our ability to solve difficult problems, and introspection. Others also feel that the ability for creativity or the feeling of joy or sorrow is uniquely human. Humans have a highly developed brain that allows us to do many of these things. But are these things uniquely human? Not necessarily. Every living in the nature has similarities with those of humans except higher level of consciousness. Animal species have lower level of reasoning, example, to find a place for safe living within the given conditions; Different species have their own language and they do communicate their expression and feeling through their own language. So also the humans who speak different languages but lack understanding each other because of not knowing the language? So also the case with different species, the difference being humans who know both languages, assist in understanding each other speaking known as the interpreter which facility does not exist with other species? Other species have also the capacity to foresee the dangers and find solutions. For example, they have the capacity to foresee the natural calamities which the human doesn't have; they also have a sense of urge to escape when attacked or one wants to capture. Humans have made and making research to understand the languages of animals and birds. As author understands, researchers have succeeded, to some extent, in understanding the language of the specific birds. Both social animals and birds are said to be capable of understanding human language. This could also be the personal experience in one's life.

Why the author has brought the topic of nature, having fairly dealt earlier? That is the temptation of the nature the author is caught in. Author is also a human being and has learnt the interaction process with the nature in life, also having been born in a tiny village. Villages are the distinct class that live in and represent the true followers of the nature. Living with nature is Life and living apart from it, makes Life not to know what the nature is in its true sense. The ways of living are different in villages and cities. The artificial appearance in cities though attracts and intends to show a better life compared to villages. Artificiality has very short presence and, to memorize it and practice it daily, one feels helpless, as the same has to be done for the sake of appearance and living. It has become a matter of habit and so the people become habituated. The life in cities does not cherish the true happiness that one derives living with nature. It is not that those living in cities cannot experience the nature. They do. Human efforts continued since long have learnt to naturalize the cities bringing to the cities a character of nature.

This is commendable because it acquaints those living in cities devoid of nature, what the nature means and how to live life together with the nature. This is receiving highest urgency and consideration among the authorities as well as the people with the authorities creating a natural environment adopting various features of the nature and the people started loving it. Most of the big and small cities are changing their landscapes in their outlook that is further changing the living style of the people. Eating habits also are showing signs of shifting towards natural products and produces beneficial for healthy living, especially for the newly born and growing children. There is also a keen competition between the natural and manmade products and produces and, to propagate the latter, the advertising agencies together with print and electronic media are making their best efforts to impress upon the manmade products and produces. Author's personal view is that it is for the people to ascertain and choose the one that is most beneficial. Author only wants to remind the readers that the Nature itself is 'The God on Earth' showering umpteen varieties of nature made products and produces for betterment and welfare of humans and every other living being on earth.

Author now deals with trust, love, kindness, compassion, forgiveness which embody the godly qualities, each individually, to enable one to know that each of them constitute godly quality and following them would confer great beneficial effects on the humans. All these qualities play a significant role in human life whether one is ordinary or rich person; whether one is employer or employee; whether one is professional or an expert; whether one is in government or private; whether one is in a school, college or university; whether one is teacher or student; whether one group of people or society; and whether one is man or woman. The entire edifice of human life in relationship with other humans and the nature including all living beings rest on the qualities mentioned and represent the essence of positivity that does always good for self and others and the opposite of which, the negativity does always harm to self and others.

Trust is important because it is the basis around which all human relationships revolve. Without trust there can be no relationship. A good husband and wife is trustworthy if they express it in words and actions. The basic needs are for human values. These values are rooted or based in trust affection. Trust, in the dictionary, is defined as being confident, believing, or relying on someone or something to do what is expected. Imagine what a world would be like without trust. Why Is Trust important in the Workplace? If a workplace is able to foster a strong sense of trust within their organisation they can see a number of benefits including: increased productivity amongst staff, improved morale amongst employees and staff. In family, people are able to trust and rely on each other for support, love, affection and warmth. Trust is the most important business and brand asset to manage, especially in relationships with customers, clients, employees, and stakeholders. Brand represents the trust.

Every interaction is an opportunity to build relationships and nurture trust.

There have been increasing complaints and reports of harassment of working class, the reasons attributed being of varying nature. Love affair is a different class not plausible to be considered under the harassment class. Author is passing through this subject not to clinically analyse but to look at it as overbearing over one or the other female class. For a female executive especially, this guards as the protecting shield in her relationship and working with the functionary of the management. That sacred sentiment should always be guarded and maintained by the management with every executive, particularly, in the case of female executive. Those who want to do harassment of female executive must remember that he acts so in utter disregard of his conscience which is done when selfishness rules negativity in mind and delinks itself with the inner Spirit.. Law, of course, takes its own course and the management may also act against the person. Yet, that is not the end in itself. A person hurting the Spirit and Conscience is bound to fall in his or her own pit. First trust in oneself and then, one will be able to trust others. Trust is the moral obligation in humans and other species. Trust and that trust turns into trustworthiness.

Mistrust or breach of trust is cheating creating chaotic psychological and physiological effects. Mistrust is individualized while breach of trust is protected in law. Law compensates the one affected due to breach of trust. Mistrust is a valid response to feeling betrayed or abandoned. But pervasive feelings of mistrust can negatively impact a person's life. This can result in anxiety, anger, or self-doubt. Mistrust normally occurs due to lack of humane, mistrust that interferes with a relationship, suspicion or anxiety about friends and family and belief that others are deceptive or malevolent without evidence. It is said that suspicion creates mistrust. The root of suspicion is lack of knowledge; as such, the remedy to suspicion was to learn more about the issue that is troubling one. It is also said that suspicion also leads to self-liquidation. Suspicion is a floating thought and, if it is to be trusted as true, it should be made true through verifiable facts or self-assessed satisfaction that convincingly concludes the suspicion or otherwise. Believe in trust unless and until the symptoms of mistrust become perceptible. The person who is entertaining mistrust in mind suffers most than the person who is causing mistrust. Mistrust and, as part of it, the suspicion is also responsible for the birth of negativity which is more painful, the reason being the mistrust and suspicion hold strongly and to displace them takes a longer time. Sometimes it leads to permanent loss of trust. One, therefore, needs to be careful in forming a mistrust or suspicion. Better to avoid them. Mistrust and suspicion act like devils. A devil is the personification of evil as it is conceived in many and various cultures and religious traditions. It is seen as the objectification of a hostile and destructive force.

Wikipedia brings out the essence and substance of love to one and all on the earth. Its purpose is to reach to everyone who is crying for it makes them loveable and liveable. The love in human has to be instinctive the way the animals and birds show their love to human; they are not asked for it, they feel they enjoy it doing so, not bothered whether the human to whom they are showing their love is responding the love with the same instinct. This is what the nature has taught them. It doesn't happen in humans. Human goes through several processes before he or she thinks of loving the other human. This kind of love is different from what the natural love means. The natural love does not distinguish the human or the other beings on earth. It is always interactive that carries the message that one is not alone and that alone is one among many around in terms of human and other species. Love is how soon one reaches to the needy or to one who is hurt and helps them to feel liveable. Love itself is not alone because when it reaches out instantly to help someone; it also makes the other person to share something what one has with him or her in kind or cash which serves as giving water when a person is thirsty. This is full of positivity making the giver and the received most happy. That is love as it characterizes the godly qualities. Absence of love need not be frustration for, the frustration flows from the lack of quality of loving. Loving keeps the loving and the loved par excellence of humanism. This thread needs to knit gently and softly so that it doesn't give chance for any hurting the feelings or the sentiments of others rather make them to feel the worth of it.

Love relationship that a couple experiences in life and extends it to its children brings not only love, also a great sense of deep affection which has the ability to absorb the pains in life. Once trust, sincerity and openness establish among the life partners and their children, it distances the dissatisfaction and develops an eagerness to care for each other to live together, the essence of life. There is nothing like differences that we talk about as could be the reason when we see soaring misunderstandings in relationship. Misunderstanding means - misinterpretation, misconstruction, misreading, misapprehension, misconception, mistake, misbelieve, to say a few. First three letters consist 'mis' as prefix. Meaning of 'mis' is said to be added to verbs and their derivatives wrongly, misapply, badly, mismanage, unsuitably. Who adds this 'mis' as prefix. One who is emotional in oneself, stubborn, uncaring, all of which adds up to 'ego'? Ego is himself or herself because it has no form of its own. It takes form the way the mental thinking is reflected – both negative and positive. Love is considered to be always positive and the one that is not love is hatred, the negative. What is stated before is formation of negatives. Negatives always lead to breaking point that is, widening the distance ship between the persons and such widening never pulls back to loveliness rather generates more and more sadness due to hatredness. Sorrows, miseries and sufferings that occur in life partners and their children or those who love each other intensely but such love doesn't materialize into a relationship. These things also occur where one thinks of failure to achieve life ambitions or what one has been aiming at.

In short, misapplication of mind is misunderstanding which, once fixes in mind, that is, within himself or herself makes one to lose love for self rather love to learn self-first which is the first lesson in love before one wants to love others, self-condemning, declining interest in life, rising dissatisfaction with whatever is done and so on. In such times, don't jump into and become victim of emotions and frustrations but listen to one's conscience within that lives with the Spirit.. That Spirit has love, kindness, compassion and forgiveness, seek for them putting aside the living in caged momentary emotional thoughts. Living life is possible both ways – with frustration and with fruitfulness of love. Frustration and sadness in life cause loneliness. As stated before, one is not lonely and one is among many all around. Open eyes and look for that all around. This consists of humans and other species – the nature. It always smoothens and soothes the life and messages to one in distress that there are others who love to help once they know grappling with problems, they extend their affection, guide one through spiritualization of mind that displaces the negativity with positivity. Once that happens, one feels joyful having liberated from the negativity and wish to live, learn and rise up in life. Make it life's motto. Being part of the nature, live with the nature. Don't search for any other way out. Come out of darkness and see the sparkling light. Look towards the godly and not ghostly qualities.

Author has attempted in this book to draw the kind attention of the readers to understand the essence of life and constantly move towards knowing 'ONE'S OWN SPIRIT CONNECTED TO THE SOUL IN EVERY BODY FOLLOWING QUALITIES OF GOD – LOVE, KINDNESS, COMPASSION, FORGIVENESS HOLDING THEM IN TRUST TO THE SOUL'; THE SPIRIT RESPONDS AND BE MOVING AS 'THE GOD ON EARTH' WHO IS AN INTEGRAL PART OF THE HUMANS AND ALL OTHER SPECIES ON

MOTHER EARTH, SO UNDERSTOOD BY FEW OF THE DIVINE LIVES WHO HAVE DONE AND ARE DOING GREAT SERVICE TO HUMANITY AND OTHER SPECIES ON EARTH IN ONE FORM OR THE OTHER.

Majority of the humans today are obsessed and driven by their ego with negativity that is causing untold injuries and miseries to humans and other species. This is also showing increasing self-abuse which is condemnation of one's own life. Self-abusing is the greatest sin and is against the wishes of God for; God has sent you to Mother Earth to feel the worth of life on earth. Self-learn and appreciate the life that opens up doors for creation of self-belief and self-confidence to move upward. Closing the eyes to existence of spirit of living distances itself from the inner Spirit and snaps relationship with godly qualities of love, kindness, compassion and forgiveness. Living with Spirit is the spring board for enthusing the life with desire to perform one's duty according to the ability, astuteness, education and skills one has acquired or enduring to acquire that confers right to live with honour and dignity of life, the Spirit embodies conscience that helps lighting up the life. Frustration in life makes one feel lonely that makes the negativity to predominate and influence one's behaviour and attitude of hopelessness and depression tending to believe that life has no meaning and to end the life as the inevitable option. This is like sitting in darkness and searching for the door.

There is no human life without difficulties, there is no human life without happiness, there is no human life without pleasure, there is no human life without relationship with co-humans, there is no human life which want to live without the presence and support of the other living beings on Mother Earth, there is no human life without going by one's Faith and the Teachings of the Saints and Sages of the respective Faiths. Then, what else the human life seeks for. In the process of the life, the positivity and negativity are integral part of the human life depending upon which one he or she chooses to live on. The consequences of both the negativity and positivity are known to each human according to his or her understanding capabilities. The only missing gap in between the positivity and negativity is one's disconnection with the Spirit [Conscience] which happens when Ego overtakes the Conscience. This is where we give place for the birth of the negativity.

The God having been there within every human being and other living beings as Spirit which extends its light to the Conscience to judge which human act is right or wrong is the fundamental basis of the humans. In between this, the Ego [self-posture] when acts superior than the Spirit and fails to consult it whether to do or not to do a contemplated act directed by the Desire of the humans, leads to the state of sorrowfulness in the form of negativity. Let us not blame God or the Soul within for such occurrences among the humans.. Other living beings do have the humanism which these exhibit to humans within one's home and outside when the humans don't intend to harm them. These do harm to the humans only when humans want to harm them. One who does act according to the Spirit, he or she doesn't know what negativity is. The negativity, by nature, persists the humans to choose the path it is showing to fulfil the Desire one is aspiring to achieve. The desire cannot be achieved through the negativity that drives the human deep into the troublesome times and fainting situations and makes the humans to hang on to self-cheating and chasing for something that wouldn't have happened but for bypassing presence of the Spirit which guides the humans solely and only towards the positivity that makes the human life worth living.

So, let the humans possess as much positivity as possible through constant consultation of the Conscience [Spirit] within that enables the humans to be part of the good deeds in life. Departing from this concept creates imbalance in the humans which happens when humans get more attached with negativity. Ego, as noted before, is the birth place of negativity for which one has to face the situations not sought for but forced upon pursuant to act the human does which are not in one's own or others' interests which stands as stumbling block in human life and births the misery.

Always wishing well and good for others will relieve the pain and agony of life. Lest, it converts into loneliness and the need for seeking the help of psychologist who has his or her own limitations and cannot offer one line solution in such cases. Be yourself, believe in yourself and never be selfish depriving the other humans which is an act of God and is the process of self-curing. Loosing balancing of the mind is like wandering in the wild forcing oneself to extremity in neither life which neither God desires nor the human life born on Mother Earth.

God cannot help when one wants to be dictated by the negativity that leads towards self-destruction rather than self-protection. When negativity strikes, don't be scared and self-misdirected but within that search for the positivity that offers the 'hope' which signals the humans to live and fulfil one's ambitions that should be spirit of life and not dispirit to make oneself self-reject the life which is precious and if one who preserves, it will have all the courage to face the challenges that confront in one's life while living in this world which sometimes becomes cruel to the humans. Never care for such world and proceed to practice your way of life guided by the Conscience and the Soul within you. That makes the life merrier.

Rash thinking and making up in mind takes one towards miserable consequences. Article given below supports this view:

**Rash Behavior: Causes, Consequences, and Strategies for Self-Control Cognitive Behavior NeuroLaunch editorial team - September 22, 2024 [Source: https://neurolaunch.com/rash-behavior/#:~:text=The%20consequences%20of%20rash%20behavior%20can%20be%20as,argument%20where%20you%20said%20things%20you%20didn%E2%80%99t%20mean%3F**

"A split-second decision can change the course of a lifetime, leaving us to grapple with the consequences of our rash behavior. We've all been there – that moment when impulse overtakes reason, and we act without thinking. Maybe it was a heated argument where words flew out of your mouth before your brain could catch up, or perhaps it was a spontaneous purchase that left your wallet significantly lighter. Whatever the case, rash behavior is a universal human experience that can have far-reaching effects on our lives and the lives of those around us.

But what exactly is rash behavior? It's more than just acting on a whim or being spontaneous. Rash behavior refers to actions or decisions made without careful consideration of the consequences. It's the kind of behavior that makes us slap our foreheads and mutter, "What was I thinking?" – usually because we weren't thinking at all.

The prevalence of impulsive actions in our daily lives is staggering. From the small things, like snapping at a loved one when we're angry, to more significant decisions, such as quitting a job in a fit of frustration, rash behavior peppers our existence like an overzealous chef with a salt shaker. It's the spice that can either enhance the flavor of our lives or completely ruin the dish.

Understanding and managing rash behavior is crucial for personal growth and maintaining healthy relationships. It's not just about avoiding regrettable tattoos or ill-advised social media posts (though those are certainly valid concerns). Learning to curb our impulsive tendencies can lead to better decision-making, improved mental health, and more fulfilling relationships. It's the difference between being the captain of your own ship and being tossed about by every passing wave of emotion.

## Common Causes of Rash Behavior: The Perfect Storm of Impulse

Let's dive into the murky waters of what drives us to act rashly. It's a complex cocktail of factors, each ingredient adding its own flavor to the mix.

First up, we have emotional triggers and heightened states. You know that feeling when your blood is boiling, and you're seeing red? That's when rash behavior is most likely to rear its ugly head. Anger, fear, excitement, and even extreme happiness can short-circuit our rational thinking processes, leading to actions we might later regret. It's like our emotions throw a wild party in our brains, and reason wasn't invited.

Then there's the issue of impulse control, or rather, the lack thereof. Some people seem to have a hair-trigger response to every stimulus, while others can maintain their cool in a volcano. This variation in impulse control is partly due to individual differences in brain structure and function. It's like some folks are born with a Ferrari engine for a brain, but the brakes of a rusty bicycle.

Environmental factors and social influences play a significant role too. Ever notice how you're more likely to splurge on a night out with friends than when you're alone? Our surroundings and the people we're with can significantly impact our behavior. It's as if peer pressure never really left the playground; it just got more sophisticated.

Lastly, we can't ignore the role of neurological and psychological conditions in impulsivity. Conditions like

ADHD, bipolar disorder, and certain personality disorders can make impulse control even more challenging. It's like trying to navigate a ship with a faulty rudder – you might know where you want to go, but steering there is a whole other story.

**Consequences of Rash Behavior: The Ripple Effect**

Now, let's talk about the aftermath. The consequences of rash behavior can be as varied as the actions themselves, ranging from mildly embarrassing to life-altering.

On a personal level, rash behavior can wreak havoc on our relationships, career, and self-esteem. That heated argument where you said things you didn't mean? It might have just cost you a friendship. The impulsive decision to tell your boss exactly what you think of them? Hello, unemployment line. These actions can chip away at our self-esteem, leaving us feeling guilty, ashamed, or inadequate. It's like playing emotional Jenga – one wrong move, and the whole structure comes tumbling down.

The legal and financial implications of rash behavior can be equally severe. From risky behaviors that land you in legal hot water to impulsive spending that leaves you drowning in debt, the consequences can follow you for years. It's like trying to run a marathon with a ball and chain attached to your ankle – you might still be moving, but progress is going to be slow and painful.

The impact on mental and physical health shouldn't be underestimated either. Chronic stress from dealing with the fallout of rash actions can lead to a host of health problems. It's like your body is keeping a tally of every impulsive decision, and eventually, it's going to present you with the bill.

Long-term, rash behavior can significantly affect personal growth and life satisfaction. It's hard to move forward when you're constantly cleaning up messes from the past. It's like trying to build a house on quicksand – no matter how hard you work; you keep sinking back to where you started.

**Recognizing Patterns of Rash Behavior: Know Thyself**

The first step in managing rash behavior is recognizing it. It's like being a detective in your own life story, looking for clues and patterns.

Common signs of impulsive tendencies include difficulty waiting your turn, acting without thinking of consequences, and frequently interrupting others. It's like your actions are always a step ahead of your thoughts, leaving your rational mind constantly playing catch-up.

Self-assessment is crucial in identifying rash behavior. Keep a journal of your actions and the emotions that preceded them. It's like creating a map of your behavioural landscape – once you can see the terrain, you can start planning your route.

It's important to differentiate between occasional impulsivity and chronic patterns.

Everyone has moments of rashness, but if it's a recurring theme in your life, it might be time to dig deeper. It's the difference between having a bad hair day and realizing you've been wearing a wig backwards for years.

Self-awareness is key in managing rash behavior. It's about understanding your triggers, recognizing your patterns, and being honest with yourself about the impact of your actions. It's like having a personal early warning system – the more attuned you are to your own tendencies, the better equipped you'll be to handle them.

**Strategies for Managing and Reducing Rash Behavior: Taming the Beast**

Now that we've identified the problem, let's talk solutions. Managing rash behavior is like training a wild horse – it takes patience, consistency, and the right techniques.

Cognitive-behavioural techniques can be powerful tools for impulse control. These methods involve identifying and challenging the thoughts that lead to impulsive actions. It's like being your own mental bouncer, checking the ID of every thought before letting it influence your behavior.

Mindfulness and meditation practices can also be incredibly effective. These techniques help you become more aware of your thoughts and emotions in the present moment, giving you the space to respond rather than react. It's like installing a pause button in your brain – when you feel the urge to act rashly, you can hit pause and consider your options.

Developing healthy coping mechanisms is crucial. This might involve finding alternative ways to express emotions, like exercise or creative pursuits. It's about giving yourself productive outlets for the energy that might otherwise fuel impulsive actions. Think of it as redirecting a river – instead of letting it flood and cause damage, you're channelling it to power a mill.

Sometimes, professional help is necessary, especially if rash behavior is significantly impacting your life. A therapist or counsellor can provide personalized strategies and support. It's like having a personal trainer for your mind – they can help you develop the mental muscles needed to control impulsive tendencies.

**Building a Support System for Long-Term Behavior Change: It Takes a Village**

Changing ingrained behavior patterns is no easy feat, and having a strong support system can make all the difference. It's like trying to climb a mountain – sure, you could do it alone, but having a team makes the journey safer and more enjoyable.

Involving friends and family in the process can provide accountability and encouragement. Let them know about your goals and how they can support you. It's like having your own personal cheerleading squad – they're there to celebrate your victories and help you up when you stumble.

Joining support groups or therapy sessions can connect you with others facing similar challenges. There's comfort in knowing you're not alone in your struggles. It's like being part of a club for impulsive behavior management – you're all working towards the same goal, sharing tips and tricks along the way.

Creating a conducive environment for positive change is crucial. This might involve removing temptations or restructuring your daily routine to avoid triggering situations. It's like childproofing your life – you're making it harder for impulsive behavior to sneak in and cause trouble.

Don't forget to celebrate your progress, no matter how small. Changing behavior is hard work, and acknowledging your efforts helps maintain motivation. It's like giving yourself a gold star for every day you resist impulsive urges – those little rewards can add up to big changes over time.

**Conclusion: The Road to Self-Control**

Understanding and managing rash behavior is a journey, not a destination. It's about progress, not perfection. Remember, every time you pause before acting, every moment you choose thoughtful response over impulsive reaction; you're rewiring your brain for better self-control.

Patience and persistence are key in this process. Behavior change doesn't happen overnight – it's a gradual process of replacing old habits with new, healthier ones. It's like learning to play an instrument – at first, it feels awkward and difficult, but with practice, it becomes more natural and effortless.

So, take that first step. Whether it's starting a mindfulness practice, seeking professional help, or simply becoming more aware of your impulsive tendencies, every action towards self-improvement counts. You have the power to change your behavior and, by extension, the course of your life.

Remember, a split-second decision can change the course of a lifetime – but so can the decision to take control of your actions. The choice is yours. Make it a good one."

Be a light within yourself so that you don't feel nor know what darkness is. Learn to live and lend help to others in whatever measure and capacity one could do. Help is like river that makes water available to one and all without trying to know who is what. That should be the object of life, that very yearning and experience makes one happy and worth living. Believe in yourself. If you don't, then no one have reason to believe. "YOU ARE ONE WITHIN YOURSELF"; it means inner peace begins the moment you choose not to allow another person or object or event to control your emotions. Believe and you will succeed, that belief guides you to move out of emotions and makes you successful in life. Helping others heals your own injury and takes you to your full positivity. That is what you need and that is what the life is for you to love and live.

**THERE IS NO EXERCISE BETTER FOR THE HEART THAN REACHING DOWN AND LIFTING PEOPLE UP." — JOHN HOLMES.**

**THE BEST ANTIDOTE I KNOW FOR WORRY IS WORK. THE BEST CURE FOR WEARINESS IS THE CHALLENGE OF HELPING SOMEONE WHO IS EVEN MORE TIRED. ONE OF THE GREAT IRONIES OF LIFE IS THIS: HE OR SHE WHO SERVES ALMOST ALWAYS BENEFITS**

MORE THAN HE OR SHE WHO IS SERVED." — GORDON B. HINCKLEY.

TO REALLY CHANGE THE WORLD, WE HAVE TO HELP PEOPLE CHANGE THE WAY THEY SEE THINGS. GLOBAL BETTERMENT IS A MENTAL PROCESS, NOT ONE THAT REQUIRES HUGE SUMS OF MONEY OR A HIGH LEVEL OF AUTHORITY. CHANGE HAS TO BE PSYCHOLOGICAL. SO IF YOU WANT TO SEE REAL CHANGE, STAY PERSISTENT IN EDUCATING HUMANITY ON HOW SIMILAR WE ALL ARE THAN DIFFERENT. DON'T ONLY STRIVE TO BE THE CHANGE YOU WANT TO SEE IN THE WORLD, BUT ALSO HELP ALL THOSE AROUND YOU SEE THE WORLD THROUGH COMMONALITIES OF THE HEART SO THAT THEY WOULD WANT TO CHANGE WITH YOU. THIS IS HOW HUMANITY WILL EVOLVE TO BECOME BETTER. THIS IS HOW YOU CAN CHANGE THE WORLD. THE LANGUAGE OF THE HEART IS MANKIND'S MAIN COMMON LANGUAGE." — SUZY KASSEM,

# SECTION [22]
# THANKFULNESS TO GOD

Thank you for your amazing power and work in our lives, thank you for your goodness and for your blessings over us. Thank you that you are Able to bring hope through even the toughest of times, strengthening us for your purposes. Thank you for your great love and care. Thank you for your mercy and grace. Thank you that you are always with us and will never leave us. Thank you for your incredible sacrifice so that we might have freedom and life. Forgive us for when we don't thank you enough, for who you are, for all that you do, for all that you've given. Help us to set our eyes and our hearts on you afresh. Renew our spirits; fill us with your peace and joy. We love you and we need you, this day and every day. We give you praise and thanks, for You alone are worthy!

[Source: https://www.crosswalk.com/faith/prayer/prayers-to-say-thank-you-to-god-today.html

**"THE BEST WAY TO SHOW YOUR GRATITUDE TO GOD AND PEOPLE IS TO ACCEPT EVERYTHING WITH JOY....WE MAY NOT BE ABLE TO GIVE MUCH BUT WE CAN ALWAYS GIVE THE JOY THAT SPRINGS FROM A HEART THAT IS IN LOVE WITH GOD. ALL OVER THE WORLD PEOPLE ARE HUNGRY AND THIRSTY FOR GOD'S LOVE. WE MEET THAT HUNGER**

BY SPREADING JOY. JOY IS ONE OF THE BEST SAFEGUARDS AGAINST TEMPTATION." - MOTHER TERESA

REFERENCES [Source References are incorporated within the Book]

# ABOUT THE AUTHOR

[Note: The recounting given hereunder is long due to misfortune and trauma that happened in my life.]

Graduate in Commerce 1961. Completed short Vigilance Course organized by the Institute of Secretariat Training & Management and in Parliamentary Procedures and Practices organized by the Bureau of Parliamentary Studies & Training, Ten days on job training in World Bank (1990), Washington. I was a Team Member of the World Bank and ADB Teams for Project Appraisal and Special Studies. Was a Member of the Loan Negotiation Team of the Government of India for ADB Loan for financing power projects in the country.

I served Rural Electrification Corporation Limited {REC} for 18 years and Power Finance Corporation Limited {PFC} for 12 years, overall 30 years.

While I was working in Rural Electrification Corporation Limited (REC) as Deputy Secretary, my services were sought by the erstwhile Ministry of Energy [now Ministry of Power] for drafting of Memorandum of Association [MOA] and Articles of Association [AOA'], other related documents and for registration/incorporation of Power Finance Corporation Ltd.[PFC]. PFC was incorporated on 16 July, 1986 under the Companies Act, 1956 after due approvals and as per the procedure prescribed under Company Law.

My services were again sought by the same Ministry on immediate basis in the first week of September, 1987 for raising Rs. 100 Cr. from the financial market [Public Issue] including its utilization for critical power projects selected by the Planning Commission by end of March, 1988 as per the mandate stated to have been given to the Ministry by the MOF/PMO. I joined PFC on 17th September, 1987 on deputation as Special Officer [Bonds] for a period of one year.

CMD was yet to be appointed. I was reporting to Joint Secretary (F) in the Ministry. CMD assumed office on 14th January, 1988.

The entire amount was mobilized by following the public Offer for Sale of printed Bonds and Interest warrants covering the said amount adopting a unique Public Offer System under the enabling provision of the Companies Act, 1956 for the first time in the history of the capital market in the country saving thereby Rs. 1.42 Cr to PFC which fact was placed before the Controller of Capital Issues [CCI] who accorded sanction of Consent for issue of Bonds.. To the best of my knowledge, in the history of the Public Sector Undertakings [PSUs] or Public Sector Enterprises [PSEs], PFC was the first financial institution to have been asked to raise funds of the value stated before simultaneously just after its incorporation. The central government contribution at that moment was Rs. 30 Cr as Equity amount as subscription to the Share Capital of PFC, to start with.

The entire amount mobilized was utilized for the projects [selected by the then Planning Commission] by the end of March, 1988 as mandated after due approvals and loan documentation by the Board of Directors [BOD] of PFC. PFC awarded to me honorarium and commendation letter. As per the desire of CMD, I absorbed in the services of PFC after one year in the same post as Employee Number One (001) of PFC. The post of Special Officer [Bonds], the post designated during my deputation period later redesignated as Senior Manager on absorption and was promoted to the post of Deputy General Manager [Finance & Financial Operations] in 1989..

As my moral duty, I wish to state that at the fag end of my services in PFC, I was implicated in a criminal case when the security scam broke out in 1992, in connection with investment transactions of around Rs. 419 Cr. made with UCO Bank, Hamam Street Branch, Mumbai during the period 1988-90 which had no relationship with security scam whatsoever for which the government established a Special Court under the Special Court [Trial of Offences Relating to Transactions in Securities] Act, 1992 in Mumbai.

The entire invested amount alongwith the interest due and payable on the said investment of Rs. 419 Cr was received back by PFC on due dates.

PFC did not file any complaint against me with the CBI. CBI registered the case suomoto.

The then CMD appeared before the Joint Parliamentary Committee (JPC) in connection with an investment of Rs. 300 Cr in March, 1992 made by him through

Harshad Mehta's Broker's Firm and invested the same in UCO Bank and Citi Bank in equal proportion, the period covered under Securities Scam even though my report on 'Money Market Survey' done at Mumbai prior thereto as per the instructions of the then CMD having been pointedly stated that the money market was not favourable for placement of Rs. 300 Cr. This report was placed before the Sub-Committee appointed by the Board and the Committee agreed with the findings of the report. The then CMD accorded approval for placement of said amount of his own even though the Director [Finance] recorded a dissenting note in respect thereof.

Due to tremendous political pressure brought upon due to JPC findings upon the then CMD, soon thereafter, I was placed under suspension in November 1992 based on the correspondence between Ministry of Energy [now Power]. On appeal in the Hon'ble High Court of Delhi and the Orders passed by the Hon'ble High Court, the suspension order was revoked in May; 1996. I remained under suspension for four and a half years.

The then CMD who was examined by JPC in connection with the issue of Bonds for Rs. 300 Cr and its investment admitted before JPC having issued the Bonds and made the investment of the same amount, accorded sanction for prosecution against me. I was not associated in whatsoever capacity at all with regard to the issue of the said amount of Rs. 300 Cr and its investment.

The Charge Sheet was filed in 1994 and the Approver's Statement was filed in 1996.The charge sheet and Approver's Statement do not mention a word about any allegation against me of any undue advantage or corruption or recovery from me or any of my relatives or of any financial loss to PFC. The Search Report given to me by the CBI which did not record any recovery from me was submitted to the said CMD the same day for his kind information.

The Statutory Auditor's Report incorporated in the Annual Report of PFC for 1992-93 {P 39, Para 1. Page 40 Para 11.6 and Page 41 Para 4, 5, 9 Point 26.1} regarding investment of Rs. 300 Cr. stated before supports the mala-fide intention of the then CMD in sanction of prosecution against me, there being no recovery whatsoever from me as aforesaid. PFC suffered financial loss of Rs.15 Cr under the above investment. The amount is stated to have been written off in the books of accounts of PFC.

On the mandate of the UCO Bank, Hamam Street Branch at Mumbai, PFC obtained quotes from the Representative of its Official Broker's firm in New Delhi, the local Branch of the Bank having stated in writing that the securities transactions are solely handled at the Hamam Street Bank as per the instructions stated to had been given by the Head Office. These investments related to the surplus funds available with PFC daily after meeting all its commitments which were invested with various other Banks and their subsidiaries based on merits of rate and absorbing capacity obtained from other empanelled Banks and their subsidiaries, duly approved by the then CMD according to the established procedure.

All the investment transactions were made by RBI Cheques (Banker's Cheques) crossed A/c Payee with all the Banks and their subsidiaries and the investments with said Branch of UCO Bank were also made accordingly initially through the New Delhi Main Branch and later, as mandated by the UCO Bank Branch at Hamam Street, Mumbai, the investments were routed through a designated foreign Bank (ANZ Grindlays Bank, Parliament Street, New Delhi) which had said to have the online money transfer through SWIFT transfer facility [Society for Worldwide Interbank Financial Telecommunication] since investment amount was to be transferred on the same day as the interest thereon was to start from the date of the cheque.

PFC had given specific written mandate in the form of letters along with the Banker's Cheque crossed A/c Payee to the said foreign Bank with copy to the Hamam Street Brach of UCO Bank at Mumbai regarding the transfer of money to the invested Bank at Mumbai. The designated foreign bank for transfer, as per the Charge Sheet, credited the proceeds of the banker's cheque to the account of the Broker's firm. It is also stated in the Charge Sheet that the forwarding letters and the banker's cheques were handed over by the concerned Officers in PFC to the local representative of the Harshad Mehta's firm, the Official Broker of UCO Bank, Hamam Street, Mumbai. This was being done by the PFC officials as per the mandate and authorization given in writing by the UCO Bank, Hamam Street at Mumbai to PFC. PFC had also received such mandates from five to six other banks and Crossed RBI Cheques handed over to their Agents under the letter of authorization. The investments made as verified from the Bank Receipts [BRs] furnished by the invested Bank and its subsidiary. The invested amounts along interest due and payable were received back by PFC on due dates from all of them. There was no default whatsoever from any Bank or its subsidiary.

The Charge Sheet states the Approver had replaced the letter given by PFC enclosing the cheques by the letter of Harshad Mehta firm as per the instructions of Harshad Mehta, the fact of which was not known to PFC which presumed the proceedings of cheques were transferred to UCO Bank, Hamam Street Branch through its designated ANZ Grindlays Bank, New Delhi since Bank Receipts [BR] for the invested funds duly signed by the authorized signatories of the said Bank were furnished to PFC with particulars of securities in which funds were invested and the invested funds along with interest payable thereon were received back by PFC on the due dates and the BR was duly discharged by PFC officials and returned to the said Bank. All these documents form part of the Documents attached by the CBI to the Charge Sheet.

The said CMD ordered special audit of the investment transactions of the value stated before. The special audit report specifically confirmed in Part III of its report to the specific queries of CMD to the effect that there were no deviations in the investment procedure followed with the said UCO Bank, Hamam Street Branch and the transactions had the approval of the competent authority i.e. the then CMD.

This report was considered by the Central Vigilance Commission (CVC) which requested the Ministry of Energy [now Ministry of Power] to forward it to the Director of CBI for taking into consideration while investigating the case. This was accordingly done by the

Ministry of Energy (now Power). CBI, except attaching a copy of the same with Charge Sheet as part of the documents (D23), did not mention a single word about the same in the Charge Sheet, thus had not taken the report into consideration during the investigation. The report would have bared the allegations made in the Charge Sheet had CBI taken same into consideration during investigation and had dealt it also in the Charge Sheet. This was biased and prejudicial on the part of the CBI.

My wife developed hypertension in 1993 which could not be controlled despite best medical treatment. She suffered brain stroke 12th May, 2005 midnight, admitted to the hospital, remained in coma for 28 days. On regaining conscious on the 29th day, the Doctors found her having completely paralyzed right side and loss of speech. She remained bed ridden for eight years and passed away on 7th Dec 2013.

The case though registered under the PCA associated with the provisions of IPC was transferred to THE SPECIAL COURT AT BOMBAY Constituted under the Special Court [Trial of Offences Relating to Transactions in Securities] Act, 1992 in Mumbai on the petitions filed by some of the accused persons residing in Mumbai sometime in 2017. On appeal by CBI in Hon'ble High Court of Delhi, in 2017, the transfer of case was stayed. Final Order is still awaited. The regular trial is yet to begin. The case has thus been pending for the last more than 30 years.

I was due for retirement on 31st December, 1996; my service was extended up to 31st July, 1997, the date on which I retired from the services of PFC. There being no Pension Scheme in PFC at that time, I served as Consultant in Multinational Consultancy Organization [a subsidiary of UK based parent company] for seven years post retirement to financially support myself and my family. I was awarded honorarium and a commendatory letter for having developed mathematical model for tariff calculation later converted into software for 33 Hydro Electric Projects in North East. PFC again engaged me as consultant in May, 2006 for assisting PFC on policy, procedural and compliance matters of SPVs set up by PFC [PFC was the Nodal Agency] under Ultra Mega Power Projects, an Initiative launched by the GOI/MOP in 2005-06, served PFC in that position for two years on contract basis. In June, 2008 joined another multinational subsidiary company (a Subsidiary of German based Parent Company) as Senior Advisor [Finance, Commercial and Regulatory Affairs], Best Professional Employee and Special Contribution Awards were given to me while working in this company.

I am now 88 years. I filed petition for discharge in the Hon'ble High Court of Delhi which, though appreciated the facts, dismissed the petition as not a fit case on the ground that other accused persons had not filed any such petition. Among the accused persons in the case, I was the oldest person.

Though I have been Employee No. 001 of PFC, I retired in the same post I was holding on the date of my suspension [DGM-Fin] while my most of the juniors retired as Director and CMD. I thus lost my entire professional future career and the consequent financial benefits.

On completion of the contract in 2018 with multinational Consultancy Company, I took up writing of books. The List of Books published by me numbering 19 is appended. .

More than thirty years are over; the trial is yet to begin. The mental and physical pain is curable by the Doctors but there is no Law under which an accused person can approach for relief for the inordinate and continuing delay in a case in which there was no recovery at all, is, according to me, also a kind of cruelty.

**THOSE WHO GRANT SYMPATHY TO GUILT, GRANT NONE TO INNOCENCE." - — AYN RAND**

## LIST OF BOOKS PUBLISHED BY PRAHALAD RAO

[The books hereunder mentioned are registered under The Copy Rights Act, 1957 and ISBNs, the details of which are incorporated therein]

1. A WAKE UP CALL FOR EVERY INDIAN {2019}

2. JAMMU & KASHMIR – THE TRUTH OF THE MATTER – 2019

3. THE LIVING GOD ON EARTH - 2019

4. PRITHVI PER JEEVIT ISHWAR {2020} {THIS BOOK WAS TRANSLATED IN HINDI LANGUAGE ON DEMAND}

5. SOUNDS OF SILENCES IN INDIA'S CONSTITUTION-DANGERS AHEAD – 2020-

6. COVID-19 – NOT A NATURAL CALAMITY – AN ANALYSIS OF ITS ORIGIN AND THE FALLOUT {2021}

7. INDIA'S POLILTICAL BLUNDERS BLEEDING ITS BOUNDARIES 2021.

8. SOCIALIST, SECULAR & RELIGION IN INDIA – THE MISCONCEPTIONS 2021

9. INDIA'S STRESSED ASSETS CONUNDRUM- SUGGESTED WAYOUT – 2021

10. ANYONE WHO CAN TELL WHERE DID COVID-19 COME FROM THAT KILLED MILLIONS HUMANS IN THE WORLD – IS SILENCE AN ANSWER? {2021}.

11. ABOUT CERTAIN DECISIONS ON TARIFF UNDER ELECTRICITY ACT, 2003 – IN RETROSPECT {2021}

12. INDIAN PARLIAMENT MONSOON SESSION {2021} RUCKUS – TIME TO THINK ABOUT COURSE OF ACTION.

13. INDIA'S FUTURISTIC DEMOCRACY – THREATS OF CONSTITUTIONAL GAPS AND DIGITAL ERA – DECEMBER, 2022.

14. INDIA'S ELECTIOIN FINANCING, FREEBIES AND WELFARE – A FISCAL DISASTEER [2023].

15. WE ARE ONE INDIA ONE PEOPLE – 2023

16. TRUTH ABOUT THE SECURITIES SCAM 1992 [2023]

17. INDIAN DEMOCRACY'S PARADOXES [2024]

18. LIFE IS TO LIVE TOGETHER [2024]

19. INDIA: "JUSTICE DELAYED IS JUSTICE DENIED" – MERE PROVERBIAL

20. FOR INDIA'S FUTURE GENERATIONS

21. GOD: ONE IN ALL AND ALL IN ONE [THIS BOOK]

[PUBLISHERS: M/S BLUEROSE PRIVATE LIMITED COMPANY]. THE ABOVE BOOKS ARE AVAILABLE WITH AMAZON, FLIPKART AND THE PUBLISHERS.

www.ingramcontent.com/pod-product-compliance
Lightning Source LLC
LaVergne TN
LVHW061606070526
838199LV00078B/7195